TENSIONS AT THE BORDER

TENSIONS AT THE BORDER

Energy and Environmental Concerns in Canada and the United States

EDITED BY
JONATHAN LEMCO

New York
Westport, Connecticut
London

Library of Congress Cataloging-in-Publication Data

Tensions at the border : energy and environmental concerns in Canada
  and the United States / edited by Jonathan Lemco.
        p.   cm.
    Includes bibliographical references and index.
    ISBN 0-275-94001-2 (alk. paper)
      1. Energy policy—Canada.   2. Energy policy—United States.
    3. Environmental policy—Canada.   4. Environmental policy—United
    States.   5. Canada. Treaties, etc. United States, 1988 Jan. 2.
    6. Canada—Foreign economic relations—United States.   7. United
    States—Foreign economic relations—Canada.   I. Lemco, Jonathan.
    HD9502.C32T46   1992
    337.71073—dc20   91-34775

British Library Cataloguing in Publication Data is available.

Library of Congress Catalog Card Number: 91-34775
ISBN: 0-275-94001-2

First published in 1992

Praeger Publishers, One Madison Avenue, New York, NY 10010
An imprint of Greenwood Publishing Group, Inc.

Printed in the United States of America

The paper used in this book complies with the
Permanent Paper Standard issued by the National
Information Standards Organization (Z39.48-1984).

10 9 8 7 6 5 4 3 2 1

Contents

Illustrations

Acknowledgments

I would like to thank Martha Lee Benz, Kim Broadhurst, Krista Kordt, Vivian Noble, Laura Subrin, Jean Wellman, and especially Kelly McClenahan for their careful reading and editing of these chapters. My colleagues at the National Planning Association gave freely of their time and wisdom. The Ford Foundation and the Donner Foundation were most generous in supporting the earlier publication of some of the papers in this volume. I would also like to thank my family for their love and support.

Introduction

Jonathan Lemco

ENERGY, TRADE AND THE FTA

Canada and the United States enjoy one of the most comprehensive and mutually profitable binational relationships in the world today. One of the most prominent shared interests includes energy/environment concerns. Environmental pollution respects no man-made boundary. Hazardous waste threatens specific areas of both nations. As a result, binational measures must be instituted to curb the impact of environmental degradation. Energy resources, such as hydroelectric power or arctic gas, can only be properly managed by both Canada and the United States working together. The 1991 acid rain agreement between the two countries is an important step toward curbing this problem. In addition, the Canada-U.S. Free Trade Agreement (FTA) offers potential guidelines for the bilateral energy relationship. Both countries share concerns about the FTA's impact on the security of energy supplies and market access and about the possibilities for infringement of the ability of each partner to establish an independent energy policy. Canadian producers of natural gas, electricity, and uranium want to expand their sales in the U.S. market, while Americans are increasingly concerned about their reliance on Middle East oil (particularly in the aftermath of the Persian Gulf Crisis). The FTA addresses these concerns.[1]

Furthermore, the energy chapter of the FTA closely parallels the stipulations for energy trade outlined under the General Agreement on Tariffs and Trade (GATT), to which both Canada and the United States are signatories. However, a historical comparison of both countries' energy policies reveals a lack of regard for GATT provisions.

From the end of World War II until the early 1980s, both the American and Canadian governments took active roles in influencing the price of energy. In 1981, the United States opted for a market approach to energy prices, and Canada followed in 1985 when it dismantled the National Energy Program (NEP), which had regulated oil and natural gas prices.

Edward Carmichael has identified three stages in North American energy policies:

1. From the mid-1950s to 1973, world oil prices fell, and U.S. and Canadian policies artificially raised prices through import restrictions.

2. From 1973 to the early 1980s, oil prices rose, and U.S. and Canadian policies artificially lowered prices through price regulation and export restrictions.

3. Since the early 1980s, both countries have deregulated prices and eliminated most import and export restrictions and have allowed the market to determine domestic oil prices.

Since 1985, there has been in effect free trade in energy between the United States and Canada. The importance of the FTA has been to offer investors the confidence that policies will not change overnight. In addition, the agreement has implications for uranium, crude oil, natural gas, and electricity. Canada is the world's largest exporter of uranium, while the U.S. uranium industry is in decline. The FTA exempts Canadian uranium from import restrictions that the United States may impose on other exporters. Cooperation is likely to grow out of this situation.

As for oil and gas, the FTA first guards against interventionist policies such as the NEP. Second, it makes U.S. protectionist measures against Canadian gas harder to sustain. Third, it may encourage U.S. buyers to view Canadian gas favorably as a relatively secure source of supply, which will lead to increased export capacity for the Canadian natural gas industry. Trade in electricity has always been tariff free, but U.S. protectionist threats have increased following rising Canadian exports in the 1970s. While electricity is covered in the FTA, it is not covered under GATT.

Although some are concerned that the FTA will subordinate national sovereignty to bilateral responsibility in policy formulation, these fears appear to have little foundation. The FTA restricts mutually harmful actions, but it allows either party to adopt beneficial, independent energy policies. Both Canada and the United States have much to gain from this relationship. The Canadian market is too small to make use of Canada's vast energy potential, and U.S. demand could make mega-projects economically viable. The United States will see an increased supply of alternative energy sources from its ally that will allow shifts away from destructive energy sources (such as coal) and from a reliance on Middle East oil.

However, important problems remain. Energy Secretary James Watkins has held hearings throughout the United States in an effort to formulate a national energy policy. In 1988, U.S. companies pumped twice as much oil from the ground as they found in new fields. In 1989, oil imports into the United States exceeded domestic production for the first time since 1977. It is estimated that the Northeast will need new capacity by 1993 and that the East Central region will lose 9,000 megawatts of existing capacity in the 1990s under the Clean Air Act.

It is here that the energy/environment trade-offs become most evident. Cost constraints rule out oil-fired plants, and environmental regulations rule out coal-fired ones. California and New England will rely increasingly on imports from Canada and the Northwest for cheap gas and hydroelectric power. Yet Hydro Quebec, in response to domestic pressure, has given notice that further sales to the United States will cease by the end of the 1990s. British Columbia Hydro does not foresee building more dams. Fortunately, some in the Department of Energy see a solution in the use of natural gas, which burns cleanly, produces relatively little carbon dioxide, and generates no ash.

During the Reagan years, federal money for alternative energy research fell more than $600 million to less than $200 million per year, and the Public Utilities Regulatory Policies Act, which had encouraged entrepreneurs to pursue alternative energy sources, fell apart as well. As Mintzer notes, the current emphasis on energy is less an economic concern than an environmental one.

BINATIONAL ENVIRONMENTAL CONCERNS

Canada and the United States have been working together on bilateral environmental issues since 1909, when the United States and Great Britain, on behalf of Canada, signed the Boundary Waters Treaty. The most important institution promoting environmental cooperation is the International Joint Commission (IJC), which consists of three commissioners from each country, created to devise guidelines for the use and management of boundary waters and to implement an antipollution clause.[2] More recently, Canada and the United States signed the UN Convention on Long-Range Transboundary Air Pollution of 1979. This too commits both countries to reducing the transboundary flow of air pollution.[3]

Coordinating bilateral environmental policies is often difficult. Canada is the smaller partner and is necessarily affected by changes in U.S. environmental policy. The United States is not always so affected, and this can be maddening to Canadian officials. In addition, there are discrepancies in the level of industrialization at different points on the border, resulting in divergent state, provincial, and federal government views on strategies for remedial action. Furthermore, opinions may differ about how much environmental damage is tolerable. Depending on the region and the kind of pollutant, environmental standards will differ. Finally, differences exist in the technical ability and economic capacity of each country's bureaucratic apparatus.

Notwithstanding these problems, most Canadians and Americans favor more-stringent penalties for polluters. In fact, the similarity of views is quite remarkable. A recent *Macleans/Decima* poll revealed that in response to the question: "Would you favor or oppose shutting down a major company which provided many jobs in your community if it was polluting the environment?," 37 percent of Canadians and 33 percent of Americans would oppose such a measure, and 60 percent of Canadians and 64 percent of Americans would support it.[4]

There are recent signs that private industry has begun to respond to public demands for environmental responsibility. For example, in the past year, International Nickel Company bought ads to announce that it had spent $500 million to clean up the air.

Industry's motives are not entirely charitable, of course. As pollution fighting becomes a leading priority for governments around the world, companies are gaining a foothold in the booming and competitive environmental market. For example, many are involved in the design of curbside blue-box recycling programs, acid rain control equipment, and engineering services. In Canada alone, pollution control is a $10 billion-per-year industry.

Acid Rain

The problem that receives the most attention in Canada is acid rain. This term is actually a misnomer. Acidic substances are deposited not only by rain and other forms of moist air, but by dry particles as well. In the southwestern United States, for example, dry deposition is a more important source of acidity than is wet deposition. Acid rain is invisible, with no discernible taste or smell to humans. It is the result of pollution made by humans mostly in the form of sulfur dioxide (SO_2) and nitrogen oxide (NO_x) emissions from cars and trucks, smokestacks of heavy industry, and coal-burning plants mixing with rain water. Of the many forms of damage inflicted by acid rain, the acidification of aquatic ecosystems is the best documented. The most studied acidified waters are in the northeastern United States, Canada, and Western Europe, although the problem is undoubtedly far more widespread. Lakes become so acidic that fish are unable to reproduce. Canada now has an estimated 14,000 of these "dead lakes," and another 40,000 are threatened.[5]

Acid rain also washes vital nutrients out of the soil, harms trees and other plants, and diminishes forest growth. It damages the surfaces of buildings and cars, endangers people who have breathing disorders, and reduces visibility.

In Canada and particularly in the United States, the federal structure of government hinders effective action to counter acid rain. In the past, all pollutants were treated as local pollutants, and the adverse regional consequences were therefore overlooked. Local jurisdictions had most of the responsibility for achieving the desired air quality, and progress was measured at local monitors. The stage was thus set for making regional pollution worse. Furthermore, the cost of reducing emissions increases with greater efforts to protect jobs in the high sulfur coal industries, an important source of acid rain.

In 1986, then U.S. Secretary of Transportation Drew Lewis and then Premier of Ontario William Davis headed a bilateral investigation that concluded that acid rain was a serious economic, political, and diplomatic problem in addition to being a major pollution concern. Furthermore, there were only a few potential avenues for achieving major reductions in acidic air emissions. Lewis and Davis recommended various innovative control technologies, cooperative activities, and research. The report acknowledged the seriousness of the transboundary environmental problem, but it did not recommend immediate action or propose specific targets for reducing acid rain at source. Canadian officials lamented the lack of concrete results, and President Reagan formally acknowledged that acid rain was a serious environmental problem. However, no specific strategies to ameliorate the problem were forthcoming.

Scientists and conservationists have suggested ways to combat acid rain, including burning less fossil fuel (specifically by conserving energy, substituting fuel sources and switching to low sulfur fuel), reducing the sulfur content of fossil fuels before they are burned, and reducing sulfur during combustion.[6] Also, politicians in both countries have expressed hopes that the goodwill associated with the Free Trade Agreement will inspire a binational effort to curb acid rain. For its part, Canada has introduced strict laws that will cut Canadian SO_2 emissions in half by 1994. As noted, the United States has now also passed clean air legislation. The Canadian government is counting on that legislation and the subsequent binational agreement to cut U.S. acid rain emissions that damage Canadian lakes.

While pollutants flow across the border in both directions, the greater amount of U.S. emissions and prevailing winds ensure that Canada is far more affected by American-generated acid rain than vice versa. Estimates are that 50 percent of the acid rain falling in Canada comes from American sources, whereas 10 to 15 percent of U.S. acid rain originates in Canada. Thus, Canada's ability to address its own acid rain problem is severely constrained by the United States.[6] This is why the new binational accord is so important. As Prime Minister Mulroney noted, there is finally "an enforceable international document." This is not an immediate cure for the problem, of course. Scientists predict that it will take 15 to 20 years before damaged North American waters are returned to complete health.[7]

Global Warming

Increasing amounts of gases such as carbon dioxide, sulfur dioxide, and nitrous oxide are being released into the air and are threatening to destroy the ozone layer which protects us from solar radiation and could raise the earth's temperature to unacceptable limits.[8] Reducing the emission of these so-called greenhouse gases to avoid global warming has become a vital issue. Neither

Canada nor the United States has adopted any target or timetable to achieve this objective.

These gases, carbon dioxide in particular, are accumulating excessively in the atmosphere and are thought to be sealing in solar heat as glass does in a greenhouse. Carbon dioxide is essential for maintaining life; without CO_2 to trap heat leaving the earth's surface that would otherwise escape into space, the earth would be permanently frozen. However, the greenhouse gas buildup could change the earth's climate dramatically. The world's temperature could rise by 1.5-4.5^0 C by the year 2030. Extreme geographic and demographic changes could result. Some scientists suggest that Canada's population could double, and industries, transportation networks, and communication facilities could follow suit. It would take decades for plant and animal life to adapt to such a climate change.

To avert this impending disaster, there is widespread consensus that efforts must be made to shift from fossil fuels, especially coal, to alternatives that do not emit carbon dioxide. One group of experts at the conference "The Changing Atmosphere: Implications for Global Security" has suggested a new tax on oil, gas, and coal as an incentive to develop other energy sources, such as solar, hydro, and wind. They recommend further that rich countries pay poorer countries to stop chopping down rain forests that suck carbon dioxide out of the air.

Chlorofluorocarbons (CFCs) contribute to the greenhouse effect by trapping heat 10,000 times more effectively than do carbon dioxide molecules. If the use of these CFCs continues at the current rate, ozone could fall to less than 90 percent of today's safe levels within 40 years. In 1987, the world's biggest CFC producers (including the United States and Canada) agreed to set a timetable for reducing dependence on CFCs. By 1999, we should be using one-half of the 800,000 tons we now use annually.

One environmentally conscious California city has passed its own law restricting the use of CFCs within its 7,000-acre jurisdiction. Other cities, notably Los Angeles, and certain corporations such as McDonald's, have restricted plastic food packaging that contains CFCs. Wise governments will take the cheapest, most cost-effective steps first, especially those that have other benefits. Complacency would be distinctly uncool.[9]

Regional Nightmares

An environmental nightmare affecting 35 million Canadians and Americans is the Great Lakes region that straddles 1,000 miles of the U.S.-Canadian border. A study by the IJC recorded toxically caused birth defects and reproductive failure in the fish and wildlife of the region. Drinking the water, eating the fish, and breathing the air exposes humans to hazardous chemicals.

In October 1989, the Mulroney government announced that it would spend $125 million for a five-year Great Lakes cleanup project. However, the cost has been estimated to be closer to $100 billion. A binational cleanup program is needed, and experts suggest the installation of modern purification plants to treat all effluent waste before it reaches the lakes.[10]

As noted, neither Canada nor the United States has been willing to set target commitments to curb greenhouse gases, stressing that they still do not know how expensive it will be to implement new regulations. Furthermore, the entire industrial consumer system is geared to energy use. Policies that in the long run would reduce energy costs and diminish air pollution such as regulations requiring new fuel standards for cars and light-duty trucks, better building insulation, and more energy-efficient appliances and lights are expensive and unpopular in a recessionary era. Reducing fossil fuels and gasoline usage will take political courage and some national sacrifice. However, it is not clear that business, industry, and the public are so convinced of dire circumstances that they are prepared to respond effectively.

Other environmental dangers that threaten the region are deforestation, which contributes to the greenhouse effect; increased soil erosion as a result of chemical changes caused by fertilizer overuse and acid rain; and, particularly threatening, waste management. Space for waste disposal grows ever scarcer, and thus its cost increases. In 1965, it cost 77 cents per ton to dispose of garbage in Toronto. Today it costs $59 per ton.[11] North American cities are seeking solutions. In Lansing, Michigan, a pay-by-the-bag system has been implemented in an effort to get residents to generate less trash. Recycling, a popular approach in the 1970s, is presently making a comeback. Nevertheless, we have not yet created sufficient incentives for most communities to tolerate landfills locally.

In this volume, Jurgen Schmandt and Lisa Chernin question what the effects of global warming will be in Canada and what impact this environmental change will have on the relationship between Canada and the United States. It is argued that global warming, with its resulting milder winters, will have a number of positive impacts on the Great Lakes region of Canada: a longer and hence more lucrative shipping season, reduced overall energy consumption, and a longer recreational season that may enhance revenues from tourism. Offsetting these benefits are the possibility of decreased water supplies and lowered hydroelectric generating capabilities and reduced overall production potential in the area's agricultural sector. In the Atlantic region, changes may include reduced supplies of potable water and a better environment for aquaculture—effects on "capture fisheries" are uncertain. In the West, part of the American breadbasket may move north to Canada—accompanied, however, by the threat of drier soils and more-frequent droughts.

Gregory Marchildon notes that since 1988, activity in the Canadian natural gas industry has accelerated, and much of it is concerned with the production and transportation of natural gas from the Canadian arctic to the United States. After years of low prices, sagging demand, as well as aboriginal, nationalist, and environmental objections to an arctic pipeline and export to the United States, large-scale energy development is going forward. The most important factor spurring this development will be Canadian and U.S. environmental legislation, both existing and proposed. In particular, U.S. utilities will be required to lessen their dependence on coal as a fuel source. As there are significant negative factors associated with alternative sources of energy, natural gas usage will increase more rapidly relative to oil, hydro, and nuclear power. While power generation using natural gas will lessen the threat of acid rain and global warming, gas drilling and pipeline development will have a negative impact on the fragile arctic ecosystem. In addition, the scale of the Mackenzie Delta mega-project will permanently alter the socioeconomic fabric of the aboriginal communities in the western Arctic. The success of the Inuvialuit in obtaining land claims settlements and the inability of the Dene and the Metis to do the same have divided the aboriginal peoples of the North on the desirability of this development, but both want to play an active role in minimizing its adverse environmental impact.

Fredric Menz acknowledges that unilateral actions by the United States and Canada are not sufficient to solve the environmental problems facing North America. Bilateral agreements are necessary. Why? 1) A common airshed may allow for more economically efficient reduction strategies. 2) Objectives of either country may change from initial agreements. 3) Further research linking emission with deposition may help in developing more cost-effective abatement measures. 4) As pollution patterns change, joint action will ensure that environmental objectives are met.

Joint action between the United States and Canada must include several elements: 1) agreement regarding the magnitude of transboundary pollution, 2) procedures to monitor deposition and emissions, 3) agreement on environmental objectives and policy instruments, and 4) procedures for resolving disputes. An effective bilateral agreement will protect individual property rights.

In order to develop effective pollution control policies, Canada and the United States must resolve a fundamental difference in their objectives. Canada's strategy aims to achieve a given level of acidic deposition in sensitive receptor areas. However, U.S. objectives emphasize atmospheric conditions, placing standards on emissions. In bilateral negotiations Canada could be expected to take the position that controls be based on environmental quality levels rather than on emission standards. Thus, Canada could better control its environmental quality. A policy based on emission controls would leave Canada at a disadvantage since it cannot control the level of emissions from the United States. Regardless of which standards are met, the objectives will ultimately depend on the costs and benefits of environmental action. Cost-effective policies will become increasingly attractive. Economists contend that a greater reliance on market-based solutions will provide more cost-effective policies, such as the credit system. The marginal costs of reducing pollution must be the same for all sources within a given airshed. Further cost savings could result if sources from both Canada and the United States could participate in transboundary trades of discharge reductions.

Alan Schwartz examines the rhetoric associated with three-quarters of a century of joint U.S.-Canadian management of the Great Lakes, and contrasts it with the actions that have resulted in improved lake quality. After a brief history of early pollution problems and the response mechanisms established by governments to deal with them, the discussion focuses on the pollution problems of the past two decades. The unique mechanism of binational management, the International Joint Commission, is examined to analyze its successes and failures in improving water quality. The progress and setbacks of recent years are contrasted with the problems that lie ahead to restore the Great Lakes system to a state where it will provide the myriad of beneficial uses that citizens of both countries desire.

In Chapter 5 Andrew Wyckoff examines the relationship between economic conditions and the use of energy. From 1972 to 1985, economic growth in the United States was sustained without an accompanying increase in energy levels used, but from 1986 to 1988 these two factors grew at the same rate. Wyckoff explains both of these trends.

The period from 1972 to 1985 was puzzling in the sense that the United States was able to maintain a significant rate of economic growth while using a constant level of energy. Just as the level of consumer spending increased during this time period due to U.S. economic growth, the mix of products purchased shifted from energy-intensive goods to less-intensive goods and services. Similarly, during this period, consumer spending increases (which imply higher levels of energy use) were offset by changing production patterns of suppliers from more energy-intensive inputs to less-intensive inputs. Furthermore, during this time, the United States made significant gains in energy efficiency, so holding all other variables constant, the United States required less energy to produce the same goods in 1985 than in 1972.

Wyckoff explains that the recent increase in energy use between 1986 to 1988 can be largely attributable to a structural shift in the U.S. economy back towards more energy-intensive industries such as steel and aluminum. This, in turn, is likely a result of the recent growth of exports and shrinking import levels.

Amy Abel and Larry Parker argue that the key element that will determine the future pattern of energy trade and types of energy traded between the United States and Canada is environmental policy. This chapter focuses on the electricity trade between the two countries, which currently faces such problems as insufficient transmission links and complicated regulations governing the establishment of such links. Legislation regarding the twin environmental concerns of acid rain and the greenhouse effect may alter the picture significantly. Acid rain legislation in both countries stands to encourage the development of sources that do not produce pollutants such as sulfur dioxide: these include natural gas-fired generators, nuclear plants, and hydroelectric plants, long the main source for Canadian electricity generation. In the United States, where more than half of total electricity generation is coal fired, plans to reduce sulfur dioxide emissions will result in higher electricity rates and likely increases in energy conservation. Such conservation may also be required to counter the greenhouse effect, and by reducing demand will lessen the need for new generating capacity and additional supply links between the United States and Canada. Natural gas exports from Canada to the United States may well increase; in addition, growing use of generating sources such as solar, hydro, and nuclear may result in additional capacity that could be traded.

Kendall Moll analyzes the two major policy options available for Canadian water resource development and export: water transfers and hydroelectricity. He documents the reasons that hydroelectric power exports will increase but water transfers to the United States will not. Electricity promises relative future investment advantages in the economic, technological, ecological, and political spheres.

Canadian environmental and national interest groups especially oppose water export, which they fear will affect the existing balances of natural vs. human habitats, and of domestic sufficiency vs. foreign interdependence. Many also oppose further hydro power development, although it poses less of a threat to alternate uses of water resources and wilderness areas in Canada. Nor is hydroelectric export likely to compromise sovereignty beyond the bounds either of historical practice of the Free Trade Agreement. Instead, it could provide new benefits to both countries under the agreement.

Barry Rabe maintains that one of the greatest problems concerning hazardous waste disposal is the NIMBY syndrome. While waste disposal sites offer widespread benefits to areas that generate such wastes, the costs incurred by such disposal sites are concentrated in a small area where the site is located. So no one wants the site located in his "backyard."

In both Canada and the United States, subnational governments dominate siting policies. However, the regulations are more centralized in the U.S. as standards imposed by the Resource Conservation And Recovery Act (RCRA) must also be met. There are two general categories of waste regulations: provincial (or state) agencies and market mechanisms. Both of these approaches have failed due to overwhelming public resistance to siting. However, one effort has succeeded in Canada under an innovative approach: the Alberta Special Waste Treatment Centre near Swan Hills. This approach emphasized cooperation between regulatory agencies, private companies, and the public.

First, Alberta established new institutions such as the Hazardous Waste Management Committee to study site proposals and potential benefits and provincial environmental agencies to set regulatory standards. Extensive public participation in the siting process was critical in easing the NIMBY syndrome by building public trust in the operations. The public was informed at all times of the site's potential dangers as well as its economic benefits. The siting decisions were all subject to public review and input. Compensation negotiations began at a very early stage offering many economic advantages to Swan Hill and securing public support. Also significant was that the policy officials were credible professionals, ensuring public trust.

Alberta's disposal site has proven very successful, but can it be copied in other areas of Canada and the United States? Manitoba and Minnesota have both tried to implement similar sites. Thus far, the Manitoba proposals have been successful. It followed Alberta's lead by establishing a crown corporation and encouraging volunteerism. On the other hand, the Minnesota siting proposals have hit many roadblocks, although Minnesota made many adjustments like Alberta, it must operate in the criteria of the national RCRA program, leaving site officials less bargaining room. Further, Minnesota's boards have been unable to harness the necessary level of public support. Although Minnesota's siting proposals have not been as successful as those in Alberta, it does not fully discredit Alberta's system, thus it must be experimented with in other states to determine its replicability.

Energy/environment issues are of vital importance to Canada, the United States, and to the world. The studies in this book will help to inform public policymakers, corporate and labor leaders, and interested citizens about the issue and to suggest alternative strategies. More concrete action is now imperative to prevent greater environmental and economic costs.

NOTES

1. The discussion in this section relies on Edward A. Carmichael, "Energy and the Canada-U.S. Free Trade Agreement," *Trade Monitor* (C.D. Howe Institute, May 1988), pp. 1-15; and "In Pursuit of Power," *The Economist*, October 28, 1989, pp. 25-26.

2. External Affairs Canada, "Canada/U.S. Environmental Issues," *Canada and the World*, September 1989, insert.

3. External Affairs Canada, "International Environmental Issues," *Canada and the World*, December 1988, insert.

4. Hal Quinn, "Trans-Border Pollution," *Maclean's*, July 3, 1989, pp. 44-45.

5. Gloria Hildebrandt, "Clearing the Air," *Canada and the World*, September 1989, supplement.

6. For a comprehensive discussion of these recommendations, see Chris C. Park, *Acid Rain: Rhetoric and Reality* (London: Methuen, 1987).

7. "Noxious Nox," *The Economist*, October 7, 1989, p. 29.

8. For a discussion, see John Eberlee, "The Problem is Blowing in the Wind," *Canada and the World*, December 1988, pp. 20-23.

9. "Rethinking the Greenhouse," *The Economist*, December 16, 1989, p. 15.

10. Michael Valpy, "Great Lakes Pollution as a Political Issue," *The Globe and Mail*, October 16, 1989; and "The Sea Fights Back, *Canada and the World*, December 1988, p. 17.

11. Angela Wheelock, "Of Trees and Trash," *Canada and the World*, December 1988, p. 15.

The Impacts of Climate Change on Canada

Jurgen Schmandt and Lisa Chernin

Canadians care about the environment. But they, as others, have often found it difficult to translate concern into action. One difficulty arises from the fact that the Canadian provinces retain principal responsibility for environmental policy. This makes it difficult for the federal government to take decisive action for the entire country. Because pollution does not respect political boundaries, action binding all or several provinces is often called for. From the 1960s on, pollution of the Great Lakes has ranked high on the environmental agenda of Canada. In this case, several provinces and two countries were directly involved. All Canadian provinces east of Ontario have a stake in the future of the Great Lakes, the world's largest body of sweet water. The same is true for the United States. Recognizing their common interest, Canada and the United States launched an ambitious and sustained international effort to clean up the Great Lakes. Two decades later, the initiative has grown into the largest international environmental program attempted anywhere in the world. Slow but steady progress was achieved. Water quality in the Great Lakes is improving. Compared to other efforts aimed at controlling pollution of international waterways, such as the Rhine or the Mediterranean, the U.S.-Canadian initiative has been more successful.[1]

In contrast, Canada and the United States are divided over the issue of transborder air pollution. This became an urgent Canadian concern in the 1970s. Initially, the causes, pathways, and effects of acid deposition were not well understood. Soon experts confirmed that sulfur dioxide, mostly from power generation, and nitrous oxides, mostly from transportation, cause acid deposition hundreds of miles downwind from the emitting sources. Both Canada and the United States contributed heavily to transborder air pollution. For many years, Canada was home to the single largest source of SO_2 emissions on the American continent. INCO's nickel smelters in Sudbury, Ontario severely damaged the ecosystem in its downwind path. Fortunately, impacts were limited to a small region. With time, the Sudbury problem became less of an irritant.

INCO scaled down its operations and emissions, partly in response to the decline of the world nickel market and partly because Canada imposed stricter pollution controls.

A much larger area is effected by industrial emissions from the U.S. Midwest. In this case, impacts are more dispersed and gradual. SO_2 and NO_x emitted from tall smokestacks in the Ohio Valley are transformed in the atmosphere and eventually come back to the surface in the form of acid deposition—rain, snow, or fog. Hundreds of miles separate emitting from receiving regions. The pollutants travel with prevailing summer winds on a northeasterly course from the Ohio Valley and reach large parts of eastern Canada, upstate New York State, and New England.

Once emission sources from south of the border had been identified as a cause of pollution in Canada, Ottawa asked Washington to curb its emissions. This can be done by switching to low-sulfur fuels or installing scrubbers. Both solutions are expensive, and the United States resisted taking either of these steps. From the end of the Carter administration throughout the Reagan presidency, the two countries were bitterly divided over the issue. At times, relations between the two neighbors deteriorated to the point that progress on other issues, such as the creation of a free trade zone uniting the two economies, was slowed down.

The confrontation was intense because Canada feared widespread damage to its lakes, streams, fisheries, forests, and buildings from activities across the border over which it had no control. When the U.S. government refused to act, Canada tried, by a variety of means, to influence public opinion south of the border, hoping to mobilize public support for new U.S. control measures. The United States, in exchange, complained about Canadian interference in domestic affairs and maintained that more needed to be known about acid deposition before expensive new control programs could be justified. No other bilateral issue has done more to undermine relations between the two neighbors. In recent years, Prime Minister Mulroney and President Bush have forsaken confrontation over acid rain. The two governments continue to give different weight to research findings about damage from acid deposition. Recently a massive ten-year research program by the U.S. government was completed. The basic findings are not disputed, yet both sides disagree on their ecological and economic significance. To this day, a bilateral solution to the problem of acid deposition has not been found. Under recently enacted revisions of the U.S. Clean Air Act, U.S. power plant emissions will have to be cut in half. Canada will benefit, but only indirectly. In a book written several years ago, we predicted that no bilateral agreement on acid rain would be reached until the United States had implemented domestic controls capable of bridging the deep differences between coal-producing midwestern and energy-dependent northeastern states.[2] This is exactly what happened.

The two cases, pollution of the Great Lakes and acid rain, suggest two patterns of bilateral environmental relations. The cases differ in one important respect. The Great Lakes issue was resolved through joint action. Both sides recognized that they contributed to the problem and needed to join forces in finding a solution. By contrast, the acid rain controversy cast one country in the role of villain while the other saw itself as the victim. Other environmental issues have divided Canada and the United States in recent times, among them fishing and drilling rights in the coastal zones, U.S. opposition to and Canadian support of the International Treaty of the Sea, and old disputes over jurisdiction over Arctic island waters and the Beaufort sea line.[3] No issue, however, has become as confrontational as the dispute over acid rain.

In this chapter we describe probable effects of global warming in Canada and ask how the expected changes may affect U.S.-Canadian relations. Given the many unanswered questions about global warming, it would be foolhardy to make detailed predictions. But it is possible to identify key issues and ask whether increased cooperation or confrontation are likely to result.

CANADA'S CLIMATE: PAST AND FUTURE

The Toronto weather station began keeping records in 1840. This reliable data set covering 150 years documents a climate that is "both harsh and unpredictable."[4] Temperatures are cold in winter and can be hot during the summer. Precipitation, on the other hand, is quite favorable, at least in those areas where most people live. In the Great Lakes region, where 8 million of the country's 27 million people live, it averages 816.4 mm a year and is evenly distributed throughout the year. "Rain and snow in the Great Lakes region are about as 'reliable' as one could find in a temperate continental climate."[5]

Past climate variability has been consistent with other regions in the northern hemisphere at similar latitudes. There have been colder and warmer periods even in the relatively recent past. As little as 250 years ago, average temperatures were about 1.2°C colder than today. Between A.D. 800 and 1300, milder temperatures reigned. During this 500-year mild phase the Gulf Stream shifted northward in the North Atlantic, Arctic pack ice retreated in the summer to north of 80°N, and the tree line in Canada was located 100 km farther north than today.[6]

What about the climate of the future? Our current understanding of global warming can be summarized as follows: There is agreement among scientists that human activities—burning of fossil fuels, rice growing cattle raising, deforestation, and use of industrially produced chlorofluorocarbons (CFCs) —cause increased concentrations of greenhouse gases in the atmosphere. As a result the climate will change worldwide. Increasing concentrations of greenhouse gases in the atmosphere have been measured for some 25 years. The data show a steady and rapid increase in carbon dioxide (now almost one-third more than in preindustrial times), methane, and CFCs—the three principal greenhouse gases.

These are the only changes in the atmosphere that have been measured so far. The rest is theory, but very strong theory. The greenhouse effect is a natural phenomenon that has shaped the Earth's climate for millions of years and accounts for the more moderate temperatures on Earth compared to other plants. Without the shield formed by greenhouse gases life as we know it would not exist. Thus, the concern with global warming is not with the greenhouse effect as such but with the probability that it will become more pronounced as a result of human activities. In addition, climatologists fear that the temperature will change faster than during past periods of climatic change.

Observed temperature data do not yet provide sufficient proof that global warming is actually occurring. Worldwide, average annual temperatures have risen 0.7°C during this century. We will not know for probably another decade whether this increase is due to regular climate variability or global warming. The same is true of recent reports by research groups from the United Kingdom and the United States that 1990 was the globe's warmest year since measurements began and that the ten warmest years since 1880 have all been experienced over the course of the last two decades.[7] At present, we can only say that these findings are consistent with the theory of global warming. It must also be noted that increases in temperature have not been measured everywhere. The 100-year increase mentioned above has not been observed on the North American continent. On the other hand, the high temperatures reported for 1990 were evident in most of the United States and southern Canada, as well as in Europe, western Siberia, and the Far East.

Compared to preindustrial times, CO_2 concentration in the atmosphere will have doubled sometime between 2030 and 2050. This assumes that energy use patterns remain similar to what they are today and population growth in the Third World continues at its current rapid pace. Because changes in energy use and population growth will be slow in coming, it is likely that "sometime in the next century, the surface of the earth will become warmer than it has been at any time in human history" (John Firor, NCAR). The International Panel on Climate Change (IPCC), in a comprehensive report on global warming issued recently, predicts that the global average temperature, under a business-as-usual assumption, will increase by 0.3°C per decade during the next century.[8] A 3°C increase in average temperatures in one century is large in absolute terms. More importantly, it will be unprecedented in terms of the speed with which it will occur. The IPCC also predicts that warming will not occur at a steady rate. This is due to the fact that other natural factors not related to global warming will continue to cause climatic variations. Because social systems find it difficult to cope with uneven change, the impact of climate change may be more severe than the numbers alone suggest.

Many areas of uncertainty remain. When exactly will we be sure that global warming is occurring? How much and how fast will temperature, windiness, and precipitation change? How long will it take for the oceans to warm and rise? Can an increase in cloud cover as a result of higher temperature and increased evaporation attenuate global warming? What policy measures are needed to stabilize the system? Can this be done at all, given continuing increases in world population and associated new demands for arable land and energy? Above all, how will the climate change in different regions?

The term *global warming* should not suggest that the climate will change uniformly. The climate of the future will be as varied as today's climate, with as much regional variation. Because people organize on a regional scale—villages, cities, provinces, nations—it is at these regional levels that the social and economic consequences of climate change will be felt and have to be coped with. Unfortunately, we know much less about regional than global climate change. This lack of knowledge will not easily be overcome. Our best tools for knowing about global climate change are general circulation models (GCMs), which simulate the movement of air masses and their interaction with the oceans. These models are highly complex. Even so, they must make many simplifying assumptions, and their spatial resolution is coarse. In the most detailed models a single grid point represents a square some 400 kilometers wide. In addition, existing models only agree with each other on increases in temperature when comparing seasonal or annual averages over large areas. Substantial disagreements become apparent as the spatial extent is reduced. Disagreements are even larger in the case of predicted changes in precipitation. Some models predict less, others more precipitation for particular areas and seasons. Grotch compared the most advanced GCMs. In order to evaluate their predictive qualities he asked how well they did in simulating current climate. He concluded that for surface air temperature and precipitation "the poor agreement between model simulations of the current climate on the regional scale calls into question the ability of these models to project the amplitude of future climatic change on anything approaching the scale of only a few gridpoints, which is essential if useful resource assessment studies are to be conducted."[9]

It is impossible, using GCM findings, to make precise predictions about the climate forty or fifty years from now in any particular region. This does not mean, however, that scenarios of future regional climates can not be constructed. Alternative methods are used for the purpose of assessing regional climates. One promising approach combines GCM predictions for large regions with historical climate data for smaller regions. Using the two sets of data, it becomes possible to identify direction and range of future regional climates. Glantz has shown the usefulness of this approach in a number of case studies that assess future climate by analogy with past experience.[10] Schlesinger uses nested simulations by linking observed data with GCM predictions.[11] Rosenberg and Crosson use the climate of the drought-prone 1930s to predict the future climate of a five-state region in the American Midwest.[12] All of these methods, by combining historical data with GCM results, make the assumption that the new climatic conditions can be superimposed on a region's historical climate. This requires special skill, but if done carefully results in reasonably accurate predictions. The reason is that future day-to-day climate variability is likely to remain relatively steady. If the assumption is correct, large-scale future climate change can be added to past or present day-to-day variability.[13]

What, specifically, can be said about the future climate of Canada? GCM-based generalizations for the northern hemisphere give a first indication of future trends. The largest increase in temperature is expected in high latitudes. Thus, Canada will see more pronounced warming than will the United States. By the same logic, the northern regions of Canada will experience higher temperature increases than areas close to the United States. Warming will also be more pronounced during winters than summers. Canada, along with northern Europe and the Soviet Union, can look forward to warmer winters. The frostline will move northwards by 150-250 miles. A warmer climate and longer growing season may increase Canada's importance as a breadbasket for the world. However, if soil moisture decreases and windiness increases at the same time, these changes may not translate into substantial benefits.

The second Villach Conference, convened in 1987 by the United Nations Environment Programme and the World Meteorological Organization, reached consensus on other likely effects of regional climate change. The southern parts of Canada, along with other regions located in the mid latitudes, may experience serious climatic stresses. Higher temperatures increase evapotranspiration. As a result, soil moisture will decrease. Summer rainfall may also decrease. Less water translates into problems for agriculture. Overall, agricultural gains and losses may even out in the mid latitudes. However, forests will adapt less well to the new environment. Tree mortality will increase. The rapid rate of climate change may overpower the natural migration capacity of forests. As a result, many forests will have to be replanted with species adapted to the new conditions. The cost will be high, and in many areas prohibitive.[14]

The northern parts of Canada, situated above 60°N, may experience winter warming two to two-and-a-half times greater than the globally averaged annual values. Cloudiness and precipitation will increase. Summer pack ice will withdraw. Permafrost will slowly disappear, resulting in increased releases of methane from the soil. Boreal soils will decay. New opportunities will open up for marine transportation, agriculture, and offshore drilling.[15]

Several Canadian authors have used these generalizations to describe expected climatic changes in Canada (Table 1.1).[16,17,18]

Using these generalizations Agnew has characterized the new Canadian climate.[19] As long as temperature alone is considered, climatic conditions will be more hospitable. But the new rainfall and storm patterns will be less benign. They are likely to increase the risk of droughts in southern Canada and of flooding in northern Canada. Given the country's huge size and diversity, Canada will not qualify entirely as either a winner or loser from climate change. A more precise look at Canada's most populated region provides additional insight.

Table 1.1

**Probable Climatic Conditions in Canada
as a Result of Global Warming**

- Winter temperatures will rise markedly.

- Soil moisture deficits during the growing season (May-September) will sharply increase.

- The extent and duration of snow and ice cover will decrease.

- More-frequent and severe droughts will occur.

Climate Scenarios for the Great Lakes Region

A number of studies have attempted to predict the future climate of the Great Lakes region. The key features of expected climatic changes are summarized in Table 1.2.

In constructing climate scenarios for the Great Lakes region most researchers used the General Circulation Model (GCM) developed by the Goddard Institute for Space Studies (GISS). Two studies also used the models developed by the Geophysical Fluid Dynamics Laboratory (GFDL).[20] Assuming that CO_2 levels are doubled compared to those of pre-industrial times, and using 10 GCM data points for the Great Lakes region, the GISS model projects that the average annual temperature in the Great Lakes will be about 4.5°C higher. Summer temperatures would be increased slightly less than 4.5°C, and winter temperatures slightly more. Annual precipitation would increase by about 8 percent in the central and western basin but be reduced by 3-6 percent in the eastern basin.[21] Evaporation would increase by 18.1 percent.[22] The GFDL model projects temperature increases of 3.1-3.7°C, precipitation increases of 0.8 percent, and evaporation increases of 6.7 percent.[23,24]

Evaporation is analyzed by Cohen. He presents several scenarios for evaporation showing the effects of increased or decreased wind speeds and vapor

---

Table 1.2

The Climate of Great Lakes Region
as a Result of Global Warming

• Summers will be warmer by 2°-5°C with a consequent increase
  of heat storage in the Great Lakes.

• The combined changes in monthly precipitation, evaporation,
  and runoff will lead to decreased water supply to the basins.

• Annual net basin supplies could fall to 15-25 percent below
  current mean values.

• This will lead to corresponding reductions in lake levels and
  water outflow.

---

pressure (humidity), and compares these effects with known data for wind and
vapor pressure collected by ships and land stations. In general, he finds that
scenarios using lower vapor pressure combined with current wind conditions, or
slightly decreased windiness, result in the greatest increases in evaporation.
Higher vapor pressure will reduce evaporation.[25]

Researchers at the Great Lakes Institute at the University of Windsor took
data from 1951 to 1980 and projected the impacts of the GISS scenario within
the Great Lakes Basin. They projected that January temperatures would rise
from the current -5°C average to 0°C in the south, and a 5°C rise would also
be seen in the north. Average January temperatures were projected to be above
0°C in much of the basin. Average July temperatures would rise to about 25°C
from a range of 15°C in the north to 21°C in the south.[26]

The same team projected that precipitation patterns would change, with
decreases of 6 percent in the southeast and increases up to 18 percent in the
northwest. Timing of precipitation would shift, with more precipitation in the
southeast in January but less in September.[27]

Impacts on Canada

Canada has been an active participant in climate research at both the national
and international levels. Climate variability and risks from drought, storms, and
floods as well as human activities were topics of concern before global warming

became a widely recognized research topic. Munn and Stewart, at the time both working for the Federal Department of the Environment, participated in the important international *Study of Man's Impact on Climate*, published in 1971. The study became one of the key documents considered at the World Environment Conference in Stockholm one year later. In 1978, the Canadian Climate Program was established. Since 1984 the Canadian Climate Change Impacts Program has conducted an important program of impact studies. Several areas have received priority attention as part of the program, among them climate change in the Arctic region, impacts on infrastructure and forestry, and policy options.[28] An important publication series, *Climate Change Digest*, is being issued under the aegis of Environment Canada (Federal Department of the Environment) and reports results of Canadian climate change studies. Environment Canada and the U.S. National Oceanographic and Atmospheric Administration are jointly sponsoring impact studies in the Great Lakes region.

The Canadian government has also been active in promoting international policy development for global warming. Among other activities, it hosted the important Toronto Conference in 1988 that proposed options for reducing CO_2 emissions.[29]

Given the size of the country, climate impact studies must cover a huge area spanning several climatic zone. In the United States, greenhouse warming will lead to different impacts and policy issues in California, Texas, or the Midwest. Similar diversity exists in Canada. The richest literature exists on the Great Lakes Region. Because the region also plays a dominant economic role, and the water resources are shared with the United States, we shall review these studies in detail and only summarize a few studies dealing with other parts of Canada.

THE GREAT LAKES REGION

The Great Lakes are the largest system of fresh water lakes in the world, containing about 23,000 km^3 of water, and accounting for 20 percent of the world's and 95 percent of the United States' fresh surface water. The entire system, from Duluth, Minn., to the Atlantic Ocean, spans 2,400 miles. An estimated 28 million people in the United States, and 8 million in Canada live in the Great Lakes Basin, which borders on eight U.S. states and one Canadian province. All Canadian provinces east of Ontario have a stake in the Great Lakes system. Major cities in the basin include Chicago, Detroit, Cleveland, and Toronto.

The location of the Great Lakes straddling Canada and the United States has given rise to several agencies in both countries that manage the resources of the lakes. The International Joint Commission (IJC), established by treaty in 1909, is the major binational agency that regulates discharges and diversions at

Lake Superior (including the outlet at Sault Ste. Marie), Chicago, and Lake Ontario (including the St. Lawrence Seaway). There are also locks at several locations for shipping. During the 1970s, the Great Lakes Water Quality Agreements were concluded, given the IJC new powers to deal with pollution of the Great Lakes.

The economic importance of the Great Lakes basin is well documented. On the U.S. side, the basin accounts for one-seventh of the U.S. population, one-sixth of U.S. national income, and over one-fifth of the manufacturing employees and capital expenditures. On the Canadian side, the basin accounts for one-third of Canada's population, one-third of national income, and more than one-half of the manufacturing employment and capital expenditures. U.S. shipping alone on the lakes has risen as high as 225 million tons in 1979, but fell to 148 million tons in 1985. Industries such as agriculture, steel, tourism/recreation, and electric utilities are largely dependent on the lakes for shipping, energy, and water requirements.

The Great Lakes region encompasses four or five gridpoints on the GDFL and GISS climate change models. Using results from the models as well as regional generalizations reviewed above, a large number of social and economic impacts have been studied, including water supply, shipping, energy, agriculture, and tourism/recreation/conservation.

Water Supply

Water supply in the Great Lakes is generally measured using "Net Basin Supply" (NBS), which is the sum of precipitation and runoff minus evaporation. Cohen defines NBS as precipitation minus evaporation plus runoff plus diversions (which may be positive or negative) minus consumptive use.[30]

There is agreement among published studies that NBS would be reduced as a result of climate change. Specific projections vary somewhat. The Great Lakes Institute team used the period 1900 to 1976 as the basis for comparison, and developed two additional scenarios: the GISS $2xCO_2$ scenario, and the GISS $2xCO_2$ scenario plus added demands of consumptive use calculated by the IJC for 2035. Comparing the base case with the third scenario, they found levels in Lake Superior reduced by 30 cm, in Michigan-Huron by 83 cm, in Erie by 68 cm, and in Ontario by 69 cm. Outflow from Superior was only reduced by a negligible amount, but outflow from Michigan-Huron was down 16.5 percent, outflow from Erie was down 20.88 percent, and outflow from Ontario was down 22.71 percent.[31] According to Cohen, overall NBS would be reduced 11.8 percent for the GISS plus consumptive use scenario.[32]

The scenario with climatic change plus consumptive use also showed that the percent of years of low lake levels (at or below 1963-65 means which are the lowest recent readings) would increase from 10 to 79 percent for Lake Superior, from 8 to 77 percent for Lake Michigan, and from 5 to 77 percent for Lake Erie.[33]

Quinn surveyed several estimates in NBS reduction made by other researchers, selected two scenarios, and applied a hydrologic model to determine the impacts on the individual lake levels. The first scenario was a 15 percent reduction in NBS, and the second a 30 percent reduction in NBS. The results for the 15 percent scenario were similar to those of the Great Lakes Institutes team. The 30 percent scenario resulted in reductions of 156 cm for Michigan-Huron, 125 cm for St. Clair, and 106 cm for Erie.[34]

Energy

A warmer climate will reduce demand for heating in winter months and increase demand for cooling in summer months. The generating capacity for hydroelectric power will decline as a result of lowered lake levels and outflows. The latter would result in added costs as other generation methods (nuclear and fossil fuel) are brought on line. The impacts of these changes vary. Studies for Canada and for New York State are described below.

The most detailed study of energy impacts was conducted by the Great Lakes Institute team led by Sanderson. Sanderson's research applies only to Canadian energy requirements (Ontario Hydro), and reports specific increases and reductions in hydroelectric generating capacity for the different plants. The changes were calculated by using the reductions in lake levels and outflows determined in the water supply portion of the study. The same three climate scenarios are used as for the water supply calculations.

Costs of adding new power sources were calculated by determining the present (1979) cost per gigawatt hour (GWh), and by applying that unit cost to the number of GWh lost as the result of the climatic change scenarios.

Costs or savings from demand were calculated by using projections of base demand from Ontario Hydro, and by creating a linear regression model of the relationship between electricity demand and temperature that was used to assess seasonal demand. The model showed that 92 percent of the variation in energy demand could be explained by temperature variations. Using this model and the Ontario Hydro projections, the team calculated the increases/decreases in energy demand of the $2xCO_2$ scenario, and showed that energy demand would be reduced because lessened winter heating requirements would far outweigh rising summer cooling demands. When annual savings from reduced demand were combined with costs of lost power generation, net annual savings were $61-92 million (1984 Can$).

Melo's study of the impact of climate change in Ontario on energy supply and demand showed similar results to Sanderson's. Melo assumed a 5°C warming during a six-month winter, and a 2.5°C warming during the summer.

The equations used by Melo to assess savings and costs were developed by Ontario Hydro, and take into account temperature averages, temperature variability, wind speed, average illumination, and dew point depression. He calculated that Ontario Hydro would save $120 million as a result of reduced winter heating and spend an additional $36 million as a result of increased summer cooling demand. A net annual savings of $84 million results from his analysis.[35]

Melo also briefly discussed other impacts of climate change such as a reduced load-carrying capacity of the system during the warmer summers and increased frequency of freezing rain storms in the winter resulting from temperatures around 0°C (higher than is now normal) which might damage the transmission system.[36]

Linder and Gibbs' study of the changes in energy demand in New York State resulting from climate change showed that in general, energy demand would increase because demand for summer cooling in the downstate region would outweigh reduced winter heating demand in the upstate regions. Their estimate of additional costs ranged from $48 to $241 million for 2015 (1985 U.S.$).[37]

Crissman examined the short and long-term impacts of reduced streamflow on hydroelectric power generation in New York State. He assumed that long-term levels in Lake Erie would be reduced by two feet over 25 years, lowering Niagara River flow to about 165,000 cfs from about 208,000 cfs. By developing a relationship between the avoided costs of replacing hydropower and the impact on hydro generation resulting from reduced streamflow, Crissman estimated that short-term annual costs (1988-2004) would be $55 million (1988 U.S.$), and that long-term annual costs would be about $160 million.[38] He also indicated that more capacity may be needed sooner than is now projected by the New York Power Authority.[39] Crissman's scenarios assumed that increased summer demand would cancel out reduced winter demand, and he did not take into account the costs of adding generating capacity to meet peak demands.

Shipping

There are two major climate-related factors influencing changes in transportation on the Great Lakes: temperature and water level. Warmer temperatures projected by the GISS model and used by Sanderson in her analysis would result in reductions in ice cover on the lakes and a much longer shipping season, up to 11 months from the present 8.5 months.[40] The level of water in the lakes influences how much the lake carriers can carry; carrying capacity can be significantly reduced by a lowering of even one inch in the water level. This is because some of the shipping locks and channels in the Great Lakes are only

27 feet deep, and these are the constraining locations for carriers plying the Lakes.[41]

Sanderson used a model created by the IJC's Lake Erie Regulation (ILER) Study Board. The model takes as input existing water levels and calculates the amount of available draft, the amount of tonnage that can be carried, the number of trips that can be made, and the costs by commodity. The four major commodities—iron ore, grain, coal, and limestone—account for 85 percent of Great Lakes shipping. Other commodities are not considered in the model. The most extreme case examined by Sanderson assumed $2xCO_2$, increased consumptive use of water, an eleven month shipping season, and a 22 percent increase in coal tonnage resulting from lowered hydro-electric capacity. Results from this scenario (compared to the base case) showed that average annual shipping costs would increase 30 percent and that costs equal to or greater than those experienced during 1963-1965 (when the lowest water levels in recent times were recorded) would rise in frequency from 10 percent to 97 percent.[42]

Raoul and Goodwin acknowledge that the danger to shipping interests in the Great Lakes lies in lower lake levels. These levels would occur, they say, if the region experiences a warmer and drier climate. Although the GISS model projects a warmer and mostly wetter climate, most researchers using GISS predictions believe that lake levels will still be reduced because the increase in precipitation will not balance the increase in evaporation and the decrease in runoff. Raoul and Goodwin state that a 2°C warming with 10 percent less precipitation would result in a 33 percent reduction in mean annual runoff, but they do not explain the method of their reasoning. Raoul and Goodwin quantify loss of carrying capacities of different sizes of vessel when lake levels are reduced up to one foot, and describe in non-quantitative terms the impacts of a two-foot decline in lake levels.[43]

The losses described by Raoul and Goodwin in carrying capacities are similar to those described by Laidlaw and Ryan, who represent major lake carrier trade associations in Canada and the United States.[44] For example, Raoul and Goodwin show that a 60,000 ton vessel loses 630 tons of capacity from a three-inch loss in draft. Ryan shows that a 69,664 ton vessel loses 267 tons per inch of lost draft. Neither of them explains how these figures were derived.[45,46]

Agriculture

This section reports results from two studies of the impacts of climate change on agriculture in Ontario, and two brief summaries of other studies on the fruit belt in Michigan, and on corn and soybean production in the Great Lakes. The Ontario study was conducted by a team at the University of Guelph led by Smit. Smit first examined the impact by region of two climate change scenarios on the agro-climate, crop yields, crop production and values, and land resources for the eight major crops now being grown in Ontario—grain corn, winter wheat, soybeans, oats, barley, fodder corn, oilseeds, and potatoes. Second, using a single climate scenario he assessed impacts at the farm, regional, and provincial level, including opportunities for new crops. The second phase differs from the first in that it takes into account the direct impacts of increased CO_2 in the atmosphere, as well as the impacts of climate variability.[47] The study assumed that the patterns of agriculture and economic and irrigation scenarios present in the base case would remain constant, so that climate change was the only variable in assessing impacts. Timmerman has criticized this "everything else will remain equal" research approach because it underestimated the resourcefulness of social responses to changed conditions.[48]

The first phase of Smit's study used climate scenarios based on the GFDL model (Scenario A) and GISS (Scenario B) model outputs. The six regions of Ontario (northern, eastern, central, south central, western, and southwestern) experience temperature increases under both scenarios, and region by region the increases are fairly similar. Precipitation and potential evapotranspiration increase more under Scenario B than under Scenario A, with evapotranspiration offsetting or more than offsetting the gains in precipitation. The growing season lengthens under both scenarios.[49]

In general, under both scenarios, lands with what Smit calls "large moisture reserves" would fare better than areas with less resistance to moisture stress. Yields would increase, generally, in the northern parts of the province and decrease towards the southern and southwestern parts of the province (where the "breadbasket" is now located). Smit calculated that annual production losses under Scenario A would be valued at $170 million, and under Scenario B would be valued at $101 million.[50] In examining land resources, the study found that grain corn, winter wheat, soybeans, and oats would be negatively affected, that barley production would remain mostly unchanged, and that fodder corn would have the most economic potential.[51]

In phase two of his study, Smit used only Scenario B (GISS), and added the effects of climate variability to his model by using monthly precipitation variability recorded from 1951 to 1981. For a "typical" cash grain farm in southwestern Ontario, Smit found that increased profits would be possible but only if the farm relied more upon a single crop, grain corn, which would increase risks substantially. Risks due to precipitation fluctuations would also be increased, but the study does not explain clearly why this would occur. The results for field crops at the regional level were similar to those in phase one, but new production opportunities would be realized for crops such as sweet corn, apples, and grapes, particularly in the southern and western parts of the province.

The overall impact of climate change at the provincial level, according to Smit, would mean increased risk particularly in years with low precipitation. Overall production potential would decline, and patterns of agriculture could shift. While some production losses might be made up in years of higher precipitation, the food supply in Ontario would be at greater risk as a result of climate change.[52]

Strommen summarized research showing positive impact of climate change on fruit production in Michigan, in particular because of the lake effect on weather patterns in the region. The lakes affect the temperature, the distribution, and severity of snow storms, and the distribution of soil moisture as a result of winter storms. He does not quantify the potential effects of climate change on the "fruit belt" but simply states that climate change could have significant impacts on agriculture because of the crop sensitivity to climate.[53]

Ritchie summarizes a study of the effects of climate change on corn and soybean production in the Great Lakes region. The study used both the GFDL and the GISS climate models as inputs. The results are generally the same as those of Smit's: decreases in yields under both scenarios (which took into account temperature and rainfall changes, but not the direct effects of increased CO_2), with more significant effects under the GFDL scenario. The study also examined the direct effects of increased CO_2 without the associated weather effects and found that the direct effects sometimes offset the decreased yields resulting from changes in the weather.[54]

Ecology

A group of researchers from the University of Alberta and the Canadian Department of Fisheries and Oceans have monitored conditions in small lakes in northwestern Ontario over the past 20 years. During this period the region has warmed by 2°C, probably for reasons other than global warming. The observed results may illustrate what will happen more generally as a result of global warming.[55]

Other climatic changes observed in the study region include a slight decline in precipitation and a dramatic increase in evapotranspiration, leading to a general drying of the watershed. Fires have become more frequent. Windiness has increased because large areas of forest have been denuded by forest fires. Forests have lost the ability to renew themselves. Ice on the lakes melts several weeks earlier in the springtime than it did at the beginning of the project. Reduced water runoff has lengthened the water replacement rate of lakes from six to 20 years. Under these conditions, higher concentrations of chemicals and deeper temperature stratification have been found. Both changes are stressful for the ecosystem of lakes. The lake chemistry is changed and will no longer support the wide variety of aquatic fauna of the past. Trout, one of the world's most desirable fish, have been extinguished. A possible reason is that the cool water strata in the lake have been compressed or entirely eliminated. Trout seek shelter in these waters to escape the summer heat. Bass, which needs to be stocked, will become the fishery of choice under these conditions.

Tourism/Recreation/Conservation

A team from the University of Waterloo studied the impact of climate change on tourism in Ontario. The results have been published by Wall. The team used the same climate scenarios as Smit (Scenario A = GFDL, and Scenario B = GISS). He assumed a warmer climate overall, with some increased precipitation offset by increased evaporation, resulting in reduced lake levels. Two wetlands near Lake Ontario, downhill skiing at two Ontario resorts, and camping at several provincial parks were selected as representative of the areas that might be affected by climate change. As did Smit, Wall's analysis held all other factors constant so that technological or social changes did not modify the impacts described in the study.

The impacts on the two wetlands areas examined by Wall were severe in one case and moderate in the other. The Point Pelee National Park has a marsh protected from the lake by beaches. Wall projected that the marsh would eventually disappear, resulting in possible disappearance of the plants and animals that now occupy the marsh during different seasons. Activities associated with the marsh such as fishing and hunting would also be reduced. The marsh in the Presqu'ile Provincial Park would not be as severely affected because it is open to the lake. Lower lake levels would probably result in a migration of vegetation toward the lake edge and a possible movement of the marsh outward from its present position.[56]

Wall selected the South Georgian Bay ski area in southern Ontario and the Lakehead ski area in northern Ontario for analysis. He states that the two areas account for a major portion of ski activity in the province but provides no supporting evidence. Base cases were developed for current snow conditions and ski expenditures, and then the two climate scenarios applied to determine impacts on the length of the ski season and resulting economic consequences. Wall used a technique developed by Crowe (cited by Wall several times) that created "temperature satisfaction criteria" on which to base the analysis of the ski and camping seasons.[57]

The southern ski area would be severely impacted under both climate scenarios, with loss of any reliable ski season. $36.55 million in skier spending per year would be lost, along with $12.8 million per year in trade at nearby Collingwood. Under Scenario A, the northern ski area at Lakehead would experience a 34.5 percent shorter reliable ski season and a 30.5 percent shorter marginal ski season. Impacts under Scenario B were even more severe. Economic losses were calculated under Scenario A to total $1.9 million annually. Wall suggested that the Lakehead resorts could diversify their activities as a response to climate change, and that they might be able to offset some losses by garnering some of the customers who were using ski areas in the south.[58]

Eight provincial parks were examined by Wall to determine impacts of climate change on camping, one of the major summer activities. Again, an analysis was done to develop a base case and to determine the appropriate temperatures for a reliable and marginally reliable camping season. Under both scenarios, all parks in the province would experience a longer reliable camping season and increased camper revenues, ranging from 9 to 31 percent under Scenario A and from 28 to 44 percent under Scenario B. A detailed description is included of how camper expenditures were obtained and analyzed. Wall recognized that the advantages of the longer camping season may be offset by increased environmental damage. He suggested that resources would have to be carefully managed to deal with this problem.[59]

Magnuson summarized a study conducted for U.S. EPA by the Center for Limnology at the University of Wisconsin-Madison, which examined the impacts of the $2xCO_2$ scenarios generated by the OSU (Oregon State University), GFDL, and GISS models, on fish that live in warm, cool, and cold waters of the Great Lakes. The study found positive impacts including increased habitat and body growth for warm, cool and coldwater fishes, and increased productivity of producers such as zooplankton. Negative effects included increased species interactions, decreased spawning areas, and increases in "exotic biota" that live in warmer waters. Policy impacts of these changes included larger recreational and commercial fisheries resulting from increased fish production, continued emphasis on lowering toxic and nutrient pollution in the lakes, and increased management of the food chain.[60]

Policy Issues

Surprisingly few policy issues were raised by the Great Lakes studies, and most that were raised (such as Smit on irrigation relating to agriculture and resulting water policy issues, Wall on resource management in parks, and Magnuson on fish resources) were simply mentioned, not discussed in detail. Below are some other specific issues mentioned.

One far-reaching policy issue raised was the need to reexamine the management plans for Lake Ontario and Lake Superior. Hare and Cohen urged that planning be undertaken now to allow for a possible reduction of net basin supply in the next few decades in the range of 15 to 25 percent of present-day values. Such reduction will have significant and largely negative results for the human economy.[61] Sanderson explained that if the current regulation plan for Lake Ontario was applied to the GISS climate change scenario, drastic drops would be experienced in the level of Lake Ontario, similar to those in the

1960s.[62] Other researchers also recognized this problem. Quinn suggested that regulation plans might have to be considered for the other lakes as well because of climate change. Quinn also shows how the policy thrust of the last few years in the Great Lakes, that is, lowering water levels, will shift to conserving water under the lower water regimes projected by climate change studies.[63]

Stakhiv and Hanchey suggest that some methods of evaluating water projects in economic terms at the policy level should be reexamined because the short time frame considered for the benefits of the projects does not take into account future changes such as climate change.[64]

Timmerman suggests strongly that we make use of what he calls "backcasting," that is, deciding how we want our future to look in 50 or 70 years, for instance and then determining what policies will get us there.[65] Timmerman also suggests that one of the most pressing policy issues relating to climate change is immigration policy.[66]

Changnon states that we need to reconsider the institutional relationships between Canada and the United States with regard to the Great Lakes, to cope with the policy changes resulting from climate change.[67] New approaches to policy making will also be needed, he argues. Institutional changes are also suggested by Totten. Botts argues that policymakers cannot afford to wait to be certain of the impacts of climate change: rather, that adaptation should be the goal of policymakers and researchers alike.[68]

Cohen describes some compensatory and substitutional strategies to mitigate the impacts of climate change. Some of these include techniques that would involve policy changes such as lake regulation, shorter forest resource rotation, reforestation, and conservation.[69] Policy changes could also influence research into technological "fixes" for the energy and water industries.

We conclude the review of published studies with a more cursory treatment of other regions in Canada.

The Atlantic Region

The most affected sectors of the economy include fisheries, marine transportation, energy development, coastal infrastructure, and tourism/ recreation. Stokoe and his team have studied expected impacts for several years. They focused in particular on small communities. The region counts more than 1,300 coastal communities with fewer than 10,000 people. Taken together, they account for a quarter of the 2 million people living in the region.[70] The study findings can be summarized as follows:

Coastal infrastructure

The coastline is vulnerable and long-term planning is needed to cope with climate-change induced change. Committees of engineers and planners should propose amendments to existing engineering standards and building codes as well as to the zoning and building permit process to ensure that sea-level rise is duly taken into account in new construction.

Freshwater supply

A combination of several factors—reduced precipitation, increased evaporation, and a lower water table—may lead to reduced supplies of potable water. Increased attention is needed to manage existing resources and protect them from contamination.

Capture fisheries

It is possible that economically important species will migrate north. On the other hand, there may be more abundance of fish in Canadian waters. Predictions are difficult to make due to the inability of existing GCMs to take into account the interaction between oceans and climate and to predict migration of maritime currents.

Aquaculture

Managed fisheries are likely to benefit. Onshore facilities will need less energy due to higher water temperatures. The danger of fish dying during the cold season will be lessened. Fish will grow faster, and more suitable locations for aquaculture will become available. One possible risk results from an increase in algae populations and bacterial outbreaks as the water temperature rises. This may make mollusks unsuitable for human consumption.

Tourism and recreation

A longer season with pleasant temperatures will extend the vacation season.

Impacts on Agriculture

It is often said that Canada's agriculture would gain from climate change. The GCMs suggest a northward shift in the world's grain belt of several hundred kilometers per °C increase in temperature.[71] A longer growing season will expand the limits of northern agriculture, and part of the American wheat-maize-soybean breadbasket may move north into Canada. Given the right soils and sufficient water, Canada's capacity to raise these crops would increase.

These are important qualifications. In the mid-latitudes, soils may become drier and droughts more frequent. Storm tracks will shift northward, and water supplies in southern Canada will decline significantly. The combined effects of less precipitation during the summer months and increased evaporation due to warming will make the grain-producing areas in the southern prairies particularly vulnerable. The droughts of 1986-87 and 1987-88 have demonstrated the vulnerability of the region to drought.[72]

Parry's study of agriculture in Saskatchewan, using different climate scenarios, also points to the risk of decreased moisture.[73] In a report to the Second World Climate Conference, Parry concludes that "increases in productive potential at higher latitudes are not likely to open up large new areas for production."[74] The potential for increased irrigated agriculture is limited. This might change if large new water projects are built. Major projects were planned in the 1960s, such as the North American Water and Power Alliance. It would have diverted surface water from Alaska to regions east of the Rocky Mountains, with a major diversion to the Midwest. Canada objected to the project. Another plan was to impound James Bay, generating twice the freshwater flow of the Great Lakes.[75] Other large water projects elsewhere in the world have led to many negative surprises, and the time of megaprojects of this type may well have passed. The cost would also be prohibitive. Moll and Rosenbrook estimate that long-distance irrigation water would cost $300 per acre-foot, at least 30 times more than the United States charges farmers today.[76]

On the prairies, farming is now being practiced near both the cold and dry margins. During the 1950s and 1960s there was concern that a decrease in temperature or rainfall would imperil prairie agriculture. Now the combination of increased temperature and reduced soil moisture is seen as a threat. But not all feel that this is the case. F. Kenneth Hare concludes that agriculture, under existing and future condition in Canada, is adaptable and less threatened than Canadian forests. "I am unimpressed when farmers are said to face ruin from changes that will give them a climate like that of eastern Nebraska . . . . Farming's deadliest current enemy is not climate . . . ."[77]

Relations with the United States

Climate change can have several impacts on relations with the United States. With higher temperatures, the United States will need more energy. Canada can produce clean energy from hydropower. Even now, the Canadian energy industry accounts for seven percent of GNP and 10 percent of exports. Technically the energy distribution systems of the two countries are highly integrated. Canada is concerned about access to the American market because its internal market is too small to develop fully its energy potential. Traditionally, the United States has been concerned not to become too dependent on foreign energy sources. With the realization of the Canada-United States free trade zone this attitude may change. Because hydropower is environmentally clean, it may become increasingly more attractive as fossil fuel-based power becomes penalized due to its roles in causing global warming and acid rain. At the same time, reduced water supply as a result of global warming may curtail Canada's energy reserves and drive up the price of electricity.

Both countries will suffer from reduced Great Lake levels. It is quite possible that they would act in concert, as they did in the case of pollution of the Great Lakes, to cope with this threat. Changes in management of the Great Lakes may hold short-term answers. Water projects designed to divert large water flows to the Great Lakes may be considered in the longer term. Such projects will be expensive and may cause environmental harm. They will certainly be highly controversial. But controversy may not be organized along national lines. Rather, environmental and economic (cost) concerns may oppose shipping and utility interests. The pro and con forces may seek allies on either side of the border.

The outlook for agriculture and forests is uncertain. On the one hand, the initial assumption may be wrong that warmer climates will lead to a stronger agricultural position for Canada. There is too much regional diversity, and the benefits of a warmer climate and longer growing season may be offset by reduced productivity as a result of reduced soil moisture. At the same time, U.S. agriculture may not be as threatened as the image of the northward move of the wheat belt may suggest. The most detailed study undertaken so far of agricultural impacts in five midwestern states comes to these results: there will be some problems because water will become less abundant. But there are several counterbalancing forces, such as the fertilizing properties of atmospheric CO_2 as well as the likelihood of development of crops adjusted to new climatic conditions.[78] Damage to forests may be extensive on both sides of the border. Natural forests would be replaced by managed forests in many location, leading to sharply increased costs.

The real controversy between the two countries may result from different views of global warming and the appropriate policy measures that need to be taken. Canada, so far, is on the side of the "progressive" countries that argue for timely action in curbing greenhouse gas emissions. Canada, along with several European countries, has committed itself to stabilize and then reduce its CO_2 emissions. The United States takes a position similar to the one it took in the acid rain case: more research needs to be done. The time for policy intervention, for example, in the form of a carbon-based tax on fuels, has not yet come. As global warming becomes an ever more central policy concern, fundamental disagreements concerning the appropriate policy response may divide Canada and the United States, as they did in the acid rain controversy.

NOTES

1.   Kenneth F. Hare and Stewart J. Cohen, "Climatic Sensitivity of the Great Lakes System," *Impacts of Climate Change on the Great Lakes Basin*, National Climate Program Office/NOAA and Canadian Climate Centre, 1989, pp. 49-60.

2.   Jurgen Schmandt, Hilliard Roderick, and Judith Clarkson, eds., *Acid Rain and Friendly Neighbors: The Policy Dispute Between Canada and the United States*, revised edition (Durham, N.C.: Duke University Press, 1988).

3.   Annette Baker Fox, "Environmental Issues: Canada and the United States," in The Atlantic Council Working Group on the United States and Canada, *Canada and the United States: Dependence and Divergence* (Lanham, Md.: University Press of America, 1986).

4.   Kenneth F. Hare, "Vulnerability to Climate," in Alberta Research Council, *The Impact of Climate Variability and Change on the Canadian Prairies*, Workshop Proceedings, Alberta, 1987.

5.   D. W. Phillips, "Climate Change in the Great Lakes Region," in *Impacts of Climate Change on the Great Lakes Basin*, National Climate Program Office/NOAA and Canadian Climate Centre, January 1989, pp. 19-42.

6.   Ibid.

7.   "2 Studies Rank 1990 as Globe's Warmest Year," *New York Times* January 10, 1991, pp. A1 and C19.

8.   International Panel on Climate Change, *Climate Change: The IPCC Scientific Assessment*, J. T. Houghton, C. J. Jenkins and J. J. Ephraums, eds. (New York: Cambridge University Press, 1990).

9.   Stanley L. Grotch, "Regional Intercomparisons of General Circulation Model Predictions and Historic Climate Data," Report DOE/NBB-0084, (Livermore, Ca.: Lawrence Livermore National Laboratory, 1988).

10. Michael H. Glantz, ed. *Societal Responses to Regional Climatic Change: Forecasting by Analogy*, (Boulder, Co.: Westview Press, 1988).

11. Michael Schlesinger, "Likely Climate Changes in the Western Hemisphere," paper presented at the Annual Meeting of the American Association for the Advancement of Science, New Orleans, 1990.

12. Norman J. Rosenberg and Pierre R. Crosson, "A Methodology for Assessing Regional Economic Impacts of and Responses to Climate Change—The Mink Study," (Washington, D.C.: Resources for the Future, 1990).

13. Michael C. MacCracken, "Scenarios for Future Climate Change: Results of GCM Simulations," in *Impacts of Climate Change on the Great Lakes Basin*, National Climate Program Office/NOAA and Canadian Climate Centre, 1989, pp. 43-48.

14. World Meteorological Organization, *Developing Policies for Responding to Climatic Change*, a Summary of Discussions and Recommendations of the Workshops Held in Villach and Bellagio, WMO/TD-No. 225, 1988.

15. Ibid.

16. H. L. Ferguson, Luncheon Address, in *Report of the First U.S.-Canada Symposium on Impacts of Climate Change on the Great Lakes Basin*, U.S. National Climate Program Office/NOAA and Canadian Climate Centre, 1989.

17. Kenneth F. Hare and Stewart J. Cohen, op. cit.

18. Michael C. MacCracken, op. cit.

19. Tom Agnew, "Canada," *EPA Journal*, (January/February 1989).

20. Barry Smit, "Implications of Climatic Change for Agriculture in Ontario," *Climate Change Digest*, Environment Canada And Canadian Climate Institute, (April 1987).

21. Marie Sanderson, "Implications of Climatic Change for Navigation and Power Generation in the Great Lakes," *Climate Change Digest*, Environment Canada and Canadian Climate Institute, (September 1987), p. 2.

22. Stewart J. Cohen, "The Effects of Climate Change on the Great Lakes," *Effects of Changes in Stratospheric Ozone and Global Climate*, 3 (October 1986), United Nations Environment Programme and United States Environmental Protection Agency, p. 168.

23. Stewart J. Cohen, "Influences of Past and Future Climates On The Great Lakes Region of North America," *Water International*, 12 (1987), p. 167.

24. Stewart Cohen, "The Effects of Climate Change on the Great Lakes," op. cit.

25. Ibid., pp. 163-183.

26. Marie Sanderson, op. cit., p. 2.

27. Ibid.

28. Tim J. Marta, "Societal Implications of Climate Change: A Review of the Canadian Perspective," *The Operational Geographer*, 7, no. 1 (March 1989), pp. 8-12.

29. Toronto Conference Report, *The Changing Atmosphere: Implications for Global Security*, June 1988.

30. Stewart J. Cohen, "Influences of Past and Future Climates on the Great Lakes Region of North America," op. cit., p. 164.

31. Marie Sanderson, op. cit., Table 1, pp. 2-3.

32. Stewart J. Cohen, "The Effects of Climate Change on the Great Lakes," op. cit., p. 168.

33. Marie Sanderson, op. cit., Table 2, p. 12.

34. Frank H. Quinn, "Likely Effects of Climate Changes on Water Levels in the Great Lakes," in *Preparing for Climate Change: A Cooperative Approach*, conference proceedings, Government Institutes, Inc., 1988, pp. 483-485.

35. O. T. Melo, "Electricity Supply and Demand in Ontario," in *Impacts of Climate Change on the Great Lakes Basin,* National Climate Program Office/NOAA and Canadian Climate Centre, 1989, pp. 140-141.

36. Melo, op. cit., p. 141.

37. Kenneth P. Linder and Michael J. Gibbs, "The Potential Impacts of Climate Change on Electric Utilities: Project Summary," *Preparing for Climate Change: A Cooperative Approach,* conference proceedings, Government Institutes, Inc., 1988, pp. 287-289.

38. Randy D. Crissman, "Impacts on Electricity Generation in New York State," *Impacts of Climate Change on the Great Lakes Basin,* National Climate Program Office/NOAA and Canadian Climate Centre, January 1989, pp. 115.

39. Ibid., p. 117.

40. Marie Sanderson, op. cit., p. 4.

41. Joseph Raoul and Zane M. Goodwin, "Climatic Changes—Impacts on Great Lakes Levels and Navigation," in *Preparing for Climate Change: A Cooperative Approach,* conference proceedings, Government Institutes, Inc., 1988, pp. 493.

42. Marie Sanderson, op. cit., pp. 4-6.

43. Raoul and Goodwin, op. cit., pp. 496-498.

44. Angus Laidlaw, "Noted on Climate Impacts on Transportation," in *Impacts of Climate Change on the Great Lakes Basin,* National Climate Program Office/NOAA and Canadian Climate Centre, 1989, pp. 119-121.

45. Ibid., p. 497-498.

46. George J. Ryan, "Impacts on Great Lakes Shipping," in *Impacts of Climate Change on the Great Lakes Basin,* National Climate Program Office/NOAA and Canadian Climate Centre, 1989, p. 123.

47. Barry Smit, op. cit., p. 1.

48. Peter Timmerman, "Everything Else Will Not Remain Equal: The Challenge of Social Research in the Face of a Global Climate Warming," in *Impacts of Climate Change on the Great Lakes Basin,* National Climate Program Office/NOAA and Canadian Climate Centre, 1989, p. 62.

49. Smit, op. cit., pp. 4-6.

50. Ibid., pp. 4, 7.

51. Ibid., pp. 7-10.

52. Ibid., pp. 11-18.

53. Norton D. Strommen, "Climate and Agriculture: Case of the Fruit Belt in Lower Michigan," in *Impacts of Climate Change on the Great Lakes Basin,* National Climate Program Office/NOAA and Canadian Climate Centre, 1989, pp. 194-195.

54. Joe T. Ritchie, "Summary: Effects on Corn and Soybean Production," in *Impacts of Climate Change on the Great Lakes Basin,* National Climate Program Office/NOAA and Canadian Climate Centre, 1986, p. 196.

55. David W. Schindler et al., "Effects of Climatic Warming on Lakes of the Central Boreal Forest," *Science* 16 (November 1990), pp. 967-970.

56. Geoffrey Wall, "Implications of Climatic Change for Tourism and Recreation in Ontario," in *Climate Change Digest*, (May 1988), Environment Canada and Canadian Climate Institute, pp. 2-5.

57. Ibid., p. 10.

58. Ibid., pp. 5-10.

59. Ibid., pp. 10-15.

60. J. J. Magnuson, "Potential Effects on Great Lakes Fishes," in *Impacts of Climate Change on the Great Lakes Basin*, National Climate Program Office/NOAA and Canadian Climate Centre, 1989, pp. 43-48.

61. Kenneth F. Hare and Stewart J. Cohen, op. cit.

62. Marie Sanderson, op. cit., pp. 3-4.

63. Frank H. Quinn, op. cit., p. 486.

64. Eugene Z. Stakhiv and James R. Hanchey, "Policy Implications of Climate Change," in *Impacts of Climate Change on the Great Lakes Basin*, National Climate Program Office/NOAA and Canadian Climate Centre, 1989, pp. 162-173.

65. Peter Timmerman, op. cit., p. 74.

66. Ibid., p. 69.

67. Stanley A. Changnon, "Climate Change and Hydrologic and Atmospheric Issues: Lessons of the Past," in *Impacts of Climate Change on the Great Lakes Basin*, National Climate Program Office/NOAA and the Canadian Climate Centre, 1989, p. 84

68. Donald Totten, Elizabeth Dowdeswell and Lee Botts, panelists, "Potential Economic and Political Problems of Climate Change," in *Impacts of Climate Change on the Great Lakes Basin*, National Climate Program Office/NOAA and Canadian Climate Centre, 1989, pp. 87-97.

69. Stewart J. Cohen, "The Effects of Climate Change on the Great Lakes," p. 181.

70. Peter Stokoe, "Implications of Climate Change for Small Coastal Communities in Atlantic Canada," *Climate Change Digest*, 1990.

71. Pierre Crosson, "Climate Change and Mid-Latitudes Agriculture: Perspectives on Consequences and Policy Responses," *Climatic Change*, 15 (1989), p. 64.

72. Tom Agnew, op. cit.

73. Martil L. Parry, T. R. Carter, N. T. Konijn (eds.) et al., "Estimating Effects of Climatic Change on Agriculture in Saskatchewan, Canada," *The Impact of Climatic Variations of Agriculture,* 1 (Dordrecht and Boston: Kluwer, 1990).

74. Martin L. Parry, "The Impact of Climatic Changes on Agriculture," paper presented to the Second World Climate Conference, Geneva, October 29-November 3, 1990.

75. K. Moll and N. Rosenbrook, "Will Free Trade Release a Flood of Canadian Water?" *Canada-U.S. Outlook*, 1, no. 3/4 (April 1990), pp. 47-59.

76. Ibid., p. 57.

77. Hare, op. cit.

78. Rosenberg and Crosson, op. cit.

2

Acid Rain and Global Warming: The Impact of Environmental Protection on Canadian Arctic Gas Development

Gregory P. Marchildon

INTRODUCTION: GAS ON THE ARCTIC HORIZON

After a decade of inactivity due to sagging demand, low prices, popular objections to northern pipeline construction, and nationalistic pressures against exporting energy to the United States, it appears that Canadian arctic gas production—and the construction of pipelines to reach lucrative southern markets—is imminent. Gas producers are gambling that the time is right to begin drilling into the huge natural gas reserves that lie underneath the permafrost and the Arctic Ocean.

The principal stimulus for this renewed activity is an increase in demand for natural gas in the United States. After years of surplus supply, the United States now faces a permanent shortfall between domestic gas production and consumption. Supplying 98 percent of imports to the United States, Canadian gas exports to that market have nearly doubled during the past four years. In 1988 alone, gas exports to the United States grew by a record-breaking 30 percent; they now constitute 37 percent of Canada's total annual production.[1]

This level of activity, augmented by the promise of an even brighter future, was the reason that three of Canada's largest gas companies recently sought permission to export 9.2 trillion cubic feet (tcf) of gas from the Canadian arctic to the United States. Their application for permission to export was the largest the National Energy Board (NEB), the Canadian government agency responsible for monitoring energy exports, had received since it was created in 1959. In October 1989, the NEB approved the companies' plan, which amounts to the export of 90 percent of the present proven natural gas reserves in the Mackenzie Delta region and 10 percent of the total of Canadian proven reserves. The estimated cost of the project is $10.9 billion of which more than half, $6.1 billion, will be spent on pipeline development alone.

As Shell Canada President Jack MacLeod has stated publicly, however, the NEB's export approval is only the first small step towards the construction of the megaproject.   The NEB's decision does not include approving the construction of an arctic pipeline, and hearings on this issue alone could take two years. Many other hurdles, including environmental hearings, aboriginal objections to the project, as well as the difficulty of raising finance for the project, must also be cleared for the project to become a reality.[2]

Nonetheless what was once a dream to some and an ecological nightmare to others will likely become a reality. The objections heard during the days of the Berger inquiry, which first considered the construction of an arctic gas pipeline in the 1970s, are appreciably muted today.[3]   Justice Thomas Berger was appointed head of a federal Royal Commission in 1974 to consider the impact of various pipeline proposals through the Mackenzie Valley region of the Western Arctic. After numerous community hearings throughout the North, the Commission concluded in 1977 that a pipeline from the Mackenzie Delta to Alberta (which would hook up to the existing southern pipeline network) could, with the appropriate restrictions and environmental safeguards, benefit the people that live in the arctic, but urged that construction be delayed for ten years to permit the settlement of aboriginal land claims.

The largest indigenous group inhabiting the gas producing region, the Inuit of the Western Arctic (the Inuvialuit), settled their land claim with the Canadian government in 1984.   According to this agreement, the Inuvialuit received title to 35,000 square miles of land in the Western Arctic.   Of this amount, 5,000 square miles involves ownership of the subsurface including natural gas and oil. An Environmental Impact Screening Committee was created pursuant to the agreement to review all economic development projects in the Inuvialuit Settlement Region.   One-half of the permanent members of the Committee must be nominated by the Inuvialuit while the other members are nominated by the Canadian government as well as the territorial governments of the Yukon and Northwest Territories.[4]

The Inuvialuit, originally the group most opposed to pipeline construction during the Berger inquiry, now support the Mackenzie Valley gas development. They do so because their land claim settlement ensures them an economic return and gives them some control over the pace and direction of development.   The Inuvialuit are also determined to protect their more traditional livelihood and can use the Environmental Impact Screening Committee to protect the ecosystem of the animals upon which this livelihood depends.   Shortly after the agreement was signed, the Inuvialuit Development Corporation purchased shares in two Western Canadian oil and gas drilling companies to begin learning about the industry.   They are considering establishing a refinery that would serve their own regional needs in place of purchasing expensive oil and gas products from the south.   These moves are intended to ensure that the Inuvialuit will have the economic opportunities that will permit them to remain in their arctic homeland. The Inuvialuit also want some of their number to continue making a living through the traditional pursuits of hunting and fishing even at the same time that many will work directly or indirectly within the hydrocarbon industry. As the chairman of the Inuvialuit Development Corporation stated in 1985:

> We're in a stage right now of developing ourselves, but the centerpoint is still protecting the land and wildlife. If all business fails, we can go out on the land and get our food. You could go bankrupt and still enjoy yourselves out on the land.[5]

The two other indigenous groups inhabiting the Western Arctic have not reached a final land claim agreement with the federal government but are likely to do so in the near future. The 13,000 Dene and Métis make up appproximately 45 percent of the total population of the Mackenzie Valley. In 1988, the government of Canada entered into a land claim agreement-in-principle with the Dene and Métis and since that time both sides have been negotiating the details. On April 9, 1990, negotiators initialed the final agreement to settle the Dene-Métis comprehensive land claim and now only ratification and signature are necessary to implement the final agreement. The terms agreed upon are a transfer of 70,000 square miles of the Mackenzie Valley to the Dene and Métis of which 3,900 will include subsurface ownership as well as a transfer of $500 million. The Dene and Métis will also share in resource royalties, the most important of which will be natural gas. They will receive 50 percent of the first $2 million of resource royalties and 10 percent of the remainder. Mirroring the environmental provisions in the Inuvialuit Final Agreement of 1984, an Environmental Impact Review Board with wide powers to evaluate economic development projects in the Mackenzie Valley will be established with half of its members nominated by the Dene and Métis.[6]

Because they have little ownership or control without the land claim agreement, the Dene and Métis are trying to stall the Mackenzie Delta gas development until the final agreement has been signed. However, both groups will likely support the Mackenzie Delta project once their claims are resolved for the same reasons as the Inuvialuit. Extremely high unemployment and grinding poverty are pressuring both groups into accepting large-scale gas development if they can be assured that they will benefit directly from the development. Only ownership of part of the land upon which the natural gas is extracted and transported can provide this type of long-term guarantee. In addition, the Dene and Métis will have some control over the nature and the pace of gas development through their participation on the Environmental Impact Board. Southern environmental groups and the nationalist Council of Canadians, although still opposed to the development, must tread carefully because of the Inuvialuits' new position and their potential conflict with the Dene and Métis after their land claims with the federal government are resolved.[7]

CANADIAN GAS EXPORTS IN GLOBAL TERMS:
THE SIGNIFICANCE OF THE AMERICAN MARKET
USING CONVENTIONAL ENERGY FORECASTS

What is under discussion in the case of the Mackenzie Delta project is a nonrenewable resource of growing global significance. Currently, natural gas is the third major source of energy in the world, only slightly behind oil and coal—and its importance will increase markedly in the years ahead. According to projections made by the International Energy Association (IEA) for 1995 and 2005, real oil prices will begin to rise as oil production capacity outside the Middle East goes down (assuming that OPEC can control production enough to permit increases in the real price of oil). Thus the world demand for natural gas will grow faster than the demand for all other major energy sources: oil, coal, nuclear, and hydro. The implications for nations such as Canada, Norway, and the USSR—all of which produce (and are capable of producing) much more natural gas than they consume—are obvious. According to conventional estimates, the production of natural gas will expand at record levels during the 1990s.[8]

Although international trade in natural gas is a relatively recent phenomenon, it may eventually rank second to oil in terms of its value in international energy transactions. Canada is the third-largest producer of natural gas in the world and is ranked ninth in terms of proven reserves. In contrast, most of the member states of the Organization for Economic Cooperation and Development (OECD) are net importers. The Western European nations are supplied by Norway, the Netherlands, Algeria, and finally the USSR, the world's leading producer of natural gas. Because it costs ten times more to transport than oil, natural gas is generally delivered through pipelines within geographically proximate regions. The current pipeline system links European customers with suppliers in Norway, the Netherlands, and the USSR, and it is likely that North Sea and arctic gas will continue to dominate the market for many years to come. Given this pipeline infrastructure, the high transport cost of gas, and the potential availability of Middle Eastern gas, it is unlikely that Canadian gas will be exported to Europe in the near or distant future. Further, although Japan's demand for natural gas is growing rapidly, delivery costs and the recent discovery of natural gas in Australia make it an improbable market for Canadian gas. Thus the future viability of Canadian arctic gas exports depends primarily on demand and supply conditions in the United States.[9]

Canadian producers have been exporting natural gas in sizeable quantities to the United States since the OPEC crisis, and to a lesser degree, so have Algerian and Mexican producers. However, the U.S. gas market has fluctuated markedly during the past decade. Demand for natural gas fell steadily from 1979 until 1986 due to sluggish economic growth, conservation efforts, and a rapid fall in oil prices.[10] The decline of natural gas consumption in America, coupled with deregulation during the Reagan administration, made the market increasingly unattractive to foreign gas suppliers. The Algerian and Mexican governments decided against lowering export prices and vacated the market; in contrast, the Canadian government began in 1984 to loosen its previously tight controls on gas exports and essentially became the only foreign gas supplier of any consequence to the United States. Rapidly expanding since 1986, growth in gas exports to the United States now represents the fastest growing component of Canadian gas production.[11] The IEA projects that there will be a gradual rise in U.S. natural gas consumption in coming years. Due to the very low level of proven gas reserves, however, production of natural gas in the United States will continue to decline.[12] The situation has obvious potential for the Canadian gas industry.

Since it went into effect in January, 1989, the Free Trade Agreement (FTA) between the United States and Canada has bolstered the trade in fossil fuels by forbidding minimum export prices or taxes, and by prohibiting either country from restricting exports except in an emergency.[13] In March, 1990, the NEB announced that Canadian gas exports would no longer have to meet the test that they are of "net benefit" to Canada before being permitted. This decision, loudly decried by the Council of Canadians and central Canadian gas consumers, removed the last nationalist restriction on energy and made NEB practice consistent with the principles enshrined in the FTA.[14]

Now that American gas consumers are guaranteed the same national treatment as Canadian consumers, American reliance on Canadian natural gas will become even greater. Not surprisingly, American energy officials are now talking about replacing some of the United States' imports of crude oil with Canadian natural gas. Constance Buckley of the U.S. Department of Energy's fossil fuels program has noted that "[t]here is a consensus that proved and potential reserves in North America are sufficient to allow [American consumption] to increase and can be used to displace foreign oil." Although deregulation has gone some distance toward creating a continental market in natural gas, Buckley points to the FTA as instrumental in galvanizing the gas industry into a "true North American marketplace."[15]

Arctic gas is expensive to produce and export, however, and according to industry analysts, the price of natural gas must rise from its present price of $2.35 (Cdn) to at least $3 (Cdn) a thousand cubic feet in order for the Mackenzie Delta megaproject to pay for itself. These prices are based on long-term contractual commitments for Canadian gas by American firms. Present short-term natural gas prices are much lower; for example, the spot-market price for gas in 1989 was as low as $1.30 (Cdn).[16] The feasibility of Canadian arctic gas exports, therefore, depends centrally on the future price of natural gas, which in turn hinges on world energy supply and demand conditions.[17] There is much evidence that these conditions will favor natural gas over other energy sources.

BEYOND THE CONVENTIONAL PROJECTIONS:
FACTORS FAVORING NATURAL GAS

The IEA's projections concerning natural gas consumption differ little from those of other international, national, and private organizations. All, however, are probably too low in their estimates of future natural gas consumption and production relative to other energy sources. In examining each energy source, it becomes evident that natural gas will be the favored alternative in most situations in the United States and Canada.

As the majority of the potential power from hydro has already been exploited in the United States, the IEA projections assumed that Canadian hydroelectric power would be available for export south at levels established during the 1980s. It now appears, however, that American utilities will not be able to import Canadian hydroelectric power in the quantities previously estimated. In the case of Hydro Quebec, Canada's largest exporter of hydroelectric energy, drought and low water levels have forced the company to cut back its export commitments for the next ten to fifteen years.[18] Moreover, oil consumption will continue to decrease *relative* to other energy sources; since the OPEC crisis of 1973 and the Gulf War of 1991, United States security interests have dictated a move away from dependence on oil imports.

Utility companies have consequently tended to rely more on the one fossil fuel that is abundant and relatively inexpensive in the United States: coal. At this time, more than 50 percent of the electricity now generated in the United States comes from coal. This trend may be logical from a short-term economic or national security perspective but it has imposed a tremendous environmental cost; coal-powered electricity generation is the main source of the sulfur dioxide (SO_2) and nitrogen oxide (NO_x) emissions, known as acid rain, in the United States.[19] These emissions are now beginning to be regulated in such a manner as to make coal a less desirable energy source relative to natural gas. Although the IEA and other energy organizations' have not yet discounted coal in their projections, it probably should be. As Canada's Energy Options Advisory Committee concedes, "conventional forecasting often does not effectively incorporate changing values (such as an increasing interest in the environment) into its analysis."[20] This conservatism is particularly striking when we examine recent shifts in opinion concerning the use of nuclear energy, the need to take action on acid rain and global warming, and major technological breakthroughs in energy generation.

These factors are not taken, or only belatedly taken, into consideration in conventional forecasting such as that employed by the IEA. All are directly or indirectly concerned with evidence of environmental damage, changing perceptions of ecological threats, and the increasing desire to change our fuel consumption patterns to lessen existing and potential threats. The argument presented here is that these environmentally-induced changes in consumption will favor natural gas relative to other fossil fuels and nuclear power. The result will be reflected in higher levels of natural gas production and consumption during the next decade or two than those levels predicted in conventional energy forecasts. This will likely result in higher natural gas prices making the Mackenzie Delta project feasible, thus increasing the pressure for large-scale exploitation of natural gas in the Canadian arctic.

THE NUCLEAR PROBLEM

The IEA projections are based on the assumption that nuclear-generated electricity consumption will actually grow faster in the 1990s than in the 1980s, because the nuclear industry will be able to reduce public concern about the safety of nuclear power.[21] This seems an unrealistic assumption at best, given the negative publicity of the Chernobyl accident and the increasing hostility of ever-larger segments of the population against the industry.[22]

It is significant that the Energy Options Advisory Committee, recently established in Canada to examine energy issues and evaluate the nation's energy options for the future, was able to agree on virtually every issue raised *except* the nuclear option.[23] Although proportionately Canadians rely more on nuclear power than Americans, the continued growth of Canadian environmental groups that are unequivocally opposed to the use of nuclear energy may soon have the same impact as anti-nuclear groups have had in the United States. Energy analysts must therefore consider the possibility that nuclear energy may eventually be removed from the Canadian portfolio of energy sources. What is more significant in terms of higher-priced Canadian arctic gas, however, is the changing balance of energy use in the United States.

Indeed, in the United States, public pressure has for some time forced policy makers to minimize the use of nuclear energy. There is little likelihood that the United States will be able to continue its nuclear program at the present level, much less expand it during the 1990s, given the degree of political opposition this would engender.[24] Any further retreat in nuclear energy usage in the United States will produce greater pressure on all the major fossil fuel energy sources: coal, oil, and natural gas. Existing and future legislation aimed at lessening acid rain and the dangers posed by global warming will load the dice in favor of increasing the use of natural gas.

THE ACID RAIN PROBLEM

The 1980s witnessed a popular mobilization against acid rain in both the United States and Canada. In Canada, the destruction of life systems in hundreds of lakes as well as thousands of acres of maple trees, attracted so much public and media attention that, by 1982, 77 percent of the Canadian population viewed acid rain as the nation's most serious environmental problem.[25] Although acid rain was not as pressing an issue in the United States, environmental groups, often joining together under umbrella organizations such as the National Clean Air Coalition, were successful in applying increased political pressure for remedial action.[26] Governments in both nations have been compelled to enact legislation that restricts SO_2 and NO_x emissions.

Between 1980 and 1984, the Canadian government spent $41 million (Cdn) on acid rain research. Total expenditures since that time have averaged about $30 million annually, more than half of which comes from the federal government. More significantly, Canada has recently introduced legislation that will halve SO_2 emissions by 1994. Since roughly 50 percent of Canada's SO_2 pollution originates in the United States, the Canadian government has tried to pressure successive U.S. administrations into taking remedial action. During the Reagan administration, the link between U.S. emissions and Canadian acid rain was flatly denied. The Bush administration softened this position sufficiently to permit the successful negotiation of a Canada-U.S. Acid Rain Accord in 1991 after American clean air legislation had been passed.[27] During the past few years, domestic pressure in the United States has produced legal measures such as mandatory scrappers for smokestacks. Only recently, however, has it resulted in a legislative scheme that would substantially reduce SO_2 and NO_x emissions in North America. After months of debate, the United States Senate and then Congress approved a Clean Air Bill in 1990, that is expected to halve acid rain emissions within 10 years.

The immediate consequence of the Canadian and American acid rain legislation will be to put severe pressure on the coal-fired utility industry in both nations—especially in the United States, where more than 50 percent of the nation's electricity is generated by coal. On a much smaller scale, Ontario, New Brunswick, and Nova Scotia, the Canadian provinces most dependent on coal-fired electricity, will also be forced to consider alternatives. Whatever fuel source is chosen, however, any change in the makeup of Canadian energy consumption will have little impact on Canadian energy production relative to the tremendous shift that will result from new clean air legislation in the United States. The immediate impact of the legislation is an increase in the relative price of coal. To a lesser but still significant degree, oil is also penalized under this new legislation relative to natural gas.

THE GLOBAL WARMING PROBLEM

Global warming has supplanted acid rain, the issue of the 1980s, as the chief environmental concern of the 1990s. The buildup of carbon dioxide (CO_2) in the atmosphere, largely the result of human activity during the industrial age, is causing the world to warm at a pace that will significantly alter ecological patterns on the planet. According to Professor Irving Minster of the Center for Global Change at the University of Maryland, "the concentration of CO_2 in the atmosphere has increased at an average annual rate of about 0.4 percent" during the past 30 years. Very recent scientific observations now suggest that the rate "may have jumped dramatically in the past two or three years, approaching 0.7-0.8 percent during 1988."[28] Although not solely responsible for the greenhouse effect—emissions of other trace gases into the atmosphere such as methane, ozone, and NO_x also influence the atmosphere—CO_2 emissions are central to the problem.

Global warming may cause small glaciers in the polar regions to melt, raising sea levels between 0.5 and 1.5 meters. This would produce flooding of extensive land regions near sea level. In addition, patterns of rainfall and snowfall will change as entire ecosystems adjust to higher temperatures. Such changes are expected to occur by the next century if CO_2 and other trace gas emissions remain unregulated.

During the past few years, environmental groups throughout the world have been actively educating the general public about the dangers posed by global warming—and have been pressuring national governments to take legislative action. Although no specific legislation has yet been introduced in the United States, the issue of global warming is being addressed in the various comprehensive environmental protection bills now before Congress. The proposed National Energy Policy Act, for example, would require a 20 percent reduction in CO_2 emissions by the year 2000, and would set the United States on a course to reduce CO_2 emissions by up to 50 percent through international negotiation and treaty. By the same token, the prospective Global Pollution Control Act would attempt to decrease CO_2 emissions by 35 percent by 2010.[29] The Canadian government has recently shown signs of concern as well. Canada's environment minister announced in 1990 that the federal government would "set a national target and timetable" for reducing CO_2 emissions as part of its strategy to combat global warming.[30]

The issue is not whether both nations will have CO_2 emission legislation in place within the next few years but how it will be framed. The U.S. and Canadian governments will be required to either lower CO_2 emissions by a tax policy that imposes the costs of these externalities on utility companies and others discharging CO_2 into the atmosphere, or they will place a cap on the amount of CO_2 that companies will be permitted to release. Coal combustion releases twice as much CO_2 into the atmosphere per unit of energy produced compared with natural gas; fuel oil releases more than 40 percent. As a consequence, either regulatory approach will translate into higher costs for coal-powered energy and fuel oil relative to natural gas. In addition, recent technology is making natural gas more efficient and flexible as an energy source than coal or oil.

GAS TURBINE TECHNOLOGY: THE NEW ENERGY-CONVERTOR

According to Robert Williams and Eric Larson, research engineers at the Center for Energy and Environmental Studies at Princeton University, we are in the midst of a revolution in electricity-generating technology that "may soon radically transform the power industry, in both industrial and developing countries."[31] New gas-powered turbine power systems, in both a portable (modular) or stationary format, have proved to be extremely energy efficient. For example, some recent gas turbines can produce electricity at an efficiency rate 50 percent higher than that achieved by conventional gas turbines. The new gas turbines are also capable of releasing substantially less SO_2, NO_x, and CO_2 into the atmosphere than coal-fired plants per unit of energy produced. Such gas turbines have been developed to the point that they are now being sold commercially.

According to Williams and Larson, the gas turbine will likely assume a significant role in central station and cogeneration power applications in both industrial and developing countries during the next 20 to 40 years:

> The gas turbine will be much more widely used both because the changing circumstances of the electric power industry are especially conducive to the gas turbine and because improvements in gas turbine technology are making gas turbines more competitive. In a wide range of circumstances, new, highly efficient, gas turbine-based power plants will be able to provide electricity at lower cost and with less adverse environmental impacts or safety problems than coal or nuclear steam-electric plants.[32]

Nonetheless, a word of caution is in order concerning the difficulty inherent in predicting the adoption of one technology over another. Rarely do we correctly predict even short-term shifts in technology, and history contains numerous examples of short-lived technologies.[33] At this time, a great deal of research and development is being devoted to cleaner coal-powered energy convertors, as well as to solar and wind-powered energy convertors. Although at present these renewable-energy convertors make up an insignificant percentage of total energy generation in North America, developments in the near future could make them an important element in the global energy portfolio. Until that time, however, it is clear that the abundance of natural gas relative to fuel oil in North America—in conjunction with gas turbines that are flexible and efficient—can only serve to increase substantially the present level of gas production. And at least for the 1990s, it is safe to assume that gas turbine technology will accelerate the shift from coal and oil to natural gas.

AN ENVIRONMENTAL TRADEOFF? SOME POLICY PROPOSALS

When the above-mentioned environmental effects and technological changes are considered, it seems clear that there will be sufficient demand for natural gas to justify the Mackenzie Delta megaproject on strictly economic grounds. Moreover, the newfound support of the Inuvialuit combined with the formal establishment of a continental market for energy through the Canada-U.S. FTA at a time when gas reserves are shrinking in the United Sates, makes the development almost inevitable. The irony may be that existing and new legislation to thwart acid rain and global warming, by providing the main stimulus to natural gas demand and thereby underwriting the Mackenzie Delta project, could also do irreparable environmental damage to the Canadian arctic.

In contrast to the Berger inquiry of the 1970s, there has been surprisingly little debate on the environmental aspect of the proposed Mackenzie Delta project in recent years. Although objections were made by a few members of Canada's Energy Options Advisory Committee concerning the economic and environmental viability of energy megaprojects in general—in a report that was intended to canvass all the major aspects of Canada's energy future—the potential threats to the arctic environment were not addressed. Those undiscussed environmental effects may be severe.

To begin with, the laying of the pipeline itself may cause a certain amount of environmental damage. Precautions will be taken so that the proposed pipeline does not interfere with migratory patterns of certain arctic wildlife, but it is impossible to know in advance the project's precise impact. In making its assessment of the various Mackenzie Valley pipeline proposals of the 1970s, the Berger inquiry placed great weight on disruption to bird and mammal wildlife caused by the construction of the pipeline itself. The proposed routes through the Yukon and Alaska were believed to be particularly damaging in this respect. The Mackenzie Valley route was favored by the Berger Commission but its environmental impact was largely unknown at the time.

Perhaps an even greater danger emanates from the nature of the drilling operations themselves. First, there is no way to eliminate the possibility of gas and water blowouts in drilling operations. Such blowouts are particularly damaging in the arctic environment. Since natural gas exploratory drilling began in the Canadian arctic, there have been at least three major blowouts. In one case, the Panarctic project at Drake Point on Melville Island, engineers worked for two weeks to cap a high-pressure gas well that blew out of control. One month later, it blew out again, but this time the company was unable to stem the flow of gas for one year with a consequent loss of 30 million cubic meters of gas. A short time later, another Panarctic well on King Christian Island near the magnetic North Pole caught fire. The 350-foot flame could not be extinguished for three months, and approximately 270 million cubic meters of gas were burned off.[34]

Vehicle activity around the drilling site can cause extensive damage to the tundra. Wheels churn up the thin, fragile layer of moss and lichen, exposing the soil underneath to the sun's heat and melting the permafrost. Within a short time, tire tracks turn into muddy channels that can remain for decades.[35] Natural gas development in the USSR has already caused precisely this form of damage to the Soviet arctic. In certain regions, the damage to the permafrost caused by vehicle traffic is so extensive that it cannot be reversed. As a consequence, thousands of miles of tundra in the Soviet arctic are permanently damaged.[36] Given that the companies operating in the Canadian arctic must rely on vehicles to transport equipment and men from landing strips and home bases to drilling platforms, we should expect similar damage to permafrost in the Canadian arctic if the Mackenzie Delta project proceeds.

Because most of Canada's arctic gas will actually be drilled in the Arctic Islands, it will have to be transported in some form to the head of the pipeline in the Mackenzie Delta. This will involve transport over or through the Arctic Ocean, one of the most fragile ecosystems in the world.[37] Although gas spills are not as destructive to polar environments as oil spills, continual transport of gas still poses a deadly threat. One attempt to transport gas through the Arctic Ocean has already failed because of environmental opposition. In 1983, the Greenland Inuit supported by some Canadian Inuit blocked a Canadian project to use an icebreaker supertanker to ship liquified gas from the Arctic islands.[38]

Despite these difficulties, there remain at least two compelling public policy reasons for arctic gas development to proceed, even from the perspective of the inhabitants of the Mackenzie Valley. The first is the economic benefit to a region plagued by unemployment, particularly if the residents of the region play a direct role in the development. As this can only be ensured on a permanent basis through land claim agreements such as the Inuvialuit Final Agreement of 1984, it follows that the land claim agreements with the Dene and Métis should be finalized before the Mackenzie Delta gas project is permitted to proceed. The land claim agreements also provide the aboriginal peoples of the arctic some control over the nature and pace of the development. This should ensure the protection of their own environment and with it the continuance of more traditional livelihoods. The land claim agreements, through the environmental review boards, are the institutional vehicle through which the Inuvialuit, Dene, and Métis will police the activities of the resource companies in the Mackenzie Valley. Given the commitment of the aboriginal groups to preserving the arctic environment for future generations, the review boards will be a more effective method of minimizing environmental damage than any agency created by the federal or territorial governments.

The second reason the project should proceed is that the replacement of coal and nuclear powered energy generation by natural gas power plants is, at present, the most effective strategy in dealing with the nuclear, acid rain, and global warming problems. To the extent that this involves an environmental trade-off, numerous safeguards should be built into the Mackenzie Delta project to minimize environmental impact to the greatest extent possible. A first step would be an in-depth study of the impact of gas development from the Urengoy gas field to the Yamal Peninsula of western Siberia. The Soviet Union did not ban travel over bare arctic tundra until 1989, and their mistakes, as well as experimentation with new tundra vehicles, might provide valuable information. The NEB will in fact be conducting an environmental assessment of the Mackenzie project, and if the project is felt to adversely affect the environment a more comprehensive review must be undertaken.[39] At this stage, the NEB should only allow the project to go ahead if the strictest environmental safeguards are imposed.

In another sense, it is very misleading to speak in terms of an environmental trade-off. If the more pessimistic predictions are realized, global warming will adversely affect the arctic regions of the world in the next few years. This melting of the polar regions will then generate major environmental disruptions throughout the world. The Inuvialuit homeland along the western Arctic Ocean as well the Mackenzie Delta itself would be on the front line of such disruptions. Although the northern aboriginal peoples did nothing to cause global warming, they may be the first to suffer the effects of it. They therefore have an inherent interest in seeing that the global warming problem is dealt with effectively and as soon as possible.

NOTES

The author is grateful for the research assistance of Mark Whitcomb and the comments of Vivian Noble on the first rough draft of this paper.

1. J. DeMont, "Opening the Tap," *Maclean's*, February 26, 1990, pp. 32-34.

2. "Natural Gas Exports get Green Light," *Montreal Gazette*, October 20, 1989, p. D-6; D. Hatter, "Conditions may Stymie Arctic Gas Export Plans," *The Financial Post*, October 18, 1989; G. Kubish, "Tapping the Delta: The NEB Approves the Largest Gas Sale in Canada's History," *Western Report*, October 30, 1989; Interviews with Jack MacLeod, *The Financial Times of Canada*, August 28, 1989 and October 23, 1989; R. Zarzeczny, "How Our Secure Gas Supplies could go Down the Pipeline," *The Financial Times of Canada*, August 14, 1989.

3. T. R. Berger, *Northern Frontier, Northern Homeland: Report of the Mackenzie Valley Pipeline Inquiry* (Ottawa: Minister of Supply and Services, 1977); T.R. Berger, "The Mackenzie Valley Pipeline Inquiry," *Queen's Quarterly*, vol. 83, no. 1 (Spring 1976). Discussion concerning the possibility

of Canadian arctic gas exports to the United States began in earnest with the OPEC crisis in 1973. Intensive exploration of the most promising arctic regions—the Mackenzie Delta and the Arctic Islands—only began in 1968, the same time that an enormous amount of oil and gas was discovered at Prudhoe Bay on Alaska's North Slope. See the report for the Canadian—American Committee prepared by Judith Maxwell, *Energy from the Arctic: Facts and Issues* (Montreal and Washington, D.C.: C. D. Howe Institute and the National Planning Association, 1973).

4.   Government of Canada, *The Western Arctic Claim: The Inuvialuit Final Agreement* (Ottawa: Indian and Northern Affairs Canada, 1984). For commentary on the legal implications of the agreement, see J. M. Keeping, *The Inuvialuit Final Agreement* (Calgary: The Canadian Institute of Resources Law, 1989).

5.   Randy Pokiak, chairman of the Inuvialuit Development Corporation, quoted in C. S. Wren, "Corporate Fever Hits the Eskimos," *New York Times*, May 26, 1985.

6.   "Agreement Reached On Dene-Métis Land Claim," Indian and Northern Affairs Canada Communique, Yellowknife, N.W.T, April 9, 1990; "Summary of the Provisions of the Dene/Métis Comprehensive Land Claim Agreement-in-Principle," Indian and Northern Affairs Canada, Dene/Métis Information Sheet No. 1, April 1989; Background to Dene/Métis Land Claim, land claims file, Canadian Embassy, Washington, D.C.

7.   The Council of Canadians, while opposing all of the NEB's energy export approvals of the last few years, were particularly opposed to the Mackenzie Delta export application: G. Koch, "Resurrecting the NEP," *Western Report*, February 5, 1990, p. 15.

8.   International Energy Agency, *Energy Policies and Programmes of IEA Countries, 1988 Review* (Paris: OECD Publications, 1989), pp. 30-31.

9.   On the significance of a single Canada-U.S. energy market to Canadian producers, see L. A. Coad and D. H. Maerz, *Continental Natural Gas Market: Canadian Export Capacity in the 90s* (Calgary: Canadian Research Institute, 1989) and G. C. Watkins, ed., *Petro Markets: Probing the Economics of Continental Energy* (Vancouver: The Fraser Institute, 1989).

10. Gas prices did not fall as much as oil prices during this period, however. While consumption of gas fell 7 percent between 1985 and 1986, gas prices fell 30 percent. The loss of consumption can be "attributed largely to fuel switching by electric utilities and large industrial users." See A. K. Waldman, "Natural Gas Imports: Federal Policy and Competition for U.S. Markets," *Natural Resources Journal*, vol. 27, no. 4 (Fall 1987), p. 789.

11. New Policy Guidelines and Delegation Orders from the Secretary of Energy to the Economic Regulatory Administration and the Federal Energy Regulatory Commission Relating to the Regulation of Imported Natural Gas, 49 Fed. Reg. 6684-6689. See A. K. Waldman, "Natural Gas Imports," p. 791;

Also see H. C. Jenkins-Smith, "An Industry in Turmoil: The Remaking of the Natural Gas Industry," *Natural Resources Journal*, vol. 27, no. 4 (Fall 1987), and L. Kummins, Congressional Research Service Issue Brief, "Natural Gas Regulation: Overview and Issues," October 26, 1989.

12. As of 1987, the United States has a Reserves/Production (R/P) ratio of 11.5. This compares with an R/P ratio for Canada of 36.8 and an R/P ratio in excess of 100 for Norway. The R/P ratio is derived by taking the natural gas reserves remaining at the end of 1987 and dividing them by that year's production. The result is the length of time that those remaining reserves would last if production were to continue at that year's level: *Oil and Gas Journal*, December 28, 1987.

13. See Chapter Nine of the FTA between Canada and the United States, in particular, article 904. The impact of the FTA on energy trade between the two nations is summarized by E. A. Carmichael, "Energy and the Canada-U.S. Free Trade Agreement," *Trade Monitor*, no. 4 (May 1988); and on pp. 48-54 of Energy, Mines and Resources Canada, *Energy and Canadians into the 21st Century* (Ottawa: Minister of Supply and Services, 1988).

14. L. Diebel, "Board Scraps Special Test on Gas Exports," *The Toronto Star*, March 16, 1990; F. Dabbs, "Maintain Analysis on Gas Export Deals," *The Financial Post*, March 20, 1990; G. Gherson, "The Rumble Over rolled-in Gas Tolls," *The Financial Times of Canada*, March 26, 1990; T. Philip, "Letting the Gas Flow," *Western Report*, April 2, 1990.

15. C. Buckley quoted in "Canadian Natural Gas Seem Key to U.S. Plan," *Toronto Star*, April 7, 1990.

16. These estimates were made by Chris Johnston, gas-marketing manager for Esso Resources Canada Ltd. U.S. energy economist Arlon Tussing, for one, believes that the natural gas price has far to go before it reaches (Cdn) \$3. See "And Miles to go For the Arctic Pipeline," *The Financial Times of Canada*, October 23, 1989.

17. The IEA was established by a group of high energy consumption nations under the auspices of the OECD. IEA participating countries include most Western European nations, Australia, Canada, Japan, Turkey, and the United States.

18. A. Abel and L. B. Parker, "The Greening of U.S. and Canadian Electricity Trade," *Canada-U.S. Outlook*, vol. 1, no. 3/4 (April 1990), p. 68.

19. In the United States in 1980 for example, 67 percent of all SO_2 emissions and 32 percent of NO_x emissions were generated by electric utilities, the majority of which used coal. This situation has remained relatively constant since that time. T. Albin and S. Paulson, "Environmental and Economic Interests in Canada and the United States," in J. Schmandt et al., eds., *Acid Rain and Friendly Neighbors: The Policy Dispute between Canada and the United States* (Durham, NC: Duke University Press, 1988), p. 109. It should be noted that acid rain is more accurately described as acid depositions because SO_2 and

NO_x more often return to the earth's surface as dry particles than through precipitation. C. C. Park, *Acid Rain: Rhetoric and Reality* (London: Methuen, 1987); J. M. Lemco and L. Subrin, "The Energy-Environment Tradeoff: The Binational Issue of the 1990s," *Canada-U.S. Outlook*, vol. 1, no. 3/4 (April 1990).

20. See the report of the Energy Options Advisory Committee: Energy, Mines and Resources Canada, *Energy and Canadians into the 21st Century* (Ottawa: Minister of Supply and Services, 1988).

21. International Energy Agency, *Energy Policies and Programmes of IEA Countries, 1988 Review* (Paris: OECD Publications, 1989), p. 14.

22. The Nuclear Energy Agency Secretariat of the OECD responded to the "fallout" of the Chernobyl disaster by preparing the report, *Chernobyl and the Safety of Nuclear Reactors in OECD Countries* (Paris: OECD Publications, 1987), however, negative public sentiment had been of concern to the Nuclear Energy Agency before Chernobyl. See *Nuclear Power and Public Opinion* (Paris: OECD Publications, 1984). On the Chernobyl disaster itself, see D. R. Maples, *Chernobyl and Nuclear Power in the USSR* (New York: St. Martin's Press, 1986).

23. Energy Options Advisory Committee, *Energy and Canadians into the 21st Century*, p. 61.

24. See J. G. Morone and E. J. Woodhouse, *The Demise of Nuclear Energy? Lessons for Democratic Control of Technology* (New Haven, CT: Yale University Press, 1989).

25. R. Egel, "Canada's Acid Rain Policy: Federal and Provincial Roles," in J. Schmandt et al., eds., *Acid Rain and Friendly Neighbors*.

26. J. L. Regens and R. W. Rycroft, *The Acid Rain Controversy* (Pittsburgh, PA: University of Pittsburgh Press, 1988); T. Albin and S. Paulson, "Environmental and Economic Interests in Canada and the United States," in J. Schmandt et al., eds., *Acid Rain and Friendly Neighbors*, pp. 116-18.

27. J. M. Lemco and L. Subrin, "The Energy-Environment Tradeoff," p. 14.

28. I. M. Mintzer, "Our Changing Climate: Challenges and Opportunities in Warming World," *Canada-U.S. Outlook*, vol. 1, no. 3/4 (April 1990), pp. 77-78.

29. Ibid., p. 74.

30. "Must Set Target, Timetable on Carbon Dioxide Emissions: Minister," *Canadian Press Wire Service* (Ottawa), April 24, 1990.

31. R. H. Williams and E. D. Larson "Expanding Roles for Gas Turbines in Power Generation," in T. B. Johansson, B. Bodlund and R.H. Williams, *Electricity: Efficient End-Use and New Generation Technologies, and Their Planning Implications* (Lund: Lund University Press, 1989), p. 503. Also see E. D. Larson and R. H. Williams, "Steam-Injected Gas Turbines," Paper No.

86-GT-47, Transactions of the American Society of Mechanical Engineers, January, 1986. I thank Irving Mintzer for making me aware of the "modular turbine" and I am indebted to Eric Larson for discussing its significance in terms of the demand for natural gas.

32. R. H. Williams and E. D. Larson, op. cit., p. 503.

33. For numerous historical examples, see D. S. Landes, *The Unbound Prometheus: Technological Change and Industrial Development in Western Europe from 1750 to the Present* (Cambridge: Cambridge University Press, 1969).

34. These examples come from S. Hall, *The Fourth World: The Heritage of the Arctic and its Destruction* (New York: Alfred A. Knopf, 1987), pp. 187-88.

35. Ibid., p. 196.

36. A popular accounting of the damage that natural gas development has wreaked in the Soviet arctic, particularly in the main producing area in the northwest of Siberia, can be found in M. Edwards, "Siberia: In from the Cold," *National Geographic*, vol. 177, no. 3 (March 1990), p. 10.

37. In 1976, the Canadian government department of Energy, Mines and Resources gave a 90 percent probability of reserves of 580 million tons of oil and 1.1 million cubic meters of gas in the Mackenzie Delta/Beaufort Sea basin; and 220 million tons of oil and 680,000 million cubic meters of gas in the Sverdrup basin in the Arctic islands. D. Sugden, *Arctic and Antarctic: A Modern Geographical Synthesis* (Totowa, NJ: Barnes and Noble Books, 1982).

38. "Tomorrow Slowly Encroaches on Harsh, Scenic Arctic," *Los Angeles Times*, October 11, 1987.

39. Canadian Press Wire Service (Ottawa), February 19, 1990; and T. Philip, "Retracting its Tentacles," *Western Report*, May 14, 1990.

3

Transboundary Acid Rain: A Canadian-U.S. Problem Requiring a Joint Solution

Fredric C. Menz

Over the last decade, the international dimensions of environmental concerns have received increasing attention. It is now widely recognized that even if the effects of pollution are felt only on a local or regional scale, their effective management often requires transboundary initiatives. It is also apparent that domestic policies for pollution control are increasingly affected by global environmental concerns. For instance, most countries have committed themselves to reducing production of chlorofluorocarbons that deplete the stratospheric ozone layer. Many are also considering policies to control carbon dioxide emissions in order to confront the problem of global climate change.

Acid rain, or acidic deposition, has been a major concern in Europe and North America since the Swedish government's report on transboundary sulfur dioxide emissions for the United Nations Conference on the Human Environment.[1] This chapter considers the acid rain policies of Canada and the United States and suggests that further bilateral Canadian-U.S. action is necessary to resolve the acidic deposition problem in North America. Coordinated action between the two countries is necessary because considerable transboundary flows of acidic emissions render unilateral policies economically inefficient and inequitable. A bilateral approach should seek to establish a mutually acceptable ambient environmental quality standard within the common airshed and to achieve the objective at minimum cost. A bilateral acid rain agreement would be more advantageous to both countries if least-cost abatement strategies allowed cross-border reductions in pollution discharges.

ACID RAIN AS A NORTH AMERICAN CONCERN

Scientific Aspects of the Problem

Acidic deposition refers to both wet and dry deposition of acidifying pollutants resulting from the transport of acidic substances from sources in one region to distant receptors. The primary chemical compounds involved in acid rain are sulfur dioxide (SO_2) and nitrogen oxides (NO_x). As of 1985, estimated man-made emissions in the United States consisted of 23.1 million tons of SO_2 and 20.5 million tons of NO_x. In Canada, annual emissions in 1985 were estimated at 4.1 million tons of SO_2 and 2.1 million tons of NO_x.[2]

In North America, industrial combustion accounts for more than 60 percent of SO_2 emissions, industrial and manufacturing processes for 21 percent, and fuel combustion approximately 13 percent. Motor vehicles account for approximately 45 percent of North American NO_x emissions. In the United States, electric utilities produce more than two-thirds of SO_2 emissions and approximately one-third of NO_x emissions. Seventy-five percent of U.S. emissions of SO_2 originate from large sources that emit at least 10,000 tons annually. Industrial processes account for nearly three-fourths of the SO_2 emissions in Canada, and nonferrous ore smelters are the major source.

Even though nitrogen oxides and other air pollutants have been implicated in the formation of acidic deposition, proposals to mitigate the effects of acid rain in both Canada and the United States emphasize the control of SO_2 emissions. The focus of concern in Canada has been on controlling discharges from smelters, while the United States has focused on further reducing emissions from electric power plants.

Since becoming a pressing concern in the 1970s, acidic deposition has been the focus of an extraordinary research effort in the United States, Canada, and Europe.[3] Much has been accomplished, but important scientific tasks remain, including: (1) defining the precise relationships between emissions and deposition and between the sources of acidifying emissions and the locations of their eventual deposition; (2) determining the extent to which acidic deposition has resulted or will result in damages to terrestrial and aquatic ecosystems, human health, cultivated crops, and materials; (3) determining whether these and other effects are reversible and over what time frame; and (4) deciding whether remedial action at sensitive receptor sites is a viable strategy to mitigate acidification damages. Another important issue is whether more-stringent controls should be required now or deferred. The question is whether to act now to control acidic deposition, given the scientific uncertainties and potentially higher costs of pollution control, or delay action until more information is available and new pollution control methods are developed, thereby risking further ecological damage.[4] These issues are central to the debate about whether to take further regulatory action; however, they are not the focus of concern in this chapter.

Canadian-U.S. Perspectives

The issue of acid rain has created a divisive atmosphere between Canada and the United States over the last decade. There are disagreements concerning scientific questions, about each country's commitment to controlling its emissions, and whether further regulatory action is warranted. Canada has continued actively to encourage the United States to impose tighter controls over emissions, but such action was deferred until just recently.

In the United States, acidic deposition is viewed primarily as a domestic political issue involving conflicting regional interests; transboundary aspects of the issue involving Canada receive little attention. States in the northeast argue that their acid rain damages are primarily the result of emissions coming from sources located in the midwest. Important issues in the domestic U.S. debate include the expected loss of jobs in the high-sulfur coal-mining industry and whether the cost of additional controls on emissions should be shared among different regions. Midwestern states hold that the additional costs should be borne by the entire country, while northeastern and western states generally believe that the costs should be assumed primarily in regions where further controls are mandated.[5]

There are similar interregional debates among Canadian provinces about how to reduce Canadian SO_2 emissions. The Atlantic provinces argue that their emissions are inconsequential compared to those from the major industrial provinces and that external sources are major contributors to their acidic deposition problems. For example, in hearings conducted by a parliamentary committee reviewing Canadian policy on acid rain, New Brunswick officials pointed out that Prince Edward Island (PEI) was wrongly credited as a low-emissions province, since PEI imported virtually all of its electrical power from New Brunswick.[6] Nova Scotia officials argued that acidic deposition in their province originated from external sources and that its own SO_2 emissions are largely deposited on nonsensitive areas (ibid., pp. 13-14). Despite such conflicts, emissions from the United States are considered to be a major cause of Canadian damages, particularly in Quebec and eastern Ontario. Thus, Canada has an important stake in reaching agreement with the United States in the task to curtail transboundary pollution.

Acid Rain Initiatives in Canada and the United States

In the past 13 years several policy initiatives at various levels of government in both Canada and the United States have addressed the problem of acid rain. Some states have enacted legislation to further control sulfur dioxide emissions, mostly for symbolic purposes in order to influence congressional action. The Canadian federal government and seven provinces east of Saskatchewan agreed to reduce significantly their emissions and have enacted programs to meet those commitments.[7] Several agreements between individual states and provinces are also in place. In addition, a group of northeastern states and the province of Ontario joined in legal action to force the U.S. Environmental Protection

Agency to respond to international transborder pollution under Section 115 of the U.S. Clean Air Act.

There has been cooperative activity at the federal level between Canada and the United States since 1978, when a bilateral research group was established to study the long-range transport of air pollutants. The group's mandate called for exchanging information, coordinating research between the two countries, and developing a joint scientific database. Both countries also signed the United Nations Convention on Long-Range Transboundary Air Pollution of 1979, committing themselves to reducing transboundary pollution. This was followed by the Memorandum of Intent on Transboundary Air Pollution, signed by Canada and the United States in August 1980, in which they consented to work toward an agreement to address transboundary pollution. Negotiations broke down in 1982, however, when Canada pressed for an immediate commitment to reduce emissions by 50 percent, but the United States said that more research was required before it would undertake further controls.   In 1985, President Reagan and Prime Minister Mulroney appointed special envoys to examine and report on the acid rain issue. The envoys' report in 1986 stated clearly that acid rain was a serious transboundary matter that should be addressed by both countries.   It also recommended that existing air pollution regulations be reviewed to identify opportunities for addressing transboundary pollution. At the Canada-U.S. summit in April 1987, President Reagan agreed to consider a bilateral accord to control acidic deposition. However, until President Bush proposed legislation in mid-1989, there was little indication that the United States was prepared to make a serious effort to resolve the problem. On July 8, 1990, President Bush and Prime Minister Mulroney announced that formal negotiations on a bilateral agreement to reduce acid rain emissions would begin the next week, even though amendments to the U.S. Clean Air Act had not received final congressional approval. In March, 1991, the two leaders signed an acid rain accord committing Canada and the United States to curb emissions and jointly monitor the transboundary problem.

Transboundary Considerations

Although many aspects of the acidic deposition problem are debated, it is widely acknowledged by scientists and officials of both governments that significant transboundary flows of acid-gas emissions occur. The major North American sources of SO_2 are concentrated in the midwestern and northeastern portions of the United States and in the eastern Canadian provinces. The spatial patterns of acidic deposition are influenced by a combination of factors, including the location of emissions, stack heights, and meteorological factors.

While the exact transboundary movement of SO_2 is not known, Canadian scientists estimated a flow of 3.2 million tons from the United States to Canada in 1985; this amount was more than three-fourths of Canada's own emissions and more than three times the flow from Canada to the United States in the same year.[8] Nearly 90 percent of the transboundary flow of SO_2 into eastern Canada originated from sources in states within 300 miles of the international border. Studies conducted for the U.S. National Acid Precipitation Assessment Program indicate that Canadian sources contribute less than 5 percent of the total sulfur deposition over most of the United States and about 15 percent over New York, Vermont, New Hampshire, and Maine; this fraction increases to nearly 25 percent in the northernmost parts of Maine.[9]

The transboundary flow of pollutants has important policy implications. One implication is that Canada cannot solve its acidic deposition problem without reductions in emissions from the United States. For instance, even if emissions from Canadian sources were eliminated entirely, the flow of SO_2 emissions from the United States would still about equal Canada's total emissions in 1980. Second, while the pollutants in question are produced in much greater quantity in the United States, damages are proportionately greater in Canada because its affected regions have less capacity to neutralize acidic deposition and thus are more vulnerable. Finally, since the costs of controlling emissions are likely to vary among sources irrespective of borders, cost-effective policies for controlling acidic deposition in the common (eastern North American) airshed will most likely involve binational sharing of source reductions.

AIR POLLUTION POLICIES IN THE UNITED STATES AND CANADA

The two countries approach the control of air pollution from stationary sources in different ways. In the United States, the federal government is responsible for developing overall air pollution policies and setting ambient air-quality standards, while each state is responsible for implementing regulations to see that the mandated standards are met. In Canada, the legal responsibility for controlling stationary source pollution rests almost entirely on provincial governments, while the federal government has the authority to deal with interprovincial and international transboundary pollution concerns.[10] Existing federal legislation in both countries concentrates on reducing local pollution and does not directly address transported air pollutants. These differences have served to frustrate efforts between the two countries to coordinate their pollution control policies regarding acidic deposition.

U.S. AIR POLLUTION POLICY

The U.S. Clean Air Act gives responsibility to the federal government to set nationwide ambient environmental quality levels and source discharge standards. While all new sources are subject to more or less uniform emissions standards nationwide, it is up to the individual states to regulate existing local sources to ensure that the national air quality standards are met. States also are responsible for monitoring and enforcing sources for compliance with environmental quality goals and with the discharge standards called for in the Clean Air Act.

Air pollution regulations in the United States emphasize setting standards for allowable emissions at individual sources. Most often this involves a "command-and-control" approach in which a specific control technology is mandated, usually by the Environmental Protection Agency (EPA), but occasionally by Congress. For example, the 1977 Clean Air Act amendments in effect required new coal-fired power plants to meet the required emissions standard by using technological means (that is, by scrubbing), thereby precluding the option of meeting the emissions standard by using low-sulfur coal or other means.

Air pollution control policies in the United States have directly contributed to the acidic deposition problem in several instances. While sulfur and nitrogen oxides have been subject to emissions standards since 1970, the primary objective of the regulations has been to meet acceptable ground-level concentrations near the point of discharge. For several years, sources were allowed to meet this objective by increasing the height of stacks discharging the pollutants, thus contributing to the problem of acidic deposition. Air pollution regulations also tend to specify limits in rates of emissions rather than total quantities.

Federal policy has further contributed to the long-range atmospheric transport problem with the so-called New Source Performance Standards (NSPS) of the Clean Air Act of 1970. The NSPS set stringent discharge standards for new industrial and electric utility sources while leaving existing sources covered by significantly less onerous regulations. The logic behind the NSPS provision was that emissions from existing sources would be reduced as plants were gradually retired. However, requiring expensive pollution controls on new sources created an incentive to postpone the retirement of older plants, and it is estimated that by 1995 over 90 percent of SO_2 discharges by utilities will come from plants constructed before 1970. The issue at hand is how quickly must existing sources be forced to reduce their emissions instead of waiting until being replaced by new sources subject to far stricter standards.

Canadian Air Pollution Policy

Air pollution policy in Canada is a joint federal-provincial program. Provincial governments are responsible for imposing regulations or legislation to control pollution within provinces, while interprovincial pollution falls under the jurisdiction of the federal government. According to Canada's Clean Air Act, the federal government formulates air quality objectives and guidelines; however, they must be incorporated into provincial environmental laws before they can be enforced.

The Canadian federal government is legally empowered to prescribe compulsory standards only when emissions present a significant threat to public health or when Canada would otherwise violate an international air pollution agreement.[11] The federal government can establish source-specific emissions guidelines, which are developed by industry-government task forces and based on "best-practicable technology." However, in order to be legally enforceable, the guidelines must be adopted by the provinces.[12]

DOMESTIC POLICIES ADDRESSING ACIDIC DEPOSITION

U.S. Policy

In the last few sessions of Congress, there were a number of proposed amendments to the Clean Air Act that would establish new limitations on SO_2 (and to a lesser extent NO_x) emissions from existing sources. These limitations would serve to extend the area of control from a single pollutant in a local area to combined pollutants with long-range effects. Most of the proposals called for a reduction of between 8 million and 12 million tons annually in SO_2 emissions from 31 states east of the Mississippi River. This would be accomplished over a ten-year period and would amount to an approximate 50 percent reduction in U.S. emissions from their existing levels. Prior to 1990, no proposal to control acidic deposition made it out of committee in the House of Representatives, nor was any seriously debated on the floor of the Senate.

The measure approved by Congress as part of the 1990 Clean Air Act amendments calls for an eventual reduction of 10 million tons in SO_2 emissions and 2 million tons in NO_x emissions annually by the year 2000. Costs of achieving this reduction will vary from about $2.5 billion to $6 billion annually in the year 2000.[4] The actual costs will depend on the methods chosen by sources to comply with the mandated standards. It is estimated that average electricity rates will rise nationwide by approximately 3 percent, and in some locations by as much as 10 to 15 percent, from what they would have been under existing policy.

Without cost-sharing among regions, most of the burden of an acid rain control program would be borne by the few states (including Illinois, Indiana, Missouri, Ohio, and Pennsylvania) that account for the largest share of SO_2 emissions. At the same time, the benefits of reduced emissions would accrue primarily to northeastern states and to southern Ontario and Quebec. To lessen the burden on the midwestern states, there have been proposals to tax all forms of nonnuclear electricity generation in the United States or for a tax on sulfur emissions. In each case, the tax revenues would be used to help defray the costs of reducing SO_2 emissions.

Some previous proposals also mandated the installation of scrubbers in the largest existing sources of emissions in order to protect jobs in the high-sulfur coal mining industry.   In addition to increasing significantly the cost of achieving SO_2 reductions, these measures also alienated the western states and some southern states. These states objected to the prospect of paying to solve a problem to which they feel they did not contribute. In addition, some of these states believed that forced scrubbing provisions would prevent them from selling their vast reserves of low-sulfur coal.

The U.S. legislation addressing acidic deposition is unprecedented in several respects. Most importantly, it acknowledges that acid rain cannot be dealt with effectively without federal action. Also, for the first time, arguments by economists appear to have exerted a significant influence on policy. Sources will be free to decide for themselves how to attain the mandated emissions standards, making use of scrubbers, lower sulfur fuel, or new technology with a lower rate of emissions.[13] Also, plants will be awarded credits for reducing emissions earlier or beyond the requirements, and owners or operators of affected sources will be allowed to transfer these credits to other sources within geographic regions as prescribed by regulation. The combination of transferable credits for reducing emissions and individual choice of pollution control methods should result in a 30 to 40 percent reduction in costs compared to what they would be if scrubbers were required.

Canadian Policy

For reasons discussed earlier, federal and provincial governments in Canada have actively pursued domestic policies addressing acidic deposition since the early 1980s. The federal government in Canada is unable to regulate directly emissions of acid rain precursors; thus, its efforts have been directed toward encouraging provincial governments and the United States to take action. Another role of the federal government has been to coordinate the overall Canadian effort and to provide financing, jointly with the provinces, for controlling SO_2 emissions from smelters.

In 1982, Canada made a formal proposal to the United States that both countries achieve a 50 percent reduction in SO_2 emissions by 1990 as evidence of a bilateral commitment to reduce acidic deposition. In 1985, although without a positive response from the United States, Canadian federal and provincial governments announced a program to cut SO_2 emissions from stationary sources by 50 percent in eastern Canada, which will result in total SO_2 emissions of approximately 2.3 million tons annually by 1994. At the same time, the federal government announced that Canadian automobile emissions standards would be brought into compliance with those in the United States.

Another noteworthy aspect of the Canadian acid rain abatement program is that the federal-provincial emissions goals were designed to comply with a specific environmental quality target. An agreement was formulated to establish a deposition objective of an annual 18 pounds per acre of wet sulfate in all vulnerable areas; according to Canadian scientific assessments, achieving this objective would halt further damages. This emphasis on specific environmental quality objectives rather than emissions standards is an important distinction between Canadian and U.S. approaches to acidic deposition. Another distinctive feature is that sources are given flexibility in deciding how to best curb emissions. Cost-effective abatement is supposed to be the guiding principle of the Canadian acid precipitation abatement program,[14] and its outcome is similar to "least-cost" strategies embodied in some U.S. acid rain control proposals.

ELEMENTS OF A BILATERAL SOLUTION

The Need for Joint Action

Since Canada and the United States have now enacted legislation controlling acidic deposition, it could be argued that joint bilateral action is no longer necessary. However, there are several reasons why further cooperation between the two nations is essential. Most importantly, it is possible that desired environmental objectives could be met at a lower cost if, when abatement strategies are developed, the common airshed includes all sources on both sides of the border. Second, both countries might initially agree that a 50 percent reduction from 1980 baseline discharges would be an appropriate standard to adopt. However, the desired objective of either or both countries might change for various reasons such as new scientific information or changes in public perceptions of the problem. Third, important questions remain regarding atmospheric processes and the spatial pattern of emissions and deposition. Knowledge linking deposition in one location to emissions originating from other locations is an important consideration in designing cost-effective abatement strategies for acidic deposition. With additional knowledge, a different spatial pattern of emissions reductions might be more effective in meeting the environmental objective. Finally, as pollution patterns change over time whether as a result of economic growth, relocation of sources, or for other reasons, changes in the pattern of emissions within the common airshed might be desired. Since pollution patterns are likely to change both within a country and between countries, joint action is needed to ensure that environmental objectives will continue to be met effectively.

An *effective* North American program to control acid rain must break new ground in finding an appropriate mechanism for dealing with the shared problem.   An institutional arrangement to deal with transboundary acidic deposition must include several important elements. Agreement will be needed on the magnitude of the transboundary pollution flow and on bilateral source-receptor relationships. Acceptable procedures will need to be established for monitoring emissions and the trends of acidic deposition over time. The two countries will also have to agree on environmental objectives and on policy instruments for equitably and efficiently dealing with the problem. Finally, procedures for resolving disputes between the two countries must also be implemented.

Determining the relationships between sources and receptors both within and between the two countries is one of the most complex issues under study.[15] While there are considerable gaps in this information, several facts concerning transboundary pollution are evident.   First, the relative quantities of transboundary flows of SO_2 between the two countries are well documented. Second, the spatial patterns of sources and receptors is diffuse in both countries, although acidic deposition is largely confined to regions in eastern North America. Finally, while total sulfur emissions from the United States to Canada are considerably greater than those from Canada to the United States, the transboundary flow is clearly a two-way phenomenon—both countries emit and receive acid rain. Thus, a common solution is more practical than would be the case if one country were the receptor and the other the source. Indeed, recognition of the shared nature of the problem has rendered a formal bilateral arrangement an obvious solution to the North American acid rain problem.

The Role of Property Rights

Property rights considerations are central to the problem of acidic deposition and other pollution concerns both within a country's own borders and between countries.   Pollution is an example of an external cost that results from inappropriately specified property rights. Economic agents pursuing welfare-maximizing behavior create external costs when they shift some of the costs of their activities to third parties. As a result they engage in a greater level of the activity than if they were forced to bear the full costs.

A variety of methods have been proposed to internalize such costs and thus take them into account. The traditional method, direct regulation, usually forces dischargers to comply with emissions standards through a mandated control technology. Other methods, including the use of effluent fees or a system of transferable permits allowing sources to discharge a certain amount of emissions, place greater reliance on market incentives. These methods effectively shift the property rights for environmental resources among various users, usually from the sources of pollutants to parties affected by the emissions.

Some might suggest that acidic deposition could be solved by individual agents if the rights and liabilities of individual citizens were clearly specified. Individuals affected by acidic deposition could then bring actions against dischargers and receive appropriate compensation for the pollution damages they suffer. However, individual litigation would be very costly since it is virtually impossible for victims to identify pollution sources and prove damages. The legal problems would be further complicated, of course, given the international dimension and scientific complexity of the acidic deposition problem.

For these reasons it is up to the two nations to negotiate a solution to the bilateral transboundary problem. In essence, the formal bilateral negotiations concern the rights and obligations of the two countries; as Anthony Scott has observed, these fundamental legal issues must be resolved prior to the establishment of environmental objectives.[16] Thus, a true sharing agreement requires a mechanism embodying a clearly prescribed set of property rights that provides the appropriate incentives to achieve a mutually acceptable environmental quality objective.[17]

Environmental Objectives

An issue that must be faced is what the appropriate bilateral acidic deposition objective should be. This is a significant matter because domestic air quality objectives differ in the two countries, particularly as they pertain to acidic deposition. Canada's abatement strategy is explicitly based on achieving an acidic deposition objective of no more than 18 pounds per acre in sensitive receptor areas. Since the regions most affected by acidic deposition (Ontario and Quebec) are also the regions in which most acid-rain precursor emissions occur, agreement on this target in Canada was fairly easy to obtain. In contrast, air quality standards in the United States, including those that address acidic deposition, are not explicitly based on meeting target levels of environmental quality at receptor sites. They emphasize, instead, atmospheric concentrations of pollutants, with emissions standards placed on sources in order to achieve the desired air quality objectives.

While it could be argued that the U.S. approach to air pollution control effectively achieves the same objective as does Canadian policy, the difference in emphasis is significant. In bilateral negotiations, Canada can be expected to take the position that environmental objectives for the common airshed should be based on environmental quality levels in sensitive receptor locations rather than on uniform emissions standards for individual dischargers. Canada would then be in a better position to control its own environmental quality, since a policy based on emissions standards would leave Canada less able to reduce the flow of emissions from the United States. Conversely, the United States is likely to focus on an objective based on emissions standards, taking the position that proportional reductions in aggregate SO_2 discharges are the most equitable solution to the problem.

Whatever the basis for choosing an acceptable standard, the objective that is ultimately selected will depend both on costs and the perceived value of environmental improvements in both countries. Perspectives of the acidic deposition problem differ widely in Canada and the United States. The reasons for these different perspectives might be economic. For example, costs for pollution control could be higher in the United States, or there could be greater risks of damages to resource-based industries in Canada, particularly forestry. This difference could also be based on environmental values. For example, in public opinion surveys, Canadians invariably place greater emphasis on environmental problems than do Americans. The difference in perspective could also be explained by the fact that Canada receives more deposition from the United States than the United States receives from Canada. Reconciling this difference in perspectives will be important in determining a mutually acceptable environmental standard.

A rough measure of the value each country places on environmental improvements is indicated by the amount they are willing to pay in order to achieve these improvements, assuming that each is willing to incur additional expenditures for pollution control as long as the benefits of those expenditures exceed their costs. The Canadian government estimates that its acid rain control program, when fully implemented, will cost $400 million (U.S.) annually and will reduce annual SO_2 emissions by approximately 2 million tons.[18] Thus, the cost of reducing sulfur emissions by 50 percent in Canada is about $200 per ton. Cost estimates for reducing sulfur emissions in the United States vary dramatically, but it is reasonable to assume annual costs of approximately $4 billion in order to achieve an additional 10 million ton reduction in annual SO_2 emissions. This amounts to a cost of approximately $400 per ton of sulfur removed, about twice as much as that in Canada, although it might be as low as $200 per ton if least-cost abatement strategies are employed.[19]

These numbers can be used as an implied measure of the damages that could be avoided if pollution levels were reduced and, thus, can provide an indication of the magnitude of damages from transboundary SO_2 pollution. Based on 1985 transboundary flows, Canada's annual emissions to the United States (approximately 1 million tons) resulted in implicit damages of about $400 million from Canadian acidic deposition in the United States. Approximately 3.2 million tons of emissions originating in the United States in 1985 resulted in about $640 million worth of implied acidic deposition damages in Canada.[20]

Cost-Effective Policies

Economic factors play a role in setting environmental objectives, but they are clearly not the only consideration. Still, the cost-effectiveness of alternative policy instruments has been the topic of considerable study by economists, and economic considerations are now playing a more important role in environmental policy. As the level of pollution control continues to rise, the cost of controlling discharges rises more than proportionately, thus making cost-effective policies even more attractive.

Economists have suggested for some time that greater reliance on market-based approaches to pollution abatement could result in considerable cost savings without sacrificing environmental quality. The inefficiency of standard regulatory approaches, such as uniform reductions in discharges from sources, is well known. Economic considerations were the reason for the U.S. Environmental Protection Agency developing its "emissions trading" program, which has allowed limited trading both within a firm (the so-called bubble, netting, and banking policies) and between firms (offsets) since the mid-1970s. The emissions reduction credit program in the 1990 amendments to the U.S. Clean Air Act call for a considerable expansion of the use of marketable permits. This innovation would give credits to sources for any reductions they make beyond those required by the law. These credits could then be applied by the owners to another source under their control or they could be transferred or leased to another source.[21] The use of market-based instruments is likely to increase in the future as abatement costs rise and additional experience is gained from their more widespread use in the United States and elsewhere.[22]

The basic rule for cost-effective pollution control is that the marginal costs of reducing pollution damages at the location of receptors be the same for all sources within a given airshed. The spatial pattern of sources and receptors plays an important role in acidic deposition because the damages caused by the emissions depend on the location from which they were discharged. Thus, cost-effective pollution control for acidic deposition requires that the location of sources as well as their pollution control costs be considered. This could be accomplished either by a system of spatially differentiated charges or by transferable discharge permits that take into account both source-receptor relationships and abatement costs.

Significant cost savings would result if individual sources in both countries could participate in transboundary trades of mandated discharge reductions. Trading among sources in both countries should result in cost savings equivalent in magnitude to those resulting when individual sources are allowed to choose a least-cost abatement strategy. Studies of the costs of meeting a mandated 10 million ton reduction in annual SO_2 emissions in the United States indicate possible savings of more than 30 percent if major sources were allowed to use coal-switching and other least-cost strategies instead of being forced to use flue gas desulfurization techniques.[23] A complete system of internationally transferable source reductions would be the most cost-effective way to manage the transboundary acidic deposition problem, but it would be difficult to design because source-receptor relationships would have to be taken into account. A zone system that allows trades within limited geographic areas, similar to that which is in the U.S. acid rain legislation but allowing bilateral trades, represents a practical alternative to a fully differentiated system and would be appropriate for managing bilateral acidic deposition.

CONCLUSION

Both Canada and the United States have taken action to deal with the problem of acidic deposition. While each country has undertaken independent efforts, a coordinated endeavor is required since transboundary flows of acidic emissions between the two countries are involved. Such an effort should go beyond simply assuring that current air quality legislation in both countries is enforced. Agreement on a common binational environmental quality standard is required and policies must be devised to achieve that standard in a cost-effective manner. A coordinated bilateral action could also be an important influence on the global debate about environmental policies regarding transboundary pollution.

The issue of acidic deposition represents an important opportunity for the two countries to work together to achieve a mutually satisfactory solution to a shared environmental problem. The "climate" in both countries is right—there is heightened awareness of environmental concerns, and the costs of controlling pollution continue to rise as more-stringent environmental regulations are imposed. Furthermore, other bilateral environmental quality problems such as toxics in the Great Lakes require integration of environmental policies. A mutually satisfactory bilateral agreement will result in environmental gains to both countries and will also achieve those gains at a lower cost than if the two countries did not collaborate.

NOTES

Work on this chapter was partially supported by a Canadian Studies Faculty Enrichment grant. I am grateful to Lisa Voss for editorial assistance.

1. *Air Pollution Across National Boundaries: The Impact on the Environment of Sulfur in Air and Precipitation* (Stockholm, Sweden: Royal Ministry for Foreign Affiars, Royal Ministry of Agriculture, 1972).

2. Marylynn Placet, "Emissions Involved in Acidic Deposition Processes," Report 1 in *Acidic Deposition: State of Science and Technology*, Summary Compendium Document, Summaries of NAPAP State-of-Science/Technology Reports 1-28, National Acid Precipitation Assessment Program (Washington, D.C., 1989).

3. For a recent comprehensive survey of the scientific aspects of acidic deposition, see National Acid Precipitation Assessment Program, *Acidic Deposition: State of Science and Technology*, (1989) op. cit. A joint assessment of Canadian-U.S. research projects can be found in NAPAP/RMCC, Joint Report to the Bilateral Advisory and Consultative Group: *Statue of Canadian-U.S. Research in Acidic Deposition*, (1987), prepared by the U.S. National Acid Precipitation Assessment Program (Washington, D.C.) and Canadian Federal-Provincial Research and Monitoring Commmittee (Downsview, Ontario).

4. For elaboration of the policy issue in the United States from this perspective, see U.S. Office of Technology Assessment, *Acid Rain and Transported Air Pollutants: Implications for Public Policy*, OTA-O-24, (Washington, D.C.: U.S. Government Printing Office, 1984).

5. For discussion and analysis of some of the distributional issues, see Congressional Budget Office, *Curbing Acid Rain: Cost, Budget, and Coal-Market Effects*, (Washington, D.C.: Congress of the United States, 1986).

6. Special Committee on Acid Rain, *First Report, Minutes of Proceedings and Evidence of the Special Committee on Acid Rain*, Issue 24, (Ottawa: House of Commons, September, 1988).

7. Special Committee on Acid Rain, op. cit.

8. Canadian Embassy, "Acid Rain Damage," *Canadian-United States Acid Rain (Washington, D.C., 1988)*.

9. Robin Dennis, "Selected Applications of the Regional Acid Deposition Model," an appendix of the State of Science/Technology Reports, no. 4, in *Acidic Deposition: State of Science and Technology*, (Washington, D.C., 1989).

10. Jurgen Schmandt, Judith Clarkson, and Hilliard Roderick, *Acid Rain and Friendly Neighbors: The Policy Dispute Between Canada and the United States* (Durham, NC: Duke University Press, 1988) pp. 138-139.

11. Special Committee on Acid Rain, op. cit., p. 3.

12. Canada, House of Commons, *Still Waters: The Chilling Reality of Acid Rain*, Committee on Fisheries and Forestry, Subcommittee on Acid Rain (Ottawa: Minister of Supplies and Services, 1981).

13. One study indicates that if electric utilities could use least-cost methods t meet the mandated reductions within the broad confines of the 1990 legislation, compliance would be achieved by switching to low-sulfur coal at approximately 30 percent of affected capacity (Temple, Barker, and Sloane, Inc., "Clean Air Act Amendments of 1989," Economic Evaluation of H.R. 3030/S.1490, Washington, D.C., 1989). The remaining sources would comply using scrubbers or some other technology-based method.

14. Special Committee on Acid Rain, op. cit., p. 9.

15. For a discussion of the current state of research into the atmospheric component of acidic deposition, see Steven E. Schwartz, "Acid Deposition: Unraveling a Regional Phenomenon," *Science* 243, no. 10, (February 1989), pp. 753-763.

16. Anthony Scott, "The Canadian-American Problem of Acid Rain," *Natural Resources Journal*, 26 (Spring, 1986), pp. 338-358.

17. Scott also argues that negotiable pollution certificates would be the best method to solve the bilateral problem. They could be issued to dischargers of each type of pollutant and exchanged at market prices with other sources or with victims of damages on both sides of the border. This scheme is similar to the tradeable emissions reduction credits in the U.S. legislation.

18. Canadian Embassy, "Transboundary Flows of Acid Rain Pollution," *Canada-United States Acid Rain*, (Washington, D.C., 1988).

19. Actually, both the Canadian and the U.S. cost estimates also include costs for controlling NO_x emissions. However, such costs are relatively small and are probably about the same proportion of total costs in both countries.

20. Maler performed a similar analysis for European countries, and in addition estimated the gains from allowing countries to trade emissions reductions to meet pollution standards. "Acid Gains," *The Economist* (November 25, 1989), p. 77.

21. Thomas H. Tietenberg, "Acid Rain Reduction Credits," *Challenge*, (March-April, 1989), pp. 25-29.

22. For a discussion of the application of market-based tools for pollution control, see Robert W. Hahn, "Economic Prescriptions for Environmental Problems: How the Patient Followed the Doctor's Orders," *Journal of Economic Perspectives* 3, no. 2 (1989), pp. 95-114.

23. Congressional Budget Office, *Curbing Acid Rain: Cost, Budget, and Coal-Market Effects*, (Washington, D.C.: Congress of the United States, 1986).

4

Great Lakes: Great Rhetoric
Alan M. Schwartz

The Great Lakes have been called "a unique national and international resource," "a truly magnificent natural resource,"[1] "an irreplaceable treasure,"[2] "an economic and environmental asset for the region, the nation, and the world,"[3] and "an important part of the physical and cultural heritage of North America."[4] But clearly the United States and Canada have not always matched this rhetoric with the protection befitting such a treasure.

This chapter will examine the rhetoric associated with three quarters of a century of joint U.S.-Canada management of the Great Lakes and contrast it with the actions that have resulted in improved lake quality. After a brief history of early pollution problems and the response mechanisms established by governments to deal with these, the discussion will focus on the pollution problems of the last two decades. The unique mechanism of binational management, the International Joint Commission (IJC), will be examined to analyze its successes and failures in improving water quality. The progress and setbacks of recent years will be contrasted with the problems that lie ahead to restore the Great Lakes system to a state where it will provide the myriad of beneficial uses that citizens of both countries desire.

The Great Lakes system (the five lakes and the St. Lawrence River) forms the largest water boundary between any two countries. Stretching for over 1,600 kilometers (1,000 miles), it contains about one-fifth of all the fresh water on the planet. The lakes cover a total area of 244,000 square kilometers (94,000 square miles). The basin is home to one of every ten Americans and one of every four Canadians. Twenty five million people depend on the lakes as their source of drinking water, and every day almost 1 billion gallons of water are withdrawn or used in stream to support residential, commercial, industrial, and agricultural requirements of both nations. The extent of this resource is so vast that only recently have people realized that it has the potential to be irrevocably degraded. Indeed, the old saying, the solution to pollution is dilution, was appropriate for the Great Lakes system for centuries. It was only after the rapid rise in population and industry that began around the turn of the 20th century and the advent of new synthetic organic pollutants after World War II that the Great Lakes began to show signs of serious degradation.

Today the lakes are subject to pollution from an unprecedented number of sources. These include both point sources (discharges emanating from a specific place) from industries, and municipal waste, as well as nonpoint sources that include leachate from landfills, seepage from industrial lagoons, agricultural runoff, and others. Although the lakes have the potential for substantial dilution of pollutants, the outflows from them are small when compared to their volumes. Pollutants that enter the lakes are retained in the system for long periods and thus are more likely to become concentrated over time. This increases the potential for the resuspension of pollutants trapped in the sediments.[5] Thus once polluted, the water of Lake Superior, which is the cleanest of the lakes both because of its volume and lower pollution loading, takes 191 years to be replaced.

The first evidence of problems with the Great Lakes came early in the 1900s in the lower lakes (Erie and Ontario), which are smaller and have the greatest concentration of people and industry. Although logging and agriculture increased siltation of the lakes during the late 19th century, the first problem that attracted the attention of the federal governments of the United States and Canada was the spread of water-borne diseases such as typhoid and cholera. People on both sides of the border were dying, and the problem was believed to be linked to contamination of drinking water. Later problems included a rapid decline in the numbers of fish and fish species, nuisance blooms of algae rotting on shorelines, and more recently the accumulation of toxic materials detrimental to fish and wildlife and potentially hazardous to human health. The threat to the integrity of the Great Lakes has been continuous for over three-quarters of a century but has never been more critical than it is today.

THE BEGINNINGS OF BINATIONAL MANAGEMENT

Because of numerous problems concerning water level changes caused by dams along the border and as a result of other minor irritants between the United States and Canada, the two countries began discussions on establishing a mechanism for the prevention and resolution of transborder disputes in the early 1900s. The International Waterways Commission, formed in 1903, made a series of recommendations calling for the creation of an international body with the authority to study and regulate the use of international waters. These discussions culminated in the signing of the Boundary Waters Treaty (BWT) in 1909 wherein each nation pledged that "boundary waters and waters flowing across the boundary shall not be polluted on either side to the injury of health or property of the other."[6]   The BWT also established an independent commission, the IJC.

The IJC was composed of six members, three from each country. It was to have final approval on all matters regarding changes in water levels (not on matters of water quality) of any boundary or transboundry body of water. Also, the commission was be an investigative body, and when asked by governments to study a problem (through a reference) it would develop recommendations to bring about resolution of the problem at hand. Although the BWT allows either nation to ask the IJC for advice, it became a custom that neither nation would do so without concurrence of the other. The commission received its first reference concerning water quality in 1912, its first year of operation. The U.S. and Canadian governments, concerned with typhoid and cholera, asked the IJC to investigate the source and extent of pollution in the lower Great Lakes (specifically the Detroit and Niagara rivers), and to determine if this pollution was causing harm to either nation, i.e., was the Boundary Waters Treaty being violated.

The commission concluded that pollution from untreated sewage, especially from the United States, was the cause of the problem. It recommended that sewage be treated and that the commission be given the power to continue to monitor this issue as it deemed appropriate.   In its very first report to governments, the commission characterized the situation as "generally chaotic, everywhere perilous, and in some cases disgraceful."[7]   Despite such blunt language, the two governments chose not to allow the IJC to continue its study of all Great Lakes concerns and did not adopt the recommendation calling for sewage treatment plants because of the large expense it would require. Their acceptance of the commission's report but the rejection of its recommendations began an eighty-year history of limited, vacillating commitment and mixed messages from both federal governments regarding the protection of the Great Lakes. The communicable disease problem was solved by the chlorination of drinking water supplies rather than by the reduction of untreated sewage. This set the stage for new problems that would be returned to the IJC decades later.

Over the next several decades concern over the quality of the Great Lakes increased, and occasional references were sent to the commission. In 1964, with lake conditions growing increasingly worse, both nations sent the IJC a broad reference to look once again at pollution of the lower Great Lakes. The effect of five decades of dealing with the symptoms of the problem rather than the problem itself had finally resulted in intolerable conditions. Ever-increasing amounts of sewage caused by rapid population increases were being dumped into the lakes without treatment. Although treatment of drinking water managed to eliminate water-born diseases, more and more beaches were being closed due to unacceptable levels of fecal coliform bacteria. Recreation and aesthetics were impaired by large blooms of nuisance algae. The accelerated input of nutrients from sewage, household detergents, and runoff from agricultural lands was causing a condition known as cultural eutrophication. This process resulted in a large increases in the amount of algae coupled with a change in the makeup of the species of algae.

Desirable forms that provided a good food source for insects and fish disappeared and were replaced by blue-green algae that were a dead end in the food chain. Because these algae were not eaten by other inhabitants of the lake, they tended to pile up on shorelines. While the algae gave off oxygen in the daylight, they, like all other organisms, used oxygen for respiration, and thus large collections of algae in still bays depleted oxygen need by fish and other organisms. The decomposition of fish killed in this manner as well as uneaten algae again greatly reduced the oxygen content of the water, causing foul-smelling nuisances. Thus, the advanced stages of eutrophication, algal blooms, and oxygen depletion and its associated fish kills, were commonplace in the lower Great Lakes by the 1960s.

The commission studied the issues for over six years before releasing its final report in 1970. The report stated the nature, severity, and causes of the problems affecting the lakes; it made specific recommendations to alleviate the problem of eutrophication. Both governments, feeling the pressure of a growing public concern for the environment, pledged themselves to a massive Great Lakes cleanup by signing the 1972 Great Lakes Water Quality agreement.

"The 1972 agreement was, with the exception of the Boundary Waters Treaty itself, the most comprehensive environmental agreement ever reached by the two countries."[8] Water quality objectives were established for each of the lower lakes. Although the commission's authority was not expanded beyond its investigative function, it was given a permanent watchdog role in Great Lake's matters; it would no longer need a reference to investigate any Great Lakes problem. It would have the responsibility for the "tendering of advice and recommendations to the Parties and to the State and Provincial Governments on problems of the quality of the boundary waters of the Great Lake System, including specific recommendations concerning water quality objectives, legislation, standards, and other regulatory requirements, programs, and other measures and intergovernmental agreements relating to the quality of those waters."[9] To accomplish this, the commission created two permanent standing boards. The Water Quality Board, composed of agency staff from both governments, would advise the commission of the status of water quality. The Science Advisory Board, composed primarily of academics, defined the research needs that provided the information the commission required to fulfill its mandate.

The rhetoric and the fanfare that surrounded the signing of the agreement had barely quieted down when the agreement received a substantial setback. One year after the signing, President Nixon impounded the U.S. Federal funds needed for the construction of sewage treatment plants. Although this was taken as a signal of wavering U.S. commitment, it was soon apparent that even without the impoundment of funds the December 1975 deadline set by the IJC for reaching water quality objectives would have been far too optimistic. While the commission, in their agreement-mandated annual reports (later to become biennial reports), noted this temporary U.S. retreat from its commitments, the tone of those reports was for the most part restrained and where possible complimentary toward efforts being made. In 1977 the IJC began its *Fifth Annual Report on Great Lakes Water Quality* by stating, "Progress towards the goals of the agreement continues to be slow and uneven. The phosphorus control program shows encouraging signs, and the total phosphorus loadings have decreased, but in general, the program is behind schedule and has not yet resulted in significant overall progress toward the anticipated improvement of Water Quality of the Great Lakes."

The 1972 agreement was to last for a period of five years. Because of the failure to meet established deadlines, and equally important, the discovery of new problems of toxic substances in the lakes, both governments decided it was in their best interests to renew the agreement. However, the process of negotiating a new agreement was not easy. Because the U.S. Water Pollution Control Act, PL 92-500, had been in effect for several years, the United States preferred to incorporate strict effluent control standards into the new agreement rather than the general water quality objectives that were in the 1972 agreement. Canada viewed this as an attempt to introduce U.S. law and environmental practice into the accord, and rejected the idea. After much debate an agreement was finally concluded and signed in 1978. It was designed to "restore and maintain the integrity of the waters of the Great Lakes."[10]

> The changes in the 1978 agreement from that of 1972 were striking. Formal deadlines of 1982 for municipal pollution abatement and 1983 for industrial pollution abatement were set. New, more stringent, overall phosphorus loading reductions were established. A long list of hazardous polluting substances were to be banned from the lakes. New tougher standards for radioactivity were established. Perhaps most significantly, the concept of an ecosystem approach was developed by the inclusion of sections dealing with airborne pollutants, and pollution from agriculture, rural forestry, and other land use activities. Article VII of the 1978 agreement continued the permanent watchdog role that the Commission first spelled out in the 1972 agreement. The new agreement held out considerable hope that a renewed committed effort on the part of both countries was to be made in cleaning up Great Lakes water quality. The IJC was generally pleased with the new agreement.[11]

Although progress was slow, the period between the two agreements was marked by the beginnings of substantial phosphorus reductions with concurrent abatement of the problems of advanced eutrophication. Steady progress on curtailing phosphorus input into the lakes was made throughout the 1970s and into the mid-1980s. By 1985 scientists could say the eutrophication problem was on the verge of solution. "As a result of phosphorus control programs which have been implemented since 1972, there have been significant reductions in the phosphorus loadings to all the Great Lakes. Lakes Superior, Huron, and Michigan, with the exception of some localized areas are considered oligotrophic [low nutrient]."[12] Lake Ontario had shown reduced phosphorus content in the water and an accompanying reduction in algal blooms. Lake Erie, said by the media to be dead in the 1960s, was still considered to be high nutrient, but the quantity of floating plant material in the open water had decreased and the composition of the algae had shifted away from the high-nutrient nuisance variety.

The 1978 Agreement set a target for large municipal sewage treatment plants on all lakes to discharge no more than one part per million (PPM) total phosphorus into the water. By 1985, although some individual plants still exceeded this target, the average of all plants on each lake had met the target.[13] Although there still must be some reductions of phosphorus from nonpoint sources to meet the goals for total loading in Lake Erie, by all measures the reduction of phosphorus and the resultant improvement in water quality looms as the single greatest achievement in the seven decades of joint lake management.

TOXICS

For most of this century attempts were made to reduce pollution to levels that would not exceed the assimilative capacity of a body of water. Since water could dilute pollutants, the task was to find and then limit inputs to a "no-effect" level. This entire concept had to be rethought when persistent toxic substances such as chlorinated hydrocarbons were found in the Lakes. The production of many of these substances, such as DDT and PCBs, was banned or greatly restricted in both the United States and Canada by 1972. The same was true for mercury, which had been shown to change from a relatively harmless inorganic form to a dangerous organic compound in lake sediments. Mirex, a close relative of PCBs, produced in New York for use as a poison for the fire ant, joined the list of banned substances by 1976. These substances were shown to cause birth defects, reduce reproductive ability, or cause cancer in laboratory animals. They were persistent in the environment, and thus even small amounts released into water were unacceptable.

Chlorinated organic chemicals are relatively insoluble in water. Thus they would not be found in most water samples but rather would sink into the sediments. Here they would be incorporated into the fat cells of plants and later into the animals that ate the plants. In this way non-detectable concentrations in water could result in very low concentrations in sediments and lower plant forms, and steadily increase as one moved up the food chain. Fish and fish-eating birds were observed to have concentrations of these chemicals over one million times greater than the water column. Because of their persistence and ability to bioaccumulate (increase up the food chain), the entire concept of acceptable releases into the environment and dilution was no longer appropriate.

The banning of many of these chlorinated organic compounds, along with the banning of mercury, resulted in precipitous declines in their concentrations in fish and fish-eating birds. However, the dramatic decreases that took place in the 1970s has leveled off and has done so for some substances at a level exceeding the objectives of the agreement. Although recent data is inconclusive, some of these substances seem to be on the increase once again. Near-shore data suggests that inputs of some of these substances are still occurring. Advisories against the consumption of many species and size classes of fish are in effect because of levels of PCBs, mercury, and mirex that are considered hazardous to human health.[14] New York State fisherman are warned not to eat any eel, catfish, lake trout, large coho salmon, or rainbow or brown trout. While smaller salmon and rainbow or brown trout are acceptable, it is alarming that even these species should be limited to no more than one meal each month and not eaten at all by women of childbearing age and children under age 15.[15]

THE REAGAN YEARS

In 1982 the United States General Accounting office (GAO), a semi-independent watchdog agency that reports to Congress, issued two reports critical of the U.S. government policy regarding Great Lakes cleanup and the government's support for the IJC. Its first report issued in May entitled *A More Comprehensive Approach is Needed to Clean Up the Great Lakes*, concluded that "although the lakes are cleaner, the United States is finding it difficult to meet Agreement [the 1978 Great Lakes Water Quality Agreement] commitments." It criticized the United Stats for "lack of effective overall strategies for dealing with Great Lake Water quality problems."[16]

The second report issued only one month later in June 1982 criticized the lack of formal response by the State Department to the recommendations of the commission. In the preceding ten years, the IJC had issued 16 reports to government that contained specific recommendations for requests for, clarification of, or information on, agreement matters. The State Department had formally responded to only three of these reports despite repeated IJC requests for response. The GAO noted that this lack of response hampered the ability of the commission to advise governments. The GAO report chastised key federal agencies for failing to give appropriate advise to the Water Quality Board of the commission.[17]

The GAO was not alone in its criticism. The IJC itself seemed to have reached an unprecedented level of frustration with the slow pace of progress. In its First Biennial Report under the Great Lakes Water Quality Agreement of 1978, the commission issued a most biting critique of government performance. Gone were the subtitles that characterized the annual reports filed under the 1972 agreement. The document cited as "important and encouraging" President Reagan's May 1981 speech to the Canadian Parliament, in which the president pledged further efforts in Great Lakes cleanup. It then pointed out the distance between the president's remarks and the actions of his administrative agencies. It included a not-so-veiled attack on the Environmental Protection Agency (EPA) for its lack of needed research and surveillance. It pointed out that at the same time the president was talking about increased cleanup efforts, his administration was proposing budget cuts that would curtail needed research. "Monitoring and research functions are essential components of the [1978] Agreement for they provide a means of assessing progress and a framework for understanding the problems of the Great Lakes Basin Ecosystem. Without such a framework, there is no rational basis for assessing whether or not there has been progress toward maintaining and restoring the physical, chemical, and biological integrity of the Great Lakes Basin Ecosystem."[18] Despite these reports and protests from environmental groups the administration continued to attempt to cut Great Lakes programs. These programs were spared by the U.S. Congress, but at considerably lower levels of funding.

Funding was not the only problem. The commission noted "A clear sense of unity and direction on issues central to the Agreement is required. The sense of drift is nowhere more apparent than with the issue of toxic and hazardous substances."[19] Annex 10 of the agreement required the parties to maintain and revise two list of hazardous substances. One list contains chemicals of unknown toxic effects on biota and the second list chemicals with potentially toxic effects. As of June 1982 neither government had begun to review or revise these lists, and no measures to minimize or eliminate the risk of release of these substances into the Great Lakes had commenced.[20]

Although the commission's frustration was well founded, the early 1980s saw the beginning of an entirely new set of circumstances in the joint management of the Great Lakes that would continue until today: the agreement was calling for advances in basic science that were moving along at a much slower pace than policymakers wanted. New methods of detection were enabling scientists to detect levels of pollutants in the range of parts per trillion, when the effects of much higher concentrations of the pollutant was not known. Hundreds of new untested chemicals were being released and/or turning up in lake sediments and biota. In addition to moving into an unknown area of science, we were moving into an unknown area of politics. The agreement mandated a coordinated integrated ecosystem approach, but agencies were not organized to address problems in this manner. They were organized to deal with problems within a given media, e.g., water pollution, air pollution, solid waste, but not with the interaction between these problems. Thus the 1980s were characterized by an administration whose lower priorities on environment were translated into reduced spending, great scientific uncertainty, and unresponsive federal bureaucracy. The rhetoric about the need for a healthy Great Lakes ecosystem continued unabated while essential scientific research and monitoring withered.

REMEDIAL ACTION PLANS (RAPs)

Following the recommendation contained in the *1985 Report of the Great Lakes Water Quality Board* to the IJC, the eight Great Lakes states and Ontario committed themselves to restore the worst areas of the lakes and to reclaim the beneficial uses these areas once supported. These 42 areas, called Areas of Concern, are the toxic hot spots in the lakes. Twenty-five of these areas are within the United States, and five more are shared U.S.-Canada sites. The commitment to restore these areas was built into the 1987 protocol which updated the 1978 agreement. "The Protocol generally strengthens and renews the bilateral commitments to further an ecosystems approach to Great Lakes management and to virtually eliminate the discharge of persistent toxic substances." [21] The RAP planning process is at the heart of current cleanup efforts and the major hope for Great Lakes restoration for the foreseeable future.

The new RAP planning process is significant for several reasons. First, in keeping with the spirit of the agreement, it is supposed to be based on an ecosystem approach in the restoration of each area. Rather than another element in the programs of the federal governments, the RAPs are community-based plans. The theory is that only by involving a wide cross-section of individuals in a grass-roots effort will the education of the public and the degree of commitment necessary be achieved. The RAP plans are to be submitted to the IJC at each of their three stages of development and implementation. The first phase is the completion of problem definition; the second phase is the selection of remedial and regulatory mechanisms; the third phase is monitoring data that indicates that impaired beneficial uses have been restored.

This process, upon which both governments are placing such critical importance, is off to a very slow start. The Fifth Biennial Report of the Commission[22] states that of the eight RAPs received by the IJC, all but one failed to achieve an adequate stage-one presentation (a definition of the problem) or to take the required ecosystem approach.[23] Most of the 42 plans have not yet been submitted, and many have made little progress. Several factors contribute to the delays, not the least of which is funding. The RAPs were to be funded primarily by state monies, and these have been in short supply. The concept of a local grass-roots planning effort may seem attractive, but clearly these efforts flounder without financial and technical support from the federal government. Limited financial help came early in the process with start-up grants to the states, but further funding in the United States is tied to FY 1991 Section 106 planning grants.[24] Ironically, section 106 grants are the major source of federal funds for water pollution control programs. This means that RAP funding is competing with funding for already designated high-priority state water pollution programs and initiatives. In short, states will have to steal from important cleanup programs if they are to receive funds for RAPs. While some praise the RAP process as a "remarkable start," thus far it has been a remarkable concept with relatively little in the way of results.[25]

Indeed some of the enthusiasm for RAPs is for what they may accomplish in the long run rather than in a belief that these plans will result in early remedies for longstanding problems. A commission staff member concluded that the importance of RAPs is to be found in the fact that they will build a local constituency for problem resolution and get local people to begin to view their local problems in an ecosystem framework.[26] This is perhaps a realistic way of viewing what will be eventually needed to bring about a restoration of these areas. For example, it will be much easier and more productive to motivate a small group of "stakeholders" to work on the restoration of the beneficial uses of Hamilton Harbor or the Massena area of the St. Lawrence River than it will be to motivate large groups of people to perceive themselves as citizens of the Great Lakes basin.

As the RAP process has developed, another concern, perhaps paramount, has emerged. Even after the first and second phases of these plans are complete, there is every reason to believe that implementation will require new legislation on both sides of the border. New environmental legislation and subsequent implementation of remediation plans require new funds. Although no hard figures are available, preliminary estimates are sure to frighten officials from the White House to the state houses, from Parliament Hill to Queen's Park. Canada's David Rapport speculated that the cost to "reestablish some semblance of ecosystem stability" may be in the tens of billions of dollars, while complete restoration may go into the hundreds of billions.[27] While no one takes these cost estimates to be definitive, the $1.8 billion price tag associated with just correcting storm water runoff discussed in the Rouge River RAP is clear evidence we are embarking on a long, expensive process.

THE "NEW" IJC

The IJC has always been praised as a low-key, behind the scenes actor that helps move governments to solutions the governments are prepared to accept. This is why the first biennial report, in 1982, with its sharp critique of government, was viewed as the beginning of a potentially new "more aggressive" role for the commission.[28] For the remainder of the 1980s, however, the commission seemed to return to its traditional operating style of gentle persuader. Indeed the second, third, and fourth biennial reports, while pointing to shortcomings in implementation of the agreement, did not have the fire of the first report. As we begin the 1990s the IJC appears to be changing tactics once again, revisiting a more active position while at the same time opening its process to the public to an unprecedented degree. While the commission has always held public hearings, many citizen groups complained that the hearings were not structured in a way to allow full open debate by the public. Indeed, many scholars viewed the strength of the commission to be its collection and synthesis of technical data, not public opinion.

The 1989 Biennial meeting in Hamilton, Ontario, was a significant departure from past practice. One environmentalist called it "the first biennial meeting of the *people* of the Great Lakes."[29] Ten environmental groups cosponsored the meeting with the commission. The commissioners set aside large blocks of time for the public and did not require written questions submitted in advance. When it was clear that only a small percentage of all who wished to speak could be accommodated in the time allocated, the commissioners extended the period several times. The commissioners present (two U.S. vacancies on the commission had still not been filled) sat and listened to public statements for over eighteen hours. Although many viewed this as a way to placate citizens and groups who felt shut out, this was not the case. This was a well thought out plan to allow the IJC to reflect public indignation back to governments. Clear evidence of this was the fact that Greenpeace, the most radical and active group in condemning the failure of governments to act, was invited. Joyce McLean, director of Toronto Greenpeace, was given the honor of delivering the luncheon address to the assembly. Rather than simply deliver an address, Greenpeace crafted a well-designed "performance" designed to capture media attention. They might have even surprised the commissioners when they called for the resignation of all the commissioners if these individuals could not motivate governments to act more decisively within the next few years.

The Commission's *Fifth Biennial Report*, published in 1989 shortly after the biennial meeting, was the first report where two commission chairs rather than the IJC staff took the lead in the drafting. These commissioners, greatly influenced by the dire warnings of potential health effects of pollutants presented in the 1989 *Report of the Great Lakes Science Advisory Board* and the outpouring of public opinion at the Biennial meeting, wrote a report that was most unusual.[30] "Hard hitting, frank, and forceful are not words one would normally associate with the biennial reports of the International Joint Commission (IJC). But the Commission's Fifth Biennial Report . . . . can be appropriately described by all of the above adjectives." [31]

The report was published in two parts, the first devoted to a summary of the public input at the biennial meeting, and the second a summary of the commission's views on six basic topics, beginning with human health and continuing to include RAPs; Spills; Exotic Species; State, Provincial, and local participation; and the federal government's response to the report. One did not have to delve into the fine print to get the commission's message. The front and back cover consisted of a single light background photo of a lake shore with two quotes dominating the pages. On the front cover appeared the words "The child that I am carrying right now has probably and is currently receiving the highest loadings of toxic chemicals that it will receive in its lifetime"; a quote attributed to an "eminent scientist" at the 1989 biennial meeting. The back cover displayed a quote from within the report that read "The Commission must conclude that there is a threat to the health of our children emanating from our exposure to persistent toxic substances, even at very low ambient levels."[32]

Until recently, the concern for the quality of the Great Lakes focused on fish, wildlife, aesthetics, and other such matters. For the last three decades there has been a concern about the potential human health problems caused by very low concentrations of persistent organic chemicals. Because so little was known about the effect of these substances, this concern was expressed by a call for more basic scientific research. As more and more data from animal studies was developed, concern for human health increased. Although animal data is still not definitive for many of the chemicals of concern, the accumulation of circumstantial evidence is cause for increased concern. "Nevertheless, in many cases, [health] problems in Great Lake wildlife have been associated with high levels of toxic contamination and some of the health effects observed have been reproduced in laboratory animals."[33] "The patterns revealed in animal and wildlife studies are ominous for humans—patterns of toxic accumulation; similar health anomalies across a wide range of species, notably generational effects in animals high in the food web; and associations between health effects and toxic substances."[34]

Human health data is still sparse, but at least one study on women who consumed large quantities of fish from Lake Michigan showed slight but statistically significant changes in infants that affected gestation period, birth weight, and development. "When the infants were retested at age seven months, the researchers found that the mothers' lifetime history of fish consumption—as well as the amount of PCBs found in the umbilical cord sera—was associated with decreased neurological development in the infants."[35] The Science Advisory Board in its letter transmittal of its 1989 report to the IJC stated "the findings and conclusions of the Board in this regard [concerning toxic and human health] warrant the Commission recommending that the Parties undertake a comprehensive binational investigation, possibly a reference, concerning the significance, nature, and extent of human exposure to toxic chemicals in the Great Lakes Basin Ecosystem. This is the first recommendation of the Board . . . . and the focus of the 1989 report."[36] Human health concerns that have been present for a long period of time will be the issues that move into the forefront in the 1990s.

Although human health concerns were certainly the keynote of the IJC Fifth Biennial, the commission also was concerned with process. Its very last recommendation was "in order for the Commission to better assist the Parties in implementing the Agreement, the Parties should respond to the Commission's recommendations following every other semi-annual meeting of the Parties. This response should include the status with respect to implementation of these recommendations or the reasons why a delay has occurred or action has not been taken." [37] This statement in various forms had been made in the past, but never by the commission itself in such an explicit fashion.[38] Gone was the gentle, subtle persuasion. In its place was the demand for real progress or an explanation of why it was not occurring. Clearly the commission was trying to rally public support and move sluggish governments.

FRUSTRATION WITH DELAY

On June 13, 1990, the Subcommittee on Oversight of Governmental Management of the U.S. Senate Governmental Affairs Committee conducted a hearing on the progress of the Great Lakes Water Quality Agreement. It had been over ten years since the agreement was signed and three years since the protocol to deal more specifically with the complex problems of toxic pollution. The senators representing Great Lakes states were outspoken in their criticism of the EPA. Senator John Glenn (D-Ohio) said that "the agreement provides a remarkable road map for restoring the good health of the Great Lakes ecosystems, but it does not remove from us the need to make the journey."[39] He claimed that while some progress was being made, the 1990 funding was still 10 percent less than that of 1980 in inflation-adjusted dollars. He cited the June 1989 GAO report on the U.S. participation in the International Joint Commission, which in many ways sounded like a rehash of many of the criticisms made by the GAO in 1982. One of the most serious findings of the GAO was that only one out every three major recommendations from the IJC was implemented by the U.S. government, and there was no process by which either government advised the IJC of its determinations relative to these recommendations. The category of recommendation least likely to get a response was "greater State and Federal cooperation."[40] Although not an ideal system, the intergovernmental cooperation appears to be working much better on the Canadian side. The Department of External Affairs has already responded to the Canadian side of the commission regarding the Fourth Biennial Report, and the response to the Fifth Biennial report is in progress. As of July 1990 the U.S. State Department had still not responded to the Fourth Biennial, which was submitted in 1988.[41]

Representative Carl Levin (D-Mich.) has pointed out that a 1989 hearing by the same Senate subcommittee found "in virtually every major Great Lake program, EPA had allowed key initiatives to stagnate. Its failures include dropping the ball on Remedial Action Plans, failing to reduce interstate disparities in water quality standards, and twiddling its thumbs on projects to demonstrate technologies to cleanup contaminated sediments. When confronted with specific program failures, EPA's witnesses promised to improve their performance." Levin went on to use the words of EPA Administrator William Reilly to emphasize the lack of progress. In October 1989, Reilly stated at a press conference "that we must redouble our existing efforts to protect and restore this vital resource [Great Lakes]." He "committed the EPA to an agency wide effort to focus on Great Lakes issues." Levin countered by claiming "[It is now] eight months later and there is little evidence that Mr. Reilly's directives have had much of an effect. With few exceptions, the EPA Great Lakes programs remain dead in the water, with progress about as murky as the sediments hauled up by the Mud Puppy [EPA's new research boat]."[42]

Perhaps the most fundamental criticism of the U.S. failure to make more progress relates to a lack of coordination among those responsible for problem resolution. A Canada-Ontario Agreement has been in place a long time and specifies federal and provincial implementation responsibilities in Canada. The Canada-Ontario Agreement Board of Review, composed of members from the Federal Ministry of the Environment and Ontario Ministry of the Environment, meets five to six times each year. Surely the matter is greatly simplified with only two players. In the United States a mechanism for clarifying responsibility between the federal government and the eight Great Lakes states is lacking and badly needed.[43] The Great Lakes Commission, an interstate compact agency with a legislative mandate to represent the collective views of the eight Great Lakes states before Congress, has called for the formation of a U.S. Policy Committee on the Great Lakes to be chaired by the administrator of the EPA and include senior policy administrators from the eight Great Lakes states.[44]

The problem of coordination is not merely between the federal government and state governments but within the federal government itself. The EPA is structured to combat pollution by the media in which the pollution is; there are people who deal with air pollution problems who may seldom speak with the water pollution specialists or hazardous waste specialists, and so on. While that system may be fine for many site-specific problems, it is antithetical to the agreement mandate for an ecosystem approach to solving Great Lakes problems. The EPA does have an internal Great Lakes Advisory Committee (GLAC) to develop an agencywide multimedia perspective on pollution, but recent EPA initiated changes are an admission of the shortcomings of the committee to date. Early in 1990 the GLAC expanded its membership to include all assistant administrators. Each of them was asked to review program and funding policies and to report back to the GLAC on specific contributions their programs can make toward a coordinated, multimedia approach to Great Lakes environmental problems. Senior-level contacts are then to be designated by each office to the EPA Great Lakes Program Office to ensure greater intra-agency coordination.[45] This is certainly a positive step, but only time will tell if a bureaucracy as big as the EPA can be remolded to met the concept of ecosystem management.

Although toxic substances, their effect on human health, and the ability of RAPs to restore the toxic hot spots in the lakes are clearly the issues that will be in the forefront of policy considerations for some time to come, a discussion of the Great Lakes ecosystem does not end with these issues. The introduction of foreign species to the lakes has in the past and threatens once again to cause serious problems. The contamination of the Great Lakes system by the sea lamprey in the 1950s decimated lake trout populations and has cost governments over $100 million for control efforts. The zebra mussel, a native of Europe, was first found in Lake St. Clair in 1987. It now is found throughout Lake Erie and in almost all of Ontario. Its clogging of water intakes, encrusting of boat hulls, and potential ecological damage points to the need for increasing efforts to control the introduction of these species through vessel ballasts.[46] Spills from shipping and shore-based industries continue to be a source of chemical contamination and have the potential to result in a catastrophic disruption of the Lakes.[47] Finally, wetland habitat, so important to both fish and wildlife populations of the Great Lakes system, continues to be degraded and developed with a resultant decline in many species.

CONCLUSIONS

The rhetoric recognizing the Great Lakes as a unique resource has been a continuous feature of government policy in both the United States and Canada throughout this century. Commitments to avoid pollution of the lakes have been bound in treaty for more than eighty years, and more-recent commitments to restore and maintain the integrity of the lakes are the basis for far-reaching government programs. Action, however, while not insignificant, is much more sporadic. Governments have often tried to deal with symptoms rather than problems, which has eventually lead to new problems. The major effort to reduce nutrient input to the lakes and virtually eliminate the eutrophication problems of five decades is a tribute to government action based on a convergence of national interests. However, "the nutrient problems were well documented--the solutions for point source discharges well known. It required the commitment of generally known technology to alleviate the problem."[48] The symptoms of eutrophication could be reversed by curtailing new input of the key nutrients.

This effort is in sharp contrast to the 1978 Agreement's pledge to use an ecosystem approach to eliminate toxic substances from the lakes. The appropriate technology to achieve this goal was not at hand in 1978, and was still not fully developed in 1990. The very definition of the word *toxic* is in dispute, and existing scientific evidence cannot provide the necessary answers regarding the degree of risk from very small quantities of chemicals known to be harmful at high concentrations. Stopping new sources of toxics will be difficult; but even if successful, this is not enough. We must deal with a legacy of "in-place" toxics now being recycled in lake sediments and organisms. In 1978 there was no agreement or even understanding of what was required for an ecosystem approach, and even today existing institutions on all levels are simply not set up to deal with ecosystem management.

In recent years there has been a resurgence of public opinion about our stewardship of the environment (or lack of it) to a degree not seen since the late 1960s. The Remedial Action Plan processes that were established to restore the lakes has built a new broader constituency for their protection. Governments have begun the process of reorganization necessary to deal with the lakes as a single ecosystem. Continued pressure from all quarters, including the IJC and nongovernmental citizens' groups, will be required to keep the process from bogging down in a web of complex scientific data and unproven remediation measures.

But even with the best of coordinated efforts and strong funding commitments (both of which are highly uncertain) the best hope for the future of the Great Lakes system will be regulations and enforcement to prevent new problems. Existing problems such as leaking waste disposal areas from practices discontinued over a decade ago will be with us for a long time.

We now recognize the ecological mandate for an ecosystems approach, but no government has ever attempted such an approach on a system as large as the Great Lakes. Our success will be measured by our ability to eliminate future degradation of the lakes and to build the political mechanisms necessary to regulate them as a single system. Our chances of success for the former are quite good; for the latter we must make the leap from controlling individual industries to changing the way all individuals live their lives. That will be a long endeavor, but one that might be successful as we increasingly realize our health and the health of our children are dependent upon it. Many consider the management of the Great Lakes to be a model for other global ecosystems. If this model is to hold out any sense of optimism, the two governments will have to match dollars and programs to their rhetoric.

NOTES

1. Gordon K. Durnil, Chairman, U.S. section of International Joint Commission, testimony before U.S. Senate Committee on Governmental Affairs, Subcommittee on Oversight of Governmental Management, June 13, 1990.

2. Carl Levin, Senator from Michigan, testimony before Senate Subcommittee on Oversight of Governmental Management, June 13, 1990.

3. M. Donahue, Executive Director, Great Lakes Commission, testimony before U.S. Senate Subcommittee on Oversight of Governmental Management, June 13, 1990.

4. Environment Canada and the United States Environmental Protection Agency, *The Great Lakes: an Environmental Atlas and Resources Book*, (Toronto: Environment Canada and Chicago: U.S. EPA, 1987), p. 3.

5. Ibid.

6. *Treaty between the United States and Great Britain Relating to Boundary Waters between the United States and Canada, 1910.* The treaty was signed and ratified by Britain, reflecting Canada's status at the time. The Government of Canada later became successor state.

7. As reported in *70 Years of Accomplishment, Report for Years 1978-1979*, International Joint Commission, p. 12.

8. J. Jockel and Alan Schwartz, "The Changing Environmental Role of the Canada-United States International Joint Commission, *Environmental Review* 8, no. 3 (Fall 1984).

9. Agreement between U.S. and Canada on Great Lakes Water Quality, 1972, Article IV, TIAS 7312.

10. Agreement between U.S. and Canada on Great Lakes Water Quality, 1978, TIAS 9257.

11. J. Jockel, op. cit., p. 243.

12. Great Lakes Water Quality Board, *1985 Report on Great Lakes Water Quality*, The International Joint Commission, June 1985, p. 5.

13. Ibid.

14. Great Lake Water Quality Board, *1989 Report on Great Lakes Water Quality*, International Joint Commission, October 1989, p. 104.

15. State of New York, *Fishing Regulations Guide*, 1989-1990, p. 1.

16. U.S. General Accounting Office, *A More Comprehensive Approach is Needed to Clean Up the Great Lakes*, May 21, 1982, CED-82-63.

17. U.S. General Accounting Office, *International Joint Commission Water Quality Activities Need Greater U.S. support and Involvement*, June 23, 1982, CED-82-97.

18. International Joint Commission, *First Biennial Report Under the Great Lakes Water Quality Agreement of 1978*, June 1982.

19. Ibid., p. 5.

20. Ibid., p. 14.

21. M. Valliante and P. Muldoon, "Annual Review of Canadian American Relations—1988," *International Environmental Affairs* 1, no. 4 (1989).

22. International Joint Commission, *Fifth Biennial Report On Great Lakes Water Quality, Part II*, 1990.

23. Ibid., p. 37.

24. Henry Habicht, II, Deputy Administrator, U.S. EPA, Testimony before Senate Subcommittee on Oversight of Governmental Management, June 13, 1990.

25. T. Colborn, et al., *Great Lakes, Great Legacy?* (Washington, D.C.: The Conservation Foundation, 1990).

26. IJC staff, personal interviews, July 1990.

27. David Rapport, "Review of Great Lakes Remedial Action Programs: What Might the RAPs accomplish and What Might it Cost," Report prepared for Statistics Canada, May 1989.

28. A. Schwartz, and J. Jockel, "Increasing the Power of the IJC," *International Perspectives* (November/December 1983).

29. *The Great Lakes United*, Newsletter of Great Lakes United, vol. 4, no. 3 (Fall 1989), p. 1.

30. IJC staff, personal interviews, July 1990.

31. P. Weeller, "IJC Criticizes Governments for Failing to act on Toxics," *The Great Lakes United* 5, no. 1 (Spring 1990), p. 1.

32. International Joint Commission, *Fifth Biennial Report*, Part II, 1990.

33. Conservation Foundation, Newsletter no. 5, 1989, p. 6.

34. Ibid., p. 7.

35. Ibid.

36. Great Lakes Science Advisory Board, Report of the Great lakes Science Advisory Board, October 1989, p. 1.

37. Ibid., p. 58.

38. IJC staff, personal interviews, July 1990.

39. John Glenn, testimony before U.S. Senate Subcommittee on Oversight of Governmental Management, June 13, 1990.

40. U.S. General Accounting Office, *The United States participation in the International Joint Commission*, June 1989, GAO/NSIAD-89-164.

41. External Affairs Staff, personal interviews, July 1990.

42. Carl Levin, testimony before the U.S. Senate Subcommittee on Governmental Management, June 13, 1990.

43. Michael Donahue, testimony before the U.S. Subcommittee on Oversight of Government Management, June 13, 1990.

44. Great Lakes Commission, resolution of executive committee, June 4, 1990.

45. Henry Habicht, II, testimony before the U.S. Senate Subcommittee on Oversight of Governmental Management, June 13, 1990.

46. International Joint Commission, fifth Biennial Report on Great Lake Water Quality, 1990, p. 49.

47. Ibid., p. 43.

48. Michael Donahue, et al., "The Great Lakes Water Quality Agreements: How to Assess Progress Toward a Goal of Ecosystem Integrity," *Post-Audits of Environmental Programs and Projects*, ed. Charles Gunnerson (New York: American Society of Civil Engineers, 1989), pp. 27-42.

5

Lessons From the Past: Energy Use, the Economy and the Environment[1]

Andrew W. Wyckoff[2]

Energy is a unique commodity. Every product sold in a modern economy either directly or indirectly uses energy. Energy is a fundamental input into our economy, essential for running the country's factories, shipping the nation's output, and ringing up the sales. Energy is also a final product consumed by itself, responsible for providing many of the most basic comforts of life—heat in the winter, light at night, cool air in the summer, mobility, and the preservation of food, to name a few.

But the use of energy is also the source of a host of environmental problems. The extraction of energy has resulted in unsightly strip mines, nuclear power plant accidents, and the damming of rivers. The distribution of energy has generated oil spills, requires pipelines which can leak, and causes the construction of transmission towers which have aesthetic and health impacts. The combustion of fossil fuels produces emissions that are linked to acid rain, urban smog, and climate change.

Energy use affects more than just the environment. Economic problems such as inflation, trade deficits, and declines in productivity are directly connected to energy and its use. Solutions to a number of these problems are associated with lowering the level of energy use through less use or more-efficient use. The worry is that policies designed to achieve this goal of lower energy use will have an adverse impact on the economy: growth will be slowed, jobs will be displaced, and income growth will suffer.

In many cases, but particularly with Canada and the United States, these issues are not limited to a country's borders. Many of the environmental problems such as acid rain or climate change are regional or global in nature. Likewise, economies are increasingly interdependent with the United States and Canada being each others' largest trading partners. It follows that solutions will depend on international cooperation.

As environmental problems increasingly demand attention, the search for ways to sustain economic growth and maintain standards of living while limiting the amount of energy used becomes crucial. This is a concern common to all industrialized countries, but particularly for Canada and the United States, two of the most energy intensive countries in the world.[3] Clues to this paradox lie in a better understanding of how energy use has shifted with changes in modern economies.

This chapter strives to improve that understanding by analyzing the period from 1972 to 1985 when energy use in the United States remained basically flat, but the economy grew by 40 percent—a sharp departure from post-World War II trends when economic growth appeared to be in lock-step with higher levels of energy use. This analysis explicitly looks at how changes in the level of overall spending, the mixture of what is being purchased, the effect of international trade, and the impact of changes in how products are made (technology) affect energy use.

The separation of economic factors is important because confusion abounds over how the United States was able to keep the economy growing during the seventies and eighties while holding energy use steady. Some observers attribute the decline in energy intensity, measured as British thermal units (Btus),[4] used per dollar of Gross Domestic Product (GDP) produced, solely to increases in energy efficiency.[5] This is only part of the story. Factors such as changing tastes, incomes, demographics, and international competition led to a shift in the makeup of the economy's output as "smokestack" industries' position declined relative to services and lighter manufacturing such as electronics.[6] This change in the structure of the economy also led to less energy used per dollar of output produced (the energy intensity). From the perspective of trying to limit energy use, these differences are critical because the factors that tend to affect efficiency gains such as mandated standards or price changes differ significantly from the policies that affect the economy's structure such as currency fluctuations or changes in income levels.

Technological advances in information processing (computers, communications, robotics, etc.) are changing the nature of the U.S. economy, making it more complex and interdependent as networks link the consumer to the retailer, the retailer to the manufacturer, and the manufacturer to his suppliers.[7] In an economy such as this one, the role of energy is less likely to be directly identified and is instead more likely to be an indirect factor that was added many steps before in the complex network that connects producer to consumer. For example, to produce all of the motor vehicles made in the United States in 1985 required relatively little direct energy, about .23 quadrillion (quad) Btus, but it required 1.22 quads of indirect energy use because the inputs into a car (steel, rubber, glass, plastic) embody a lot of energy consumed in their manufacture and fabrication. Thus, most of the energy associated with making a motor vehicle is not at the assembly plant but was added a few steps before at the steel mill, tire plant, or glass factory. From this perspective, a change in the nonenergy inputs used to make a product (e.g., material substitution) could indirectly affect energy use. The analysis presented in this chapter separates direct from indirect energy use.

This division between direct and indirect energy use is especially appropriate when the energy associated with international trade is considered. Most of the calculations presented in this analysis as well as most conventional measures of U.S. energy use include only direct energy imports such as barrels of oil or megawatts of electricity from Canada. Nevertheless, as production networks continue to extend beyond a country's borders, the inclusion of the indirect energy embodied in the trade of nonenergy products is increasingly important in calculating a country's total energy use. For example, including only the direct energy needed to make a U.S. automobile might miss the energy embodied in the steel axle that was imported from Japan.

This chapter makes no attempt to explain why these changes in the economy or in energy use occurred. Instead, only the question of how shifts in the economy affected energy use is explored. As a result, although the industrial structure of the economy and the implementation of technology is undoubtedly affected by changes in tastes, incomes, government regulations, and the relative prices of products, especially the huge changes in the prices of energy, these factors are not explicitly addressed.[8]

Nevertheless, a number of lessons can be drawn from the 1972-1985 period that add insight on how the United States was able to keep its use of energy level over a 13-year period. This analytical framework is then applied to the post-1985 period when U.S. energy use began once again to parallel economic growth. The chapter concludes with a series of findings that provide background for businesspeople and policymakers trying to walk the tightrope between environmental protection and continued economic development.

HISTORICAL TRENDS OF ENERGY USE AND ECONOMIC GROWTH

Figure 5.1 gives an overview of the relationship between economic growth and energy use in the United States. After World War II, growth in our economy as reflected by the GDP[9] and increases in energy, measured in Btus, appeared to be in lock-step. From 1950 to 1971, energy use and GDP both increased at an average annual rate of 3.5 percent. Although deviations from this trend occurred in the mid-1950s and mid-1960s, growth in the two factors were highly correlated.[10] Economic growth was assumed to be linked to increases in energy use, and public and private investments were made that rested upon this assumption.[11]

In the early 1970s the apparent link between increasing GDP and rising energy use came unraveled. Between 1972 and 1985, 20 million homes were added to the country's housing stock, the fleet of vehicles on America's roadways had increased by 50 million, the number of business establishments

Figure 5.1

**Index of U.S. Energy Use, GDP,
and Energy Intensity**

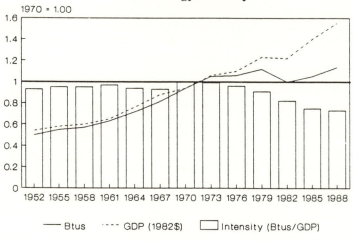

Btus ···· GDP (1982$) ▢ Intensity (Btus/GDP)

Source: U.S. Department of Commerce, *National Income and Product Accounts*, Table 1.8, various years and U.S. Department of Energy, Annual Energy Review, Table 1.4, various years.

had risen by 1.5 million, and the GDP had grown by 39 percent in real terms.[12] But energy use had remained basically flat.

Although the average growth rate of GDP was 2.5 percent per year over this period, energy use increased at an annual rate of only 0.3 percent.[13] The energy intensity or units of Btus used to produce a dollar's worth of the economy's output (GDP), which was relatively flat from 1950 to 1971, fell by 2.4 percent per year from 1972 to 1985, resulting in an overall drop in U.S. energy intensity of over 25 percent from 1972 to 1985.[14]

This trend of decreasing energy use per dollar of GDP ended in 1986 for the United States. From 1986 to 1988, the two factors began to grow in parallel again with energy use increasing at a 3.9 percent annual rate and GDP growing at 4.1 percent. The energy intensity of the U.S. economy fell at a meager annual rate of 0.2 percent between 1986 and 1988.

Although an exact parallel between the United States and Canada is difficult to draw because Canada enjoys access to more-reliable energy supplies, has an economy that is much more dependent upon natural resource-based industries, and has a significantly different climate, the two countries have both experienced a decline in their energy intensities during the 1970s and 1980s (Figure 5.2).

Figure 5.2

**Index of U.S. and Canadian
Energy Intensity**

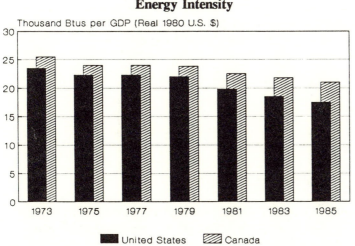

Thousand Btus per GDP (Real 1980 U.S. $)

■ United States   ▨ Canada

Source: U.S. Department of Energy, *Energy Conservations Trends*, September 1989,
Table 14, p. 36.

The main difference is that the U.S. decline has been longer and larger. Steady
Canadian declines in energy intensity did not appear until 1980 while U.S.
declines started in the early 1970s. As a result,Canada only achieved an annual
drop of 1.4 percent in its energy intensity between 1972 and 1985, while the
United States achieved a 2.4 percent annual decline. For both countries, this
decline is due to a combination of energy efficiency improvements and structural
changes in the sectoral composition of the economy as the mix of industries
moved away from energy intensive industries and toward less intensive services.

To better understand how these changes in efficiency and structure affect
energy use and what some of the implications are, the U.S. situation was
examined in greater detail using input-output data.[15] The following sections
present the findings of this analysis in a top-down manner where the broad
factors are discussed so as to establish an overview, and then each factor is
individually analyzed in greater detail. Implications stemming from these
findings are drawn in the final section.

ECONOMYWIDE CHANGES IN ENERGY USE: 1972-1985

Energy is used both as an intermediate input in the production of goods and services, such as GM's use of electricity in making a car; and it is also consumed as a final product itself—consumers filling up their cars with gasoline. On an aggregate level, the consumption of energy can be thought of as having two components that roughly correspond to supply and demand:

- Energy is used directly by final consumers as they demand energy products such as gasoline as well as through indirect use stimulated by demand for goods and services such as clothes or food that require energy to be used in their production. The sum of demand for all products in a particular year equals the GNP.

- Energy is also used by businesses as they supply products to meet consumer's demand. Each businesses' production process directly uses energy to run motors and power lights and indirectly uses energy through the use of other inputs such as steel or rubber that embody energy. This mixture of inputs and how they are combined into a company's product is an implicit reflection of technology.

Together these factors dictate the amount of energy that is used to operate the economy in any given year. The consumers decide what and how much will be consumed, while businesses decide how these products will be made. When these variables are evaluated over time, the simultaneous change in these factors creates a third variable, an interaction term, that cannot be attributed to either spending or the production process. As can be seen in Figure 5.3, these three factors—spending, production processes, and the interaction of the two—have caused energy use to change from 1972. Spending and the interactive term have led to increases in energy use, while changes in production processes have caused a reduction. Together, the factors tend to offset one another so that by 1985, U.S. energy use was only slightly higher than it was in 1972.

Changes in spending have increased energy use, with the magnitude of its effect growing in every year except for 1982, a severe recession year. Over time, the size of the U.S. economy reflected by the overall amount of spending has increased along with increases in population, motor vehicles, and homes, leading to an increase in energy requirements. If more people buy more things, everything else being equal, more energy will be used.

But the way these things are made has changed dramatically. To produce the same mix and level of products using 1985 technology and practices used nearly 20 quadrillion Btus less energy than what would have been used if 1972 practices and technology were employed. If these changes had not occurred between 1972 and 1985, the United States would have used about 25 percent

Figure 5.3

**Changes in U.S. Energy Use
1972 to 1985**

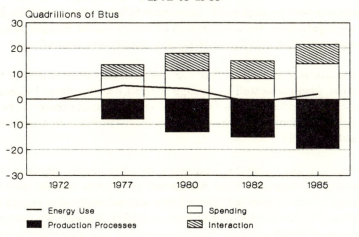

more energy in 1985. Assuming that this marginal increase would have been obtained from foreign sources, this would mean that the U.S. level of energy imports would be more than double what it was in 1985.

THE CONSUMER'S EFFECT ON ENERGY USE

Consumer demand or spending is a broad category that can be broken down into components that better illustrate how demand affects energy use.

The Level and Mix of Spending

The effect of increases in the sheer size of spending can be separated from changes in the mix of what is being purchased. If a consumer simply buys more of everything, keeping the proportions of spending the same across all products purchased and not allowing the process by which those products are produced to change, energy use will increase. But if the overall level of spending stays constant and the mix of what is being bought changes, the energy use associated with that market basket of products will change depending on how energy intensive the products are. When both factors are allowed to change individually over time, an interactive effect is derived.

From 1972 to 1985 the increase in energy use associated with spending came from the increased level of spending and the interactive effect generated between changes in level and mix. Changes in the mix of spending resulted in a decline in energy use in every year examined (see Figure 5.4). As the level of spending has grown, the mix of what is being purchased has shifted to less energy intensive products, such as health care instead of gasoline. If the mix had not shifted between 1972 and 1985, the United States would have used 8 percent more energy in 1985 than what was actually used.

Although it is hard to draw firm conclusions from only five data points, the impact of changing levels of spending on energy use appears to be offset by changes in the mix of spending. In other words, just as an uptick in economic growth causes an increase in energy use, it also frequently causes a shift in what is bought towards a less energy intensive array of products, causing the two factors, level and mix, partially to cancel one another. Likewise, in the lean economic years of 1980 and 1982, the increase in energy use due to growth was reduced, but the mix of products purchased became more energy intensive. This suggests that as consumers are pinched by tough economic times, their market basket of products consumed shifts towards relatively more energy intensive products, probably basic necessities such as heating fuel or gas for cars.

During periods of relative prosperity, the mixture of purchases shifts back to a less energy intensive collection of items of a more luxurious nature such as

Figure 5.4

**Changes in U.S. Energy Use
due to Spending, 1972 to 1985**

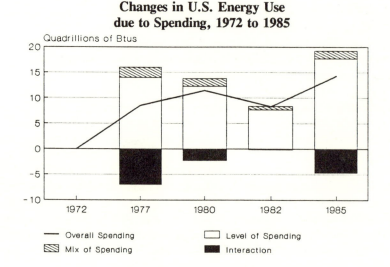

electronics, sporting events, or clothes.[16] Definitive conclusions cannot be drawn because of the sparseness of the data points, but the responsiveness of the mix of spending is indicative of a flexible buying pattern that can reduce the change in energy consumption by as much as 7 quads (1972 to 1977 change) or as little as 0.2 quads (1972 to 1982), depending on the time interval chosen.

The tilt in the mix of products purchased towards less energy intensive goods and services is reflective of a whole group of events that occurred between 1972 and 1985: income growth, demographic change, new government regulations, changing prices, the end of the Vietnam War, and technological innovations, to name a few. The fuel economy of new passenger cars nearly doubled over this period. Consumers turned down their thermostats. Purchases of energy intensive products such as automobiles, stoves, and washers, and energy intensive infrastructure such as roads and factories hit saturation points, limiting the market for these items mainly to replacement.[17] As expenditures on energy products and energy intensive goods drop, money is left to be spent on products that are less energy intensive. The next section explores this further by breaking spending into five broad groups of products and tracing how changes in spending on each group affected energy use.

Spending by Broad Product Groups

The influence of spending on energy use becomes less abstract when spending is broken down into tangible goods and services that can be purchased. In this study, spending was broken into five broad groups: energy, natural resources,[18] manufacturing, transportation services,[19] and services. This separation of purchases of energy products from other products allows exploration of questions such as:

- If spending caused an increase in energy use between 1972 and 1985, what type of purchases led to this increase?

- How much of the increase in energy use due to spending was caused by direct purchases of energy, and how much of the increase was the result of indirect uses of energy as consumers buy products such as food or clothing that embody energy?

Direct purchases of energy products by final consumers have been constant or falling since 1977 (see Figure 5.5). Only 1.1 quads or 8 percent of the overall 1972 to 1985, 14.4-quad increase in energy use due to spending came from direct demand for energy products. This would not seem to be small if the share of the increase was commensurate with the share of the overall base the product held in 1972. But for the energy product group, this increase translates

Figure 5.5

Changes in U.S. Energy Use due to
Spending on Different Product Groups

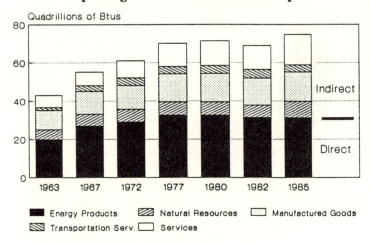

into a disproportionately low 8 percent share of the 1972 to 1985 increase since energy products represented 48 percent of the energy associated with 1972 spending (Figure 5.6). The energy product group was the only group substantially to lose share over this period.

The engine behind the growth in energy use due to spending was the indirect use of energy associated with purchases of services (Figure 5.6). Forty-four percent of the increase was due to services, more than double the energy associated with the 1972 spending on services. By 1985, spending on services used more energy than the energy associated with spending on manufactured goods. Although individual services are not very energy intensive, the large segment of the economy they constitute coupled with the dramatic growth they have experienced mean that they are an important demand-side factor in energy use.

Sources of Spending

Consumers of final products are a heterogeneous group, composed of households, governments, businesses, [20] and international trade.[21] The overall consumption of a particular product is calculated by summing the expenditures made on that product from each of these sources. But spending by each source depends on widely differing factors. For example, household expenditures are

Figure 5.6

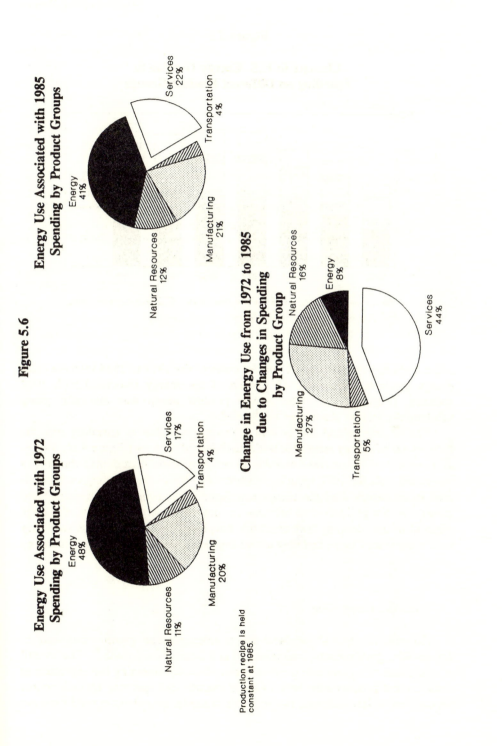

Energy Use Associated with 1972 Spending by Product Groups

Energy 48%
Services 17%
Transportation 4%
Manufacturing 20%
Natural Resources 11%

Energy Use Associated with 1985 Spending by Product Groups

Energy 41%
Services 22%
Transportation 4%
Manufacturing 21%
Natural Resources 12%

Change in Energy Use from 1972 to 1985 due to Changes in Spending by Product Group

Natural Resources 16%
Energy 8%
Services 44%
Manufacturing 27%
Transportation 5%

Production recipe is held constant at 1985.

affected by changes in wages, governments depend on taxes, businesses rely on revenues, while foreign trade is influenced by fluctuations in the value of currencies. The policy levers that affect each group are also very different. Given these differences, it is important to isolate how each group's demand for energy, both direct and indirect, contributed to the increase in energy use due to spending.

Figure 5.7 shows how energy use would have changed as a result of changes in spending from households (personal consumer expenditures) and government, which together constitute 85 percent of the 1985 GNP. Direct personal consumer expenditures on energy rose steadily from 1963 to 1977 and then leveled off while the indirect use of energy associated with purchases of nonenergy products steadily grew from 1963 to 1985. By 1985, households' indirect energy use was nearly as large as the energy directly consumed. The indirect use of energy is even more apparent in government spending where the indirect use of energy has always exceeded direct energy purchases.

Imports and exports constitute the other major source of demand for energy. Tracking the effect of trade on energy use through the U.S. economy is a difficult task, complicated further by the fact that conventional energy use accounting does not reflect the indirect energy embodied in nonenergy imports. Obviously, accounting for the energy used to produce every import would be a herculean task, but a rough approximation of the energy that would have been used if that imported product were produced domestically can be estimated.[22]

Figure 5.7

**Direct and Indirect Energy Use
by Households and Government
1963 to 1985**

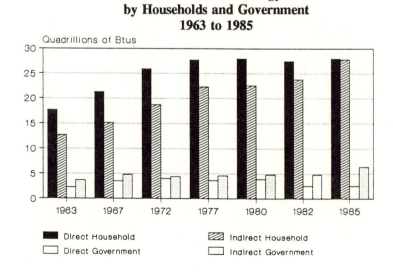

Figure 5.8

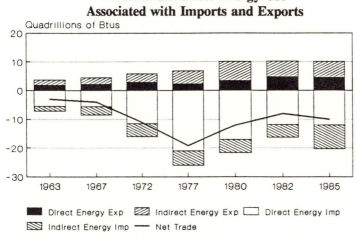

**Direct and Indirect Energy Use
Associated with Imports and Exports**

Production process held constant
at 1985 level.

Without this correction, it would be easy to achieve a decline in the economy's energy use simply by importing energy intensive goods such as steel or aluminum. Such a decline is illusory because businesses have not changed their products or adopted new technologies, they just import inputs that embody energy that would have required direct energy use if the inputs were produced domestically. Given that nonenergy imports have doubled their share of GNP since 1970, the need to make this distinction has grown in importance.[23] Policies that advocate mandating a certain reduction in a country's energy intensity for efficiency or environmental reasons should be aware of the ability of companies to outsource components from foreign sources, effectively circumventing the intent of domestic policies.[24]

When the correcting adjustment for the energy embodied in 1985 nonenergy imports is made, U.S. use of imported energy rises by over 50 percent from 13 quads to 20 (see Figure 5.8).[25] While the indirect energy embodied in exports has stayed relatively steady in the 1980s, the indirect energy embodied in imports has increased as the U.S. trade deficit has deepened. The net trade line in Figure 5.8 reflects this situation. From 1977 to 1982, the net trade balance of energy, including both direct and indirect energy, was improving. This improvement was due to reductions in the level of direct imports of energy and a balance between the indirect energy associated with imports and exports. After 1982, the net trade line began to fall. This turnaround was not due to increased direct imports of energy; they stayed roughly constant over this time period. The cause of the decline was a increase in the indirect imports of energy. Not surprisingly, this deficit mirrors the current account trade balance (dollars), which went from a surplus of $26 billion in 1982 to a deficit of $104 billion in 1985.[26] The lack of post-1985 data may skew this picture since the trade balance has improved as exports have increased with the decline in the value of the dollar, and increases in the level of imports have been more modest.[27]

BUSINESSES' IMPACT ON ENERGY USE

Spending on goods and services triggers the production of output as businesses try to satisfy consumer demand. Whether it is something as mundane as the gasoline in the car that delivers the pizza or as sophisticated as the laser used in surgery, every product requires some energy, directly or indirectly, along the complex network that connects the extraction of raw materials with processing plants, assemblers, distributors, retailers, and finally the ultimate consumer.[28]

The term *production process* refers to the ingredients and methods used to make a product. To track how energy is used, the production process has been split into two parts:

- the energy portion of production processes show the use and manipulation of direct energy inputs such as coal, oil, gas, and electricity; and,

- the nonenergy portion of production processes which contain inputs such as steel, plastics, advertising, and financial advice that indirectly embody energy.

On a dollar value basis, the direct use of energy products in production processes represents only about a fifth of all inputs.[29] The remaining four-fifths of inputs, however, include significant amounts of indirect energy use. As mentioned before, to produce all of the cars sold in 1985 required relatively little direct energy, about .23 quads, but 1.2 quads of energy were indirectly used because the inputs into a car (steel, rubber, glass, plastic) embody a lot of energy. Changes in the nonenergy inputs (e.g. material substitution) of a production process indirectly affect the energy use.

Estimates of the amount of energy associated with changes in production processes requires that the level and mix of spending be kept constant. Under this experiment, any changes in energy use are attributed to the production process or the interaction of the production process with spending. Changes in production processes can be examined in more detail by breaking ingredients for production into two broad categories of inputs—energy and nonenergy—and then selectively varying each component to see how much of the change can be attributed to each factor. Changes in energy use associated with changes in the energy portion of production processes are indicative of changes in energy efficiency: it requires fewer direct energy (Btus) inputs to make the output needed to satisfy a constant set of demand. Variations in the nonenergy portion of production processes are a partial reflection of the structural change occurring in the United States as technology, prices, and tastes increase the demand for some inputs and slacken the demand for others.[30] For example, as substitutes for steel are discovered, such as high-strength polymers, the relative position of the plastic industry will rise in the economy while the steel industry declines.

Energy Inputs

Both the energy and nonenergy components of production changed so that U.S. industry used less energy in 1985 than in 1972 to produce the same mix and level of products. Nevertheless, over three-quarters of the decline was attributable to changes in the direct use of energy inputs, indicative of improvements in energy efficiency (Figure 5.9).

Forty percent of this drop came from the manufacturing sector. This change is disproportionately large given that using 1972 production processes,

Figure 5.9

**Changes in U.S. Energy Use due to
Changes in Production Processes
1972 to 1985**

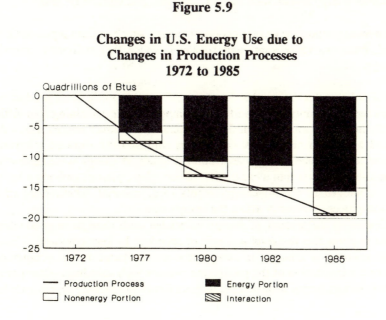

manufacturing only used 27 percent of the total energy required. A number of technological advances and process changes such as sensing and control systems, heat recovery systems, use of variable speed motors, continuous casting of steel, and the application of new membrane technologies for the separation and purification of materials have improved the energy efficiency of manufacturing production processes.

The energy sector itself and the services sector each contributed about 20 percent of the 15.4 quad drop in energy use due to changes in the use of energy inputs (energy efficiency). Unlike the manufacturing sector, this change was not disproportionately large given their 1972 consumption.

Non-Energy Inputs

Although less significant in magnitude than the changes occurring in the energy portion of production processes, the indirect energy savings associated with changes in nonenergy inputs have grown in size and have reinforced the energy savings gained from pure energy efficiency. By 1982, over a quarter of all the decline due to production process changes from 1972 to 1982 was due to changes in non-energy inputs.[31]

These declines are a result of the shifting mix of nonenergy inputs in the production process. Less energy intensive inputs are being used relatively more than energy intensive inputs. For example, of the inputs that registered a gain in share between 1972 to 1980, wholesale and retail trade was the largest. Number two was business services. Both of these inputs have relatively low energy intensities. The input with the largest decline in share was primary iron and steel, one of the most energy intensive industries.[32] Shipments of steel from U.S. plants fell by 41 percent from 1972 to 1985.[33] Since the bulk of the coal that is not used by the electric utility industry is used to make steel, a decline in domestic production of this magnitude would have a large indirect effect on the use of coal.

Nearly all of the indirect decreases in energy use due to nonenergy changes in production from 1972 to 1985 occurred in the manufacturing sector (Table 5.1). Three of the sectors, energy, transportation services, and services, actually had nonenergy changes that led to an increase in energy use from 1972 to 1985.

Examples of how changes in the nonenergy portion of the production process can decrease energy use include the automobile industry where lighter materials such as high-strength plastics have been substituted for metals. From the mid-1970s to the mid-1980s, the iron and steel content of a car fell by 30 percent while the amount of plastics and composites increased by 33 percent.[34] Automated manufacturing technologies such as computer-assisted design (CAD), becoming more commonplace in industries such as the motor vehicle industry,

Table 5.1

Changes in Primary Energy Use from 1972 to 1985 by Sector due to Energy Production Process Changes

(Quadrillion Btus)	Energy	Nonenergy	Total
Energy	-3.0	0.2	-2.8
Natural Resources	-2.7	-0.4	-3.1
Manufacturing	-6.3	-3.9	-10.2
Transportation Services	-0.4	0.1	-0.3
Services	-3.0	0.2	-2.8
Total	-15.4	-3.7	-19.1

NOTE: Total may not add due to rounding.

allow products to be designed so that fewer parts are required, reducing the amount of material that is wasted and energy that is required for assembly. Fiat's recent investments in automation means that the Fiat Uno has over a third fewer major body parts, reducing the number of welds required for assembly by 43 percent from the previous generation model, the Fiat 127.[35]

Advances in information technologies have made it possible to substitute information for materials, leading to changes in the production that indirectly save energy. Instead of creating dozens of prototypes, Levi Strauss is using computers to test out new fabrics, patterns, and designs before ever cutting a piece of cloth.[36] Ten years ago, four-fifths of the value of a computer was embodied in its hardware, the remainder being associated with software. Today, these are ratios are reversed, resulting in a drop in the energy associated with a dollar's worth of output.[37]

TECHNOLOGY V. STRUCTURAL CHANGE

Most studies that analyze the declining energy intensity of the economy normalize for changes in the sheer growth of demand and split up the interactive effects across identifiable factors.[38] By rearranging and adding the results of this analysis, the findings can be made to conform to this framework. The sum of the change in energy use due to the changing mix of spending and the changes in nonenergy production processes can collectively be called a "sectoral shift" or the "structural" effect. The change attributed to the energy portion of production processes is frequently called the "efficiency improvement" or the "technology" effect. When measured using these classifications, more than a third (38 percent) of the decline in energy consumption from 1972 to 1985 is attributed to structural changes, the remainder being due to efficiency improvements. As Figure 5.10 illustrates, the bulk of this decline due to changes in structure is attributable to changes in the mix of spending.

Without these changes in energy use due to shifts in structure and gains in energy efficiency, energy use in 1985 would have been nearly a third higher than it actually was that year (Figure 5.11).

THE RECENT PAST: 1985-1988

The trend of constant energy use established from 1972 to 1985 was broken between 1985 and 1988 when energy use increased by 8 percent (6 quads). Although the energy intensity of the economy continued to decline from 1986 to 1988, it did so at a meager 0.2 annual rate as opposed to the 2.4 percent

Figure 5.10

Reduction in Energy Use 1972 to 1985

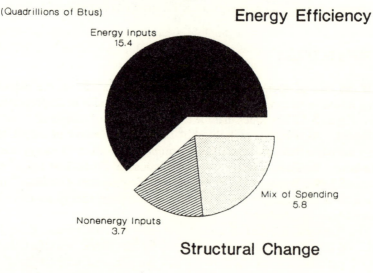

(Quadrillions of Btus)   Energy Efficiency

Energy Inputs
15.4

Mix of Spending
5.8

Nonenergy Inputs
3.7

Structural Change

Controlling for economic growth and
interactive effects.

Figure 5.11

Changes in Energy Use from 1972

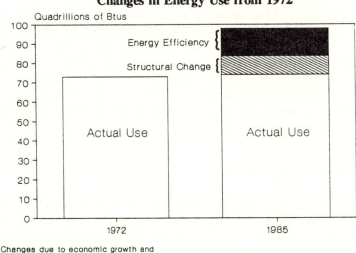

Changes due to economic growth and
interactive effects are not shown.

decline achieved from 1972 to 1985. The lack of detailed data preclude answering the question of what factors caused this increase, but it appears that an increase in the level of spending coupled with a shift in the mix of consumption towards more energy intensive products contributed to the increase.

Shifts in Output

If the mix of spending became more energy intensive, the output from energy intensive sectors such as manufacturing should also be disproportionately large. Figure 5.12 illustrates that the energy intensity of industries is not evenly distributed. As a result, a slight shift in the composition of output towards energy intensive industries could have a pronounced effect on energy use. Two data sources, the Federal Reserve Board's Industrial Production Index[39] and the Bureau of Labor Statistics (BLS) Output and Employment Database,[40] indicate that a shift in the composition of output towards these energy intensive sectors occurred between 1985 and 1988.

The Industrial Production Index (IPI) grew by 10.6 percent from 1985 to 1988. Of the three major sectors covered by this index, manufacturing grew by 13.2 percent, mining declined by 5.0 percent, and utilities grew by 1.8 percent. Within manufacturing, the largest percent gains in the index from 1985 to 1988 occurred in lumber (21.5 percent), printing and publishing (19.6

Figure 5.12

Ranking of Primary Energy Intensities
(Top 60 out of 88 Products)

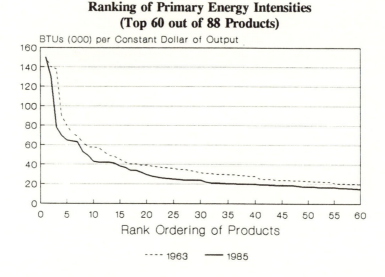

BTUs (000) per Constant Dollar of Output

Rank Ordering of Products

---- 1963   —— 1985

percent), chemicals (19.6 percent), rubber and plastic products (18.6 percent), nonelectrical machinery (which includes computers) (17.8 percent), and paper and paper products (17.4 percent).

The BLS database has shipment (gross output) data on every sector in the economy. Of the ten major (one-digit Standard Industrial Classifications) sectors, manufacturing increased its share of total shipments the most from 1985 to 1988, growing from 32.9 percent of all shipments to 33.8 percent. The service sector was second, growing from 13.8 percent to 14.2. The 0.9 percent gain in share by manufacturing sounds small but translates into a $50 billion increase in real shipments over the three-year period.[41] This gain in share breaks a trend where manufacturing fell from a 35.8 percent share of output in 1972 to 32.9 in 1985.

Within manufacturing, the three industries experiencing the largest gain in share of manufacturing's total output were machinery, except electrical (which includes the computer industry) whose share grew by 1.4 points, chemicals (0.5 gain), and primary metals (0.3 gain). Chemicals, primary metals, and to a lesser extent machinery are all relatively energy intensive industries.

Changing Mix of Spending

This shift in output reflects a shift in the mix of spending. A shift in the mix of spending would occur if a product's share of growth between 1985 and

1988 were different than the share of spending it represented in 1985. The main changes occurred in the household, government, and international trade sectors.

A shift in the mix of household purchases (personal consumer expenditures) occurred between 1985 and 1988, tilting spending towards durable goods as opposed to nondurable products. Although durable goods, such as furniture and home electronics, only represented 15 percent of all household consumption in 1985, they were responsible for 24 percent of the increase in household spending from 1985 and 1988. This disproportionate growth of durables came at the expense of nondurable goods such as clothing and food. Nondurable spending represented only 23 percent of the growth, below their 1985 share of 36 percent.

Data limitations restrict the analysis of the changing mix of government expenditures to the federal government where the mix underwent a radical realignment from nondefense purchases to defense purchases.[42] In real terms, nondefense purchases declined by 16.2 percent from 1985 to 1988, while defense purchases increased by 10.2 percent.[43] The disproportionate growth occurring within defense has been in durable goods (aircraft, missiles, tanks, etc.) which have been responsible for 51 percent of the 1985 to 1988 growth in defense expenditures from a 1985 share of 30 percent.[44] Thus, government spending at the federal level has undergone a shift from nondefense to defense purchases which are about one-and-a-half times as energy intensive.[45]

Of all the sources of demand that make up the GNP, the one that showed the most pronounced disproportionate growth during this period was exports. Although net trade was still in deficit in 1985, exports were responsible for 30 percent of the real, gross increase in GNP between 1985 and 1988 even though exports' share of GNP in 1985 was only 10 percent.[46] Between 1985 and 1988, exports grew by 44 percent while imports increased by only 28 percent. This gain in exports is probably attributable to the sharp devaluation of the dollar that occurred after 1985, making U.S. exports more attractive overseas.[47] For example, exports of steel mill products increased by 121 percent from 1985 to 1988 while imports of steel mill products decreased by 14 percent.[48] Aluminum also rebounded with exports increasing by 44 percent and imports falling by 5 percent.[49]

Instead of offsetting the increase in energy use due to a rise in the level of spending, the mix of spending changed between 1985 and 1988 in such a way that energy use increased, reversing the trend set in the 1972-1985 period. Thus it appears that the industrial structure of the economy shifted into a more energy intensive configuration.

Changes in Energy Efficiency

The other factor that has traditionally acted as a brake on increases in energy use due to growth has been energy savings associated with changes in the way products are made. From 1972 to 1985, nearly four-fifths of the energy savings attributed to changes in the process of production were due to changes in the way energy was used as an input.

Given that energy efficiency improvements were the dominant factor behind the leveling of energy use between 1972 and 1985, could energy efficiency gains have stopped or even reversed themselves between 1985 and 1988? Evidence indicating how energy efficiency has changed is very limited. In theory, some inefficiencies would be expected as the economy continues to expand and plant utilization begins to hit capacity constraints. For example, as demand for steel continues to rise, old, mothballed facilities using outmoded technology such as open-hearth furnaces, might be brought back online, causing the energy efficiency of steel production to dip.[50]

At least for the steel industry this has not been the case. The percentage of steel made from relatively inefficient processes such as open-hearth or blast-furnace methods declined between 1985 and 1988, with the most energy efficient mode, electric arc, gaining.[51] More generally, the Federal Reserve Board reports that capacity utilization in manufacturing did increase from 80 to 83 percent from 1985 to 1988[52] and that the bulk of this jump occurred in the more energy intensive primary processing portion of manufacturing where the capacity utilization rate jumped from 81 to 87 percent.[53] Nevertheless, these capacity utilization levels are below the rates set from 1978 to 1980 when manufacturing hit 86.5 percent of capacity and primary processing climbed to 89.1.[54] Even at these high levels set between 1978 and 1980, efficiency gains were still achieved.[55] It is thus unlikely that the 1985 to 1988 levels of capacity utilization led to significant inefficiencies in energy use.[56]

In fact, this notion that businesses might reactivate old, inefficient modes of production might need to be updated for the 1982 recession that led some manufacturers, especially those in the "smokestack" industries, to permanently retire their oldest facilities or transfer operations to offshore sites.[57] Thus, in some cases, the old capacity no longer exists. For example, Pittsburgh was once thought of as the U.S. capital of steel production, but today many of the old U.S. Steel facilities have been torn down, and the local economy has shifted towards financial services. U.S. Steel has diversified into retail, transportation, and oil industries.[58]

Coupled with this is the fact that investment in new equipment by businesses usually results in energy efficiency gains as old equipment is replaced by new.[59] The investment rate by businesses during 1972 to 1985, a period of energy efficiency gains by business, was an annual rate of 4.7 percent, significantly below the 1985 to 1988 rate of 6.9 percent.[60] It is unlikely that these new investments hindered energy efficiency; rather, they are likely to have improved efficiency.

Lastly, the real price of energy dropped from 1985 to 1988 reducing the incentive for making energy efficiency improvements (Figure 5.13). The price for crude oil and gas, for example, fell from $27 per barrel (current dollars) in 1985 to $14 in 1988.[61]   But falling energy prices do not necessarily result in declines in energy efficiency gains due to changes in the production.[62]   Figure 5.9 shows that savings in energy due to the production process were achieved from 1982 to 1985, another period of declining energy prices.[63]   Likewise, fuel efficiency improvements were made between 1958 and 1971, another period of low and falling fuel prices, albeit not as steep a drop as what occurred between 1985 and 1988.[64]   Nevertheless, the U.S. energy intensity started to decline before the 1973-1974 Arab oil embargo caused the price of energy to increase.

Energy efficiency gains are frequently associated with modernization efforts undertaken to achieve objectives other than energy savings such as improving quality, boosting yields, or increasing the flexibility of production.[65]   Thus, energy savings are often an unintended dividend of investments made to obtain other goals.   Canada's National Energy Board concludes that most of the industrial energy efficiency gains achieved have "resulted from the adoption of new processes, motivated by concerns for competitiveness and productivity, rather than energy costs."[66]   The U.S. Department of Energy projects that industrial energy efficiency will increase more under a low price scenario that under a high price scenario because low energy prices result in a higher level of economic growth which stimulates greater investment in new, more efficient capital equipment.[67]

Figure 5.13

**Composite Price for Fossil Fuels
1982 Dollars**

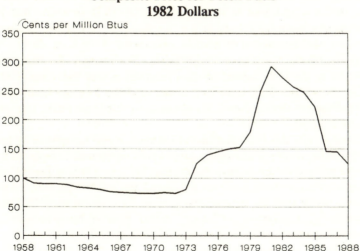

Although a conclusive answer cannot be reached, it appears from the data available that the rise in energy use from 1985 to 1988 was largely due to strong growth in the overall size of the economy and a shift in economic activity towards more energy intensive industries. No evidence was found that would indicate that businesses' energy efficiencies have declined during this period. Rather, it appears that structural shifts toward energy intensive production could not be countered by energy efficiency improvements, leading to a net increase in energy use. It is important to note that changes in economic structure are not as permanent as the word *structure* would suggest. Trends in both industrial structure and energy use can be reversed in a relatively short time.

LESSONS AND IMPLICATIONS FOR POLICY MAKERS

Policies to limit energy use in the 1970s were designed to lessen the dependence on the use of oil because of concerns surrounding national security and the economic consequences (e.g., inflation, lower productivity) associated with price shocks and oil shortages.[68] These concerns still exist in the 1990s, but they are secondary to the environmental problems associated with energy use.   Nevertheless, significant progress on reducing energy use for environmental gains will not be achieved unless the two issues,   economic growth and environmental quality, are joined. This requires an understanding of how energy use and the economy interact.

The analysis presented above uses the recent history of the United States (1972 to 1985) as a case study of how a developed economy can keep its energy use constant but still sustain economic growth. Several lessons about how the economy and energy use interact, that apply to most countries, can be drawn from this example.

Economic growth is not necessarily contingent upon using more energy. Although the economic conditions of the 1970s and early 1980s were certainly not ideal, being marked by double-digit inflation and unemployment, the period did sustain an annual GDP growth rate of 2.5 percent while energy use increased at an annual rate of only 0.3 percent. In fact, slow economic growth tended to cause changes that impeded strides towards improving energy efficiency. Although sheer growth, holding all other changes constant, does increase energy use, economic growth never occurs in a vacuum; rather, growth is likely to be associated with other factors such as shifts in the mix of spending towards less energy intensive products such as services, and investments in new capital equipment, which tend to be more energy efficient. Between 1972 and 1985, the amount of energy used to produce a dollar's worth of the economy's output fell by over a quarter. Although energy is a fundamental input into a modern economy, its relative importance has diminished. In terms of policy, claims of economic Armageddon   associated with efforts to reduce energy use underestimate the dynamic nature of the U.S. economy.[69]

The United States made significant gains in energy efficiency between 1972 and 1985. If the energy efficiency gains achieved between 1972 and 1985 had not been obtained, the nation would have required 20 percent more energy in 1985 to produce its output than it actually used. This source of energy is frequently overlooked or not given the recognition it deserves. Claims of environmental gloom and doom should be tempered by the successes that have been achieved. The recent past provides proof that society is capable of making significant changes in energy use patterns.

Contrary to some widely held beliefs, the leveling of energy use from 1972 to 1985 was not solely due to improvements in energy efficiency but was also caused by structural shifts in the economy. Nearly two-thirds of the decline was because of energy efficiency improvements; the remaining third was due to a realignment of the industrial composition of the economy, shifting towards less energy intensive industries such as services. Policymakers should acknowledge that energy use has two broad factors: changes in efficiency and changes in the structure of the economy. Efforts to affect one factor could be reduced, offset, or enhanced by a change in the other.

Due to the increasing complexity of the U.S. economy, energy is increasingly being consumed indirectly, embodied in nonenergy products such as clothes, tires, and automobiles. At the same time, growth in the direct use of energy such as gasoline and heating fuel has been relatively small. This means that efforts to influence decisions involving energy use might be less effective since in many cases energy use decisions are made many steps away from the immediate user.

The bulk of the increase in indirect energy use between 1972 and 1985 came from demand for services. Although the energy intensity of the service sector is low, its size and rapid growth have meant that its total energy use is larger than manufacturing's. The somewhat myopic focus of energy analysis on the five leading users of energy in the industrial sector should be broadened to include the huge, growing "second tier" of manufacturing industries and the service sector that is rapidly investing in capital equipment that requires energy. For example, modern office equipment such as a laser printer requires five to ten times as much electricity as an old impact printer; more-powerful desk-top computers such as the IBM AT use almost twice as much electricity as the previous generation IBM PC.[70]

The United States indirectly uses energy as it is embodied in goods and services imported into this country. As the trade deficit has deepened, so has this indirect energy use. It is estimated that in 1985, the United States consumed roughly 7 quadrillion British thermal units (Btus) of energy in nonenergy imports such as cars and steel, a 50 percent increase in the amount of energy that was directly imported. Because this indirect use of energy that is embodied in imports is not counted in the energy use accounts, some of the United States' reduction in energy intensity is illusionary. Policies designed to achieve reductions in a country's energy intensity should take the embodied energy in imports into account. Otherwise, efforts to lower the nation's energy intensity could be achieved simply by importing energy intensive products such as steel or aluminum, eliminating the need to make any efficiency improvements. Ford Motor Company is already using its global connections to assist it in achieving domestic corporate average fuel efficiency standards (CAFE).[71]

Energy savings can also be achieved indirectly. Nearly a fifth of the reduction in energy use achieved from 1972 to 1985 because of changes in businesses' production processes came indirectly as less energy intensive inputs such as plastic were substituted for more intensive inputs such as steel. To a large degree, these improvements are a reflection of technological developments where new, high-strength polymers can now be substituted for steel, or improvements in microprocessors makes it possible to place sensors and controls on a wider array of products and processes. In this sense, technological advancement should not always be seen as a threat to the environment but as a potential solution.

The price of energy is not the only factor that affects energy use. The fact that the energy intensity of the economy began to decline before the first oil shock and continued to fall during periods of declining energy prices supports the idea that decisions about energy use are not solely contingent upon price. Increasingly, it appears that energy efficiency gains are an unintended dividend of pursuing other productivity improvements such as increased quality, more-flexible modes of production, and lower labor costs. Policies that aim to boost competitiveness through the improved transfer of technology, lower interest rates, or incentives to conduct research and development should indirectly contribute to improvements in energy efficiency. Thus, policies designed to modernize industries for competitiveness purposes should also indirectly improve energy efficiency.

The complex interconnections of the economy mean that policy goals will frequently be in conflict with one another. Some of the recent increase in energy use between 1985 and 1988 is due to a shift in the structure of the U.S. economy back toward more energy intensive industries such as steel and aluminum. Many of these increases are the result of a rise in the growth of exports and a decline in the growth rate of imports. This phenomenon creates a dilemma for policymakers who want a strong manufacturing sector and a reduced trade deficit, but also want to avoid some of the consequences associated with increased energy use.

NOTES

1. This chapter is drawn from an Office of Technology Assessment background paper entitled *Energy Use and the U.S. Economy*, released in June 1990.

2. Andrew A. Wyckoff is a project director at the U.S. Congress' Office of Technology Assessment. The views expressed here are the author's and do not necessarily reflect those of the Office of Technology Assessment or any individual members of OTA, its board, or advisory group.

3. Based on fossil fuel equivalencies per unit of gross domestic product, Canada ranks first out of the 24 OECD countries, and the United States ranks third. National Energy Board, *Canadian Energy: Supply and Demand 1987 to 2005*, September 1988, Table 10-2.

4. A British thermal unit (Btu) is the amount of heat required to raise the temperature of one pound of water one degree Fahrenheit. A Btu equals 252 calories.

5. For example, see C. Komanoff, "Increased Energy Efficiency: 1978-1986," *Science* 239, no. 4836 (January 8, 1988): 128; U.S. Department of Energy, Oak Ridge National Laboratory, *Energy Efficiency—How Far Can We Go?*, ORNL/TM-11441, January 1990, p. 1; and World Resources Institute, Press Release, "U.S. One of the World's Least Energy-Efficient Countries," November 20, 1989.

6. For more on how the structure of the U.S. economy has changed over the last decade and a half, see U.S. Congress, Office of Technology Assessment, *Technology and the American Economic Transition: Choices for the Future* OTA-TET-283 (Washington, D.C.: U.S. Government Printing Office 1988), ch. 5.

7. For example, DuPont has initiated a "Quick Response" system that ties the clothing retailer to the apparel manufacturer to the textile producer. See U.S. Congress, Office of Technology Assessment, *The U.S. Textile and Apparel Industry: A Revolution in Progress* OTA-TET-332 (Washington, D.C.: Government Printing Office, April 1987), p. 23.

8. The analysis of the economy over time requires that output be converted into constant dollars, otherwise it would appear that the energy used to produce a dollar's worth of output is falling simply because inflation has increased the level of output. This conversion to constant dollars allows an analysis of changing energy intensities and shifts in structure but prevents an explicit analysis of the effect of price. For two different analyses of the how changes in the price of energy affect the economy, see Douglas R. Bohi, *Energy Price Shocks and Macroeconomic Performance* (Washington, D.C.: Resources for the Future, 1989) and Sam H. Schurr, "Electricity Use, Technological Change, and Productive Efficiency," *Annual Review of Energy* 9 (1984), pp. 409-425.

9. GDP is the sum of all output produced in a year that was sold in the formal market (GNP) minus net payments paid to foreigners as returns on their investments in the United States and the return gained by U.S. citizens on their investments overseas. All GDP figures used in this report are in constant 1982 dollars.

10. The correlation coefficient of Btus and GDP was .992 from 1950 to 1971 which is statistically significant at the .01 level.

11. W. Walker, "Information Technology and The Use of Energy," *Energy Supply* (October 1985), pp. 460-461. Some analysts argue that a strong link still exists. See Culter J. Cleveland, Robert Stanza, Charles A. S. Hall, and Robert Kaufman, "Energy and The U.S. Economy: A Biophysical Perspective," *Science* 225 (August 1984), pp. 891-893.

12. For comparison, the number of housing units in 1970 was 63.4 million, the number of cars and trucks stood at 98 million in 1970, and there were 4.1 million businesses established in 1975. Housing and vehicle data comes from U.S. Department of Energy, *Energy Conservation Trends* (Washington, D.C.: Office of Policy Planning and Analysis, September 1989), p. 2, and the U.S. Department of Commerce, *Statistical Abstract of the United States, 1989* (Washington, D.C.: U.S. Government Printing Office, 1989), Table 1243, p. 706, and Table 1011, p. 594, respectively; business establishment data is reported in the *Statistical Abstract of the United States 1989*, op. cit., Table 858, p. 523; energy use data is from U.S. Department of Energy, Energy Information Agency, *Annual Energy Review, 1987* (Washington D.C.: U.S. Department of Energy, 1988), Table 4, p. 13; the source for GDP data is U.S. Department of Commerce, Bureau of Economic Analysis, National Income and Product Accounts (July 1989 revision), Table 1.2.

13. U.S. Department of Commerce, Bureau of Economic Analysis, National Income and Product Accounts (July 1989 revision), Table 1.2, and U.S. Department of Energy, Energy Information Agency, *Annual Energy Review, 1987* (Washington D.C.: U.S. Department of Energy, 1988), Table 4, p. 13.

14. This phenomenon is not unique to the United States. It has also been found to have occurred in the United Kingdom, France, Germany, Japan, and Austria. See J. Dunkerley, "Energy Use Trends in Industrial Countries," *Energy Policy* 8 (June 1980).

15. For a description of this model, see U.S. Congress, Office of Technology Assessment, *Energy Use and the U.S. Economy* OTA-BP-E-57 (Washington, D.C.: U.S. Government Printing Office, June 1990).

16. Indirect energy use is also positively correlated with income. See *A Time to Choose* (Cambridge, Mass.: Ballinger, 1974), p. 127.

17. R. H. Williams, Eric D. Larson, and Marc Ross, "Materials, Affluence, and Industrial Energy Use," *Annual Review of Energy* (1987), p. 114.

18. Includes agriculture, mining, and construction.

19. This group includes freight and passenger transportation services. Transportation provided by personal vehicles would not be included in this category because the transportation service in this case in not being purchased but is instead being supplied outside of the formal market by the individual himself-self service. The fuel purchased to run the vehicle would be counted as a purchase of an energy product.

20. Businesses are categorized as final consumers only when they buy products that are not reprocessed for further sale. Final products consumed include buildings and durable equipment such as machine tools, not intermediate purchases of inputs such as steel or rubber that are purchased for further processing.

21. The change in business inventories represent a fifth category, but is excluded for simplicity.

22. This estimate does assume that it would be possible to produce all imports in the United States that would not hold for some products (e.g., bananas), and it also assumes that the production process used for domestic products would be identical to the one used for imported products--obviously the production process needed to make a Lamborghini is much different than the average U.S. automobile production process. But this assumption is preferable to the implicit assumption that the United States does not consume energy embodied in imported goods.

23. U.S. Department of Commerce, National Income and Product Accounts, Tables 1.2 and 4.4. Measured in constant 1982 dollars.

24. See W. U. Chandler, H. S. Geller, and M. R. Ledbetter, *Energy Efficiency: A New Agenda* (Springfield, Va: GW Press, 1988), p. 21, for an example of such a policy.

25. This estimate matches the 1984 estimate produced by the Department of Energy in its 1985 report entitled U.S. Department of Energy, *Energy Use Trends in the United States 1972-1984* (Office of Policy Planning and Analysis, May 1985), p. 25, and is roughly in line with the 8 quads estimated for the energy embodied in 1984 exports in U.S. Department of Energy, *Energy's Role in International Trade: Structural Change and Competitiveness* (Office of Policy Planning and Analysis, July 1989), pp. 1-7.

26. Measured in constant 1982 dollars. U.S. Department of Commerce, National Income and Product Accounts, Table 1.2.

27. From 1985 to the second quarter of 1989, the constant dollar share of exports to GNP increased from 10.1 percent to 14.2 percent, imports grew more slowly, increasing from 13.0 percent in 1985 to 15.5 in 1989. U.S. Department of Commerce, National Income and Product Accounts, Table 1.2, July 1989.

28. See Cleveland et al., op. cit., for thermodynamic perspective.

29. Based on the 1982 U.S. Input-Output matrix.

30. The other component of structural change is a changing mix of consumption.

31. Data limitations restrict the endpoint of the analysis of nonenergy changes in production processes to 1982, since a 1985 Input-Output table did not exist when this analysis was being performed. The 1985 table was published in January 1990.

32. *Technology and the American Economic Transition* op. cit., p. 155.

33. U.S. Department of Labor, Bureau of Labor Statistics, "Historical Input-Output Time series Data Base," unpublished, January 1989.

34. Based on weight. Williams, Larson, and Ross, op. cit., p. 120.

35. D. Jones, "Future Perspectives on the Automobile Industry," *Information Technology and Economic Perspectives* (Paris: OECD, 1985), cited in Walker, p. 470.

36. "Computer Graphics are Animating Another Market," *Business Week* (March 16, 1987), p. 92.

37. Office of Trade Representative, "U.S. National Study on Trade in Services," (Washington, D.C., December 1983).

38. For example, the occurrence of an interactive factor in a divisia analysis is noted by in Boyd et al. where they allocate the interaction effect equally to each factor. G. Boyd, DA Hanson, and M. Ross, "The Market for Fuels in the U.S. Manufacturing, 1959-81: Effects of Sectoral Shift and Intensity Changes," prepared for the Energy Modeling Forum, Study 9 (September 1987), p. 32.

39. Data for 1985 is from the U.S. Department of Commerce, Bureau of Census, *Statistical Abstract of the United States, 1989*, Table 1273, p. 730. The 1988 data is from the U.S. Department of Commerce, Bureau of Economic Analysis, *Survey of Current Business*, 69:9, pp. s1-s2.

40. U.S. Department of Labor, Bureau of Labor Statistics, "Historical Input-Output Time series Data Base," unpublished, January 1989.

41. Based in constant 1982 dollars, the total value of gross output for the whole economy in 1988 was $7.3 trillion.

42. The National Income and Product Accounts do not have expenditure data for state and local government for 1988 and do not publish any constant dollar figures for state and local expenditures by item.

43. U.S. Department of Commerce, National Income and Product Accounts, Table 1.2.

44. U.S. Department of Commerce National Income and Product Accounts, Table 3.10.

45. Hannon, B., "Analysis of the Energy Cost of Economic Activities: 1963 to 2000," *Energy Systems and Policy Journal* 6:3 (1982), p. 261.

46. This gross figure excludes the losses in GNP attributed to imports.

47. The real dollar index of the dollar where 1973:Q1 is 100, fell from 117 in June 1985 to 90.5 in June 1988. Federal Reserve Bank of Dallas, RX-101 Real Dollar Index: Monthly, 1976-88.

48. Measured in net tons. American Iron and Steel Institute, Annual Statistical Report, 1988, 1989, tables 14 and 18, pp. 34 and 44.

49. Measured in millions of pounds.   The Aluminum Association, Aluminum Statistical Review for 1988, no. 94, 1989, p. 5.

50. In some cases, higher levels of operating capacity result in greater energy efficiencies since many uses of energy are fixed inputs that are not strictly proportional to increases in the volume of production.   Thus as production increases the energy used per dollar of output falls, resulting in efficiency gains.

51. American Iron and Steel Institute, Annual Statistical Report, 1988, Table 1B.

52. Second quarter of 1988.

53. U.S. Department of Commerce, *Statistical Abstract of the United States* (1989), Table 1274, p. 730, primary processing includes textiles, lumber, paper and pulp, petroleum, rubber, stone, clay, glass, primary metals, fabricated metals, and a portion of chemicals.

54. Federal Reserve Bulletin, Board of Governors of the Federal Reserve System (Washington, D.C., November 1989), Table 2.12, p. A48.

55. Boyd et al., op. cit.

56. Given that many of the industrial uses of energy are to run "fixed" rather than "variable" modes of production (e.g., motors), it is likely that high utilization rates result in an increase in energy efficiency. See U.S. Department of Energy, *Energy Conservation Trends* (Office of Policy Planning and Analysis, September 1989), p. 11.

57. R. S. Whishart, "Comments to the Office of Technology Assessment Workshop: Energy Use in Industry," (May 11), 1989.

58. Barry Bluestone and Bennett Harrison, *The Deindustrialization of America* (New York: Basic Books, 1982), pp. 6, 40.

59. U.S. Department of Energy, *Energy's Role in International Trade: Structural Change and Competitiveness* (Office of Policy Planning and Analysis, July 1989), pp. 2-11.

60. U.S. Department of Commerce, National Income and Product Accounts, Table 5.7.

61. Landed cost of imports. *Monthly Energy Review* (August 1989), Table 9.1, p. 91.

62. U.S. Department of Energy, *Energy Conservation Trends* (Office of Policy Planning and Analysis, September 1989), p. 10.

63. Crude oil decline from $33 per barrel to $27. Landed cost of imports. *Monthly Energy Review*, (August 1989), Table 9.1, p. 91.

64. Marc Ross, "The Potential for Reducing the Energy Intensity and Carbon Dioxide Emissions in U.S. Manufacturing," unpublished (1989), p. 2.

65. H. C. Kelly, P. D. Blair, and J. H. Gibbons, "Energy Use and Productivity: Current Trends and Policy Implications," *Annual Review of Energy* 14 (1989), p. 345.

66. National Energy Board, "Canadian Energy: Supply and Demand, 1987-2005," (September 1988), p. 46.

67. U.S. Department of Energy, *Energy Conservation Trends* (Office of Policy Planning and Analysis, September 1989), p. 28.

68. G. Bruce Doern and Glen Toner, *The Politics of Energy: The Development and Implementation of the NEP* (Toronto: Methuen, 1985).

69. For example, see *Economic Report of the President* (Washington, D.C.: Government Printing Office, February 1990), p. 214.

70. L. Norford, A. Rabl, J. P. Hariss, and J. Roturier, "Electronic Office Equipment: The Impact of Market Trends on End-Use Demand," in *Electricity*, T. B. Johansson, B. Bodlund, and R. H. Williams, editors (Lund, Sweden: Lund Press, 1989), p. 432.

71. See *Energy Use and the U.S. Economy*, op. cit., p. 25.

6

The Greening of U.S. and Canadian Electricity Trade

Amy Abel and Larry B. Parker[1]

One of the Free Trade Agreement's (FTA) major accomplishments was to establish a sense of certainty that future regulations will not discourage energy trade and that the status quo will be preserved. Indeed, this has been the case for electricity, coal, and natural gas transfers. Additionally, immediately preceding ratification of the FTA there were effectively no barriers to crude oil trade. There was concern, however, that future U.S. energy policy may include an oil import fee or tariff that would include Canadian imports. Under the FTA, this is forbidden.

If the FTA is effective in eliminating taxes, tariffs, and regulations limiting trade, what will be the main factor determining the future type and amount of energy trade between the United States and Canada? Current legislation in the U.S. Congress and the Canadian Parliament point to environmental issues driving fuel choices and energy trade. In additional, physical barriers such as insufficient capacity for electricity transmission or inadequate oil and gas pipelines will place a limit on the amount of energy transfers. This chapter concentrates on issues surrounding electricity trade between the United States and Canada.

THE CURRENT SITUATION

Current Generation Mix and Plans for the Future

The United States and Canada have developed electric generation capacity that reflects each country's natural resources.[2] The United States has large reserves of coal and, in the past, has developed coal-fired generating technology as the economic choice for large capacity additions. Canada has vast water resources well-suited for large hydroelectric facilities. In many regions of

Figure 6.1

**Electric Utility Generation by Fuel Type
in Canada and the United States, 1988**

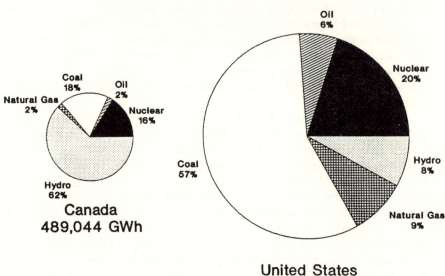

Canada, therefore, water is the "fuel" of choice. Figure 6.1 illustrates electric utility generation by fuel type in Canada and the United States. Whereas the United States is 72 percent dependent on fossil fuels, Canada is only 22 percent dependent on fossil fuels.[3]

Hydropower is the least-cost method of generating electricity, assuming an economical source of capital is available, since there is no fuel cost. In 1988, 62 percent of Canada's total generation was produced from hydropower. In contrast, in 1988, United States hydropower generated 8.3 percent of total domestic utility generation. Canada has the largest quantity as well as the highest proportional use of hydropower for electricity generation in the major industrialized nations.[4] Therefore, Canada has a natural competitive advantage in electricity trade with the United States.

In the United States, concern regarding the regulatory and economic impacts of future environmental legislation have made some utilities and nonutility generators leery of depending on coal for future capacity additions. In addition, slow electricity demand growth, regulatory delays, cost overruns, and public opposition have created substantial reluctance among electric utilities to order new nuclear units.

Instead of building large (greater than 500 MW) base-load coal or nuclear plants as was the case in the 1970s, additional capacity is being built and planned in smaller increments. In general, these plants are being designed to burn natural gas and sometimes an additional fuel such as coal or oil. Smaller gas-fired units such as the natural gas combined cycle (GCC) are economically competitive and have a relatively short construction time. Short lead times are important in the current uncertain regulatory environment. In addition, short construction periods are ideal for nonutility generators (NUGs) which are contributing an increasing proportion of capacity additions. In the United States, nonutility electricity generation accounts for approximately 5 percent of total U.S. generation.

In Canada, increasing demand for electricity will require construction of additional generating capacity. The National Energy Board of Canada projects that the generating capacity fuel mix will remain fairly constant through the year 2000 with hydropower continuing to be the main source of electricity.[5] Quebec, New Brunswick, Manitoba, and British Columbia expect to sign firm export contracts with the United States so additional capacity to supply Canadian domestic needs can be prebuilt and the capacity can temporarily be used for export purposes. Provinces with varied generating capacity and long construction lead times, such as Ontario, are planning to rely more extensively on demand-side management for adequate and reliable electricity supply until large facilities are built. In addition, nonutility generators are expected to supply increasing amounts of electricity in Canada. Currently, NUGs provide about 8 percent of total electricity production in Canada, and this is expected to grow to about 10 percent in the next fifteen years.

U.S. Imports from Canada

Several regions of the United States, including the Northeast/New York, the Midwest, and the Northwest, import significant quantities of electricity from Canada. In 1988, net imports of Canadian electricity were 29,729 gigawatt-hours (Gwh), 1.1 percent of total U.S. production. Nearly two-thirds of U.S. power imports from Canada are delivered to New York and New England (31 percent to New York and 34 percent to New England).[6]

New England imports most of its Canadian electricity from New Brunswick. Quebec and Ontario supply New York with electricity; the Midwest imports electricity from Ontario, Manitoba, and Saskatchewan; and the Northwest, including California, imports electricity from British Columbia.

Ontario's electricity exports are largely coal generated, and most of the coal comes form the United States (about 68 percent in 1986). Saskatchewan's electricity exports are all coal generated. The Canadian National Energy Broad has stated that one-seventh of the 35 billion kilowatt-hours imported by the

United States in 1986 was produced from United States Coal.[7] In contrast, Quebec's exports are entirely hydroelectric, and British Columbia exports electricity generated mostly in hydroelectric facilities.   Table 6.1 shows all generating sources for Canada exports.

The bulk of current U.S. electricity imports are interruptible with no firm commitment from the supplying utility for duration and amount of electricity supplied. A shift to firm contracts is occurring and is expected to continue, thus formalizing power transactions between the United States and Canada.

Gas Trends

In 1988, the United States consumed 18.6 quadrillion Btus (quads) of natural gas. The U.S. Energy Information Administration projects that domestic natural gas consumption will grow at an annual rate of 1.1 percent through the year 2000 to 20.9 quads. If the United States continues to meet a significant portion of new generating capacity with natural gas, additional natural gas supplies will be necessary. Two potential sources for additional natural gas supply are increased liquified natural gas (LNG) imports and additional gas imports from Canada.

If the market calls for it, approximately 3 to 4 quads per year of LNG could be imported by the United States during the 1990s. In the past, gas prices and demand have not been sufficient to link Canadian natural gas deposits. Continued growth in U.S. natural gas demand could provide the impetus to

---

Table 6.1

Energy Sources of Canadian Electricity Exports, 1988
(Percent)

Province	Oil	Coal	Nuclear	Hydro	Other*
New Brunswick	28	18	40	14	0
Quebec	0	0	0	100	0
Ontario	3	81	2	13	1
Manitoba	0	1	0	29	70
Saskatchewan	0	100	0	0	0
British Columbia	0	14	0	86	0

Source: Energy Mines and Resources Canada, *Electric Power in Canada,* 1988.
* refers to U.S. electricity imports that are subsequently exported.

continue expanding Canada's natural gas pipeline system. Similarly, Canada's recent effects to build pipeline systems to the Arctic could result in more trade in gas than generally predicted.

Transmission Capabilities

The quantity of electricity transfers between the United States and Canada and the practice of wheeling[8] within the United States are limited by transmission capability between regions. Table 6.2 shows the current interties between the United States and Canada. Most transmission lines are currently operating at or near capacity.

The National Energy Board of Canada estimated a 1990 interconnection capacity with New England of 3,435 megawatts (MW), with New York/ New Jersey of 7,300 MW, with the Midwest/North Central states of 4,275 MW, and with the Northwest of 2,300 MW.[9] Only small amounts of imported Canadian power are wheeled within the United States. The exceptions to this are British Columbia (BC) hydropower sales to California, and Ontario Hydro and Hydro Quebec sales of power to Consolidated Edison of New York City.

There are many areas in the United States and Canada that could benefit from increased transmission links to other regions. Wheeling electricity between regions can increase reliability of the system. This is possible by allowing for power exchanges in emergencies, and economy transfers between regions. However, there are many technical and nontechnical impediments to siting and construction of new transmission lines. One example of a technical constraint is an engineering problem associated with local terrain.

One nontechnical impediment to transmission line additions is the complicated approval process. Each state has its own procedure, and in most states, siting and certification requires approval of several agencies. Any proposed transmission line would need to repeat the approval process in each state that is entered. The entire process, at best, takes several years.

Environmental issues are also considered during state approval. Questions of health effects caused by electromagnetic fields have resulted in the delay or cancellation of planned transmission additions and the removal from service of existing lines. Health effect concerns have surfaced in the regulatory arena in Arizona, California, Colorado, Florida, Maryland, New York, Texas, Washington, and Ontario. These concerns have affected both planned and existing transmission facilities.[10]

U.S. Regulatory Requirements

U.S. regulation of imported Canadian electricity primarily addresses transmission. Any transmission line that crosses the U.S. international border requires a presidential permit under the Federal Power Act.[11] Currently, the

Table 6.2

Existing Transmission Lines Greater than 35 MW
Between the United States and Canada

State	Province	Numbers of Lines x Voltage (Kilowatts)	Design Capability (Megawatts)
Maine	New Brunswick	1x345	600
	New Brunswick	1x138	60
	New Brunswick	5x69	155
Michigan	Ontario	1x230	535
	Ontario	1x230	515
	Ontario	2x345	1,470
Minnesota	Ontario	1x120	35
	Manitoba	1x230	175
	Manitoba	1x500	1,000
New Hampshire	Quebec	450(DC)	690
New York	Quebec	1x765	2,300
	Quebec	2x120	300
	Ontario	1x230	470
	Ontario	1x230	400
	Ontario	2x230	600
	Ontario	2x345	2,300
	Ontario	2x69	132
	Ontario	2x115	200
North Dakota	Manitoba	1x230	150
	Saskatchewan	1x230	150
Vermont	Quebec	2x120	275
Washington	British Columbia	1x230	300
	British Columbia	1x230	400
	British Columbia	2x500	4,300

Department of Energy (DOE) is responsible for issuing these permits. DOE receives input from the Departments of Defense and State as to whether the transmission line in question will protect the "territorial integrity" of the United States and will be consistent with the public interest. DOE bases its final evaluation on 1) a technical reliability assessment that addresses whether the transmission line or lines will adversely affect U.S. power systems, and 2) an environmental impact statement. Presidential permits are required for proposed additional construction but not for increased transmission over existing lines.

Other federal laws that may affect transmission line construction projects include 1) Coastal Zone Management Act of 1972 (16 U.S.C. Sec. 1451-1464); 2) National Wilderness Act (16 U.S.C. Sec. 1131 et. seq.); 3) Resource Conservation and Recovery Act of 1976 (16 U.S.C. Sec. 6901 et. seq.); 4) Endangered Species Act of 1973 (16 U.S.C. Sec. 1531-1543); and, 5) Wild and Scenic Rivers Act (16 U.S.C. sec. 1274 et. seq.). The U.S.-Canada Free Trade Agreement did not affect prevailing domestic policies regarding transmission of Canadian electricity to the United States.

Canadian Regulatory Structure

Unlike most utilities in the United States, Canadian electric utilities are generally owned by the province in which they are located. In Canada, most regulation of electric utilities is done on a provincial level rather than by the federal government. Provinces have jurisdiction over production and distribution of electricity. However, exports are controlled by the federal government.

The National Energy Board Act extends federal jurisdiction to regulate international transmission lines and licensing electricity exports.[12] When considering a proposed international transmission line, the National Energy Board must determine whether the transmission line "is and will by required by the present and future public convenience and necessity."[13] This requirement is similar to those of the U.S. Federal Power Act.

BACKGROUND: AIR POLLUTION REGULATIONS

A major question raised concerning the U.S.-Canada Free Trade Agreement has been the environmental standards of Canadian coal-fired electric generating facilities. The FTA requires fair and equal treatment in both countries. Some have suggested that Canada's lack of scrubbers on their coal-fired plants gives them an unfair advantage both economically and environmentally. This may have some relevance in the future, but if the current U.S. standards for utility emission were applied to Canadian utilities now, very few scrubbers would need to be installed in Canada, because few Canadian coal-fired plants commenced construction after 1978, the beginning of the revised U.S. New Source Performance Standard (NSPS).[14]

Federal Canadian source emissions requirements fall into three categories. First, there is regulation of specific industries emitting designated substances hazardous to human health such as asbestos and lead. These federal standards are legally binding on those industries affected; however, as SO_2 and NO_x are not classified as hazardous contaminants, no federal standard has been promulgated.

The second category is national emission guidelines for pollutants not designated as hazardous substances. Set on an industry-by-industry basis, these guidelines are similar in purpose to the U.S. NSPS. However, the Canadian guidelines are not legally binding on provincial governments, while U.S. standards are directly enforceable by the federal government. For SO_2 and NO_x, such guidelines have been established for powerplants constructed after 1971.

These federal objectives are guidelines for the provincial governments; provinces are not bound by them. For example, Ontario's source emission requirements are derived from their ambient air standards. Depending on land use, topography, or other site-specific circumstances, special standards requiring greater control may be necessary to main ambient standards. Thus, Ontario's source emission requirements do not strictly focus on total pollutant loadings per se, as U.S. NSPS standards do or the Canadian federal guidelines suggest. Instead, they focus on maintaining ambient air standards. The result is that source emission requirements in Ontario may vary from site to site and climatic condition, permitting the use of intermittent control techniques not allowed in the United States.

U.S. SO_2 ambient standards are a little less stringent than Ontario's, although the Ontario government has promulgated a short-term, one-hour standard that the United States has not. For NO_x, the United States has not issued a short-term standard while the Ontario government has.[15]

In the United States, the Clean Air Act of 1970 and the later amendments in 1977 required New Source Performance Standards for emissions from electric generating facilities. Plants that commenced construction after 1978 must meet stricter emission rates standards than those that began construction between 1971 and 1978. In addition, those plants that began construction after 1978 must reduce their SO_2 emissions through technological means, generally scrubbers. Any plant that began construction prior to 1971 is not subject to NSPS. Each state implements a plan in order to comply with the federal ambient air standards, and older plants must comply with the plan's requirements.

The third category is mobile standards. As of model year 1988, Canadian NO_x standards for automobiles and light-duty trucks are similar to U.S. standards. The U.S. 1.0 gram per mile NO_x standard has been in effect since model year 1981.

These basic air pollution regulations are being fundamentally reassessed and changed by emerging environmental concerns. Environmental issue of bilateral concern related to energy consumption include air pollution (acid rain and greenhouse), water pollution (Great Lakes), and land use (electric transmission). The energy future of both Canada and the United States will be heavily influenced by emerging environmental issues, particularly electricity supply and demand. This chapter focuses on the two air pollution issues: acid rain and the greenhouse effect.

Acid Rain

Acid rain is a major international issue, particularly in Europe where there is great concern over damages to aquatic ecosystems in Scandinavia and forest ecosystems in central Europe. Acid rain has also been a contentious issue between the United States and Canada. Eastern Canada contains thousands of lakes that are sensitive to acid rain. With U.S. SO_2 emissions crossing the boundary to Canada in amounts estimated at nearly equal to Canada's total SO_2 emissions—approximately 4 million tons annually—the Canadian government has been pressing Washington to take control action. After several years of fruitless negotiations with the United States on a common SO_2 and NO_x control program, the Canadian government announced a two-part acid rain control program in 1985. The first part involves an agreement among the eastern provincial governments to institute new SO_2 standards on existing stationary sources. The program's objective is to reduce 1994 SO_2 emissions in eastern Canada by 50 percent from 1980 permitted levels. The government's overall objective, to reduce deposition to no more than 18 lb/acre/year, would require parallel action by the United States, although the Canadian program is not contingent on such action. The second part involves new Canadian regulations with respect to emission of NO_x, carbon monoxide, and hydrocarbons from mobile sources. Since 1985, most provinces, including Ontario and Quebec, have promulgated the necessary regulations to achieve their share of the reductions.

A major portion of Canada's SO_2 emissions result from nonenergy related activities. For example. nonferrous smelters account for about 46 percent of the country's SO_2 emissions in 1986. Because smelters represent cost-effective sources of SO_2 control, the Canadian acid rain control program focuses on smelters for much of the reductions. The effects on energy production will be mostly felt in control measures necessary by Ontario Hydro and the prevention of increased emissions in the maritime provinces of Nova Scotia and New Brunswick.

Despite the limited role energy facilities play in Canada's SO_2 control program, the acid rain regulations have begun to run up against energy policy considerations in several provinces. In Ontario, the need to maintain SO_2 and

NO_x emissions at a reduced level, along with adverse water conditions and record electricity consumption, has caused Ontario Hydro to begin importing power from Ohio, the largest SO_2-emitting state in the United States. In addition, Ontario Hydro has raised the possibility of doubling the size of its four-reactor nuclear facility at Darlington to meet future demand with no SO_2 or NO_x emissions. In Quebec, adverse water conditions have caused Hydro Quebec to "buy-back" heating power from 6,750 clients and cut off industrial consumers with self-generation capacity. With many of these consumers reverting to oil for heat, Quebec is projected to exceed its 1990 SO_2 target by about 60,000 tons. The adverse conditions have also halted Quebec attempts to increase exports to the United States. Such conflicts can only be expected to increase as the 1994 target is imposed and the emissions cap is maintained over time.

For the United States, the prospect for acid rain control changed with the election of George Bush. In November 1990, the President signed P.L. 101-549, the Clean Air Act Amendment of 1990, requiring reductions by January 1, 2000, of about 8.5 million tons below 1980 levels from electric utilities. The bulk of those reductions will come from existing coal-fired powerplants above 75 MW that emit at greater than a 1.2 lb. of SO_2 per million Btu rate. Perhaps more important from an energy policy standpoint, the new law requires maintenance of the reduced emission level by mandating that new facilities offset their SO_2 emissions by further reductions at existing facilities, i.e., an emission cap.

The upshot of the acid rain provisions in the two countries is to encourage development of non-SO_2 emitting sources of electricity, including natural gas-fired generation, nuclear, renewable, and conservation; and lower SO_2 emitting coal-fired technology such as newer generation scrubbers and pressurized fluidized bed combustion. For Canada, increased hydroelectric development in provinces with significant untapped potential—Quebec, Manitoba, and British Columbia—would seem a possibility, with additional nuclear capacity a possibility in Ontario and New Brunswick. Nova Scotia is already planning to use circulating atmospheric fluidized bed combustion at a new facility, and western provinces may also consider clean coal technology as SO_2 control becomes a critical issue in those provinces.

For the United States, the importance of coal to electricity generation (over 50 percent of total generation) places some emphasis on reducing SO_2 emissions from that source. However, acid rain legislation may also confirm the current trend in new capacity toward the use of natural gas. It would seem at the current time that acid rain legislation, even with its SO_2 cap, will be insufficient to revive the nuclear option. The increased price of electricity, however, may prove a significant incentive to increase conservation in the United States.

Given both countries' commitment to acid rain control regimes to restrict SO_2 emissions, maintenance of the emission cap may encourage further electricity and trade on both sides of the border. As noted earlier, Ontario

Hydro has already found such trade useful in meeting its control commitments. In addition, the potential increase in natural gas demand for electricity generation in the United States may increase prospects for Canadian exports of that resource. However, as both countries accept SO_2 caps as part of their environmental and energy policy, some coordination between the two countries in planning and constructing facilities, particularly the choice of fuel, may be useful in improving the cost-effectiveness of SO_2 control.

The Greenhouse Effect

If acid rain was the environmental issue of the 1980s, then the greenhouse effect may be the environmental issue of the 1990s. If CO_2 controls becomes a necessary part of a greenhouse control strategy, the effect of such control on both countries' energy policy can hardly be underestimated. Both countries are heavily dependent on fossil fuel for transportation, and the United States, as noted above, is heavily depended on fossil fuel for electricity generation. Indeed, on average, the United States creates about 700 tons of CO_2 per Gwh of electricity generated, while Canada creates about 270 tons of CO_2 per Gwh of electricity generated.

Like the acid rain threat, the effect of the greenhouse projections is to emphasize non-fossil fuel electricity generation, conservation, and more efficient coal-fired technologies. The priority for each of these fuel sources will depend on the perceived urgency of the problem. If serious stabilization or reduction in CO_2 emissions are determined necessary in the short term (ten years), then the emphasis of a CO_2 control strategy will have to be conservation and natural gas substitution. Conservation, by reducing electricity demand growth, would lessen the need for new electricity generating capacity and additional energy supply links between the United States and Canada.

For natural gas, the potential for exports to the United States would appear significant. Yet domestic Canadian use of natural gas may also increase under possible greenhouse controls. Currently, Alberta prohibits the use of natural gas for electricity generation in that province, reserving that job to its low-sulfur coal resource. Greenhouse considerations may force a reassessment of this position if CO_2 reduction in Alberta is determined to be a prudent policy. Coordination of natural gas exports may result in more cost-effective CO_2 reductions through the export of natural gas to the United States, but as with the acid rain situation, integrated planning between the two countries would be useful.

Other non-fossil fuel sources may also profit from a coordinated North American response to greenhouse fears in the longer term. In particular, nuclear power, generally built in large increments, would profit from a larger pool of consumers. Canada, particularly New Brunswick, has attempted to attract U.S.

utility interest in building reactors for many years. Greenhouse concerns may increase U.S. interest in such coordinated action. Development of renewable and clean-coal technology may also profit from coordinated U.S.-Canadian efforts.

In summary, enactment of the FTA opened the door to a more coordinated North American energy market. The emerging regional and global environmental issues will tend to increase the need for coordination of North American energy responses to ensure environmental control on the most cost-effective basis. The speed and predictability at which this will occur will depend on the environmental urgency perceived by Canada and the United States and their willingness to build on the foundation of the FTA.

NOTES

1. Amy Abel is an analyst in energy policy and Larry B. Parker is a specialist in energy policy at the Library of Congress, Congressional Research Service. Views expressed in this chapter are those of the authors and not necessarily those of the Congressional Research Service or of the Library of Congress.

2. For a detailed discussion on the Free Trade Agreement and electricity see U.S. Library of Congress, Congressional Research Service, *Canadian Electricity: The U.S. Market and the Free Trade Agreement* 88-427 ENR, Amy Abel (July 5, 1988).

3. Nuclear powered electric generation is not considered to be fossil fuel-fired generation.

4. Electricity Consumers Resource Council, *Canadian Hydropower Potential Resources and Implications for U.S. Industrial Competitiveness* (Washington, D.C., 1987).

5. National Energy Board, *Canadian Energy Supply and Demand 1987—2005.*

6. Energy, Mines and Resources Canada, *Electric Power in Canada 1988* (Ottawa, Ontario, 1989).

7. The total contribution of U.S. Coal exports to Canadian domestic supply of electricity is more than 2 million tons.

8. *Wheeling* is defined as the use of transmission facilities of one system to transmit power produced by another entity to a third party.

9. National Energy Board, *Canadian Energy Supply and Demand 1987-2005* (Ottawa, Ontario, September 1988) p. 80.

10. For a discussion of electromagnetic fields, see U.S. Congress, Office of Technology Assessment, *Electric Power Wheeling and Dealing: Technological Considerations for Increasing Competition*, OTA-E-409 (Washington, D.C.: U.S. Government Printing Office, May 1989).

11. Federal Power Act of 1935. 16 U.S.C. 792.

12. R. S., cn-6 amended by cc. 10,27,44 (1st Supp.) c. 10 (12 Gd Supp.), 1, 973-4, c. 52.

13. National Energy Board Act, C. 46, s.44.

14. For a detailed discussion see U.S. Library of Congress, Congressional Research Service, *Canada's Progress on Acid Rain Control: Shifting Gears or Stalled in Neutral?* Mira Courpas and Larry B. Parker, (Washington, D.C., April 20, 1988).

15. See U.S. Library of Congress, Congressional Research Service, *Canada's Acid Control Program: Catching Up or Pulling Away?* Larry B. Parker (June 7, 1985).

7

Water and Hydroelectric Exports from Canada to the United States

Kendall D. Moll

WATER DEVELOPMENT: A TRADE DILEMMA

Diverse economic, political, environmental, and technological forces that appeared in the 1980s are now influencing Canadian and U.S. water resource policies. Economic interdependence, observable in rapidly rising international trade statistics and integration of the European Community, has appeared in North America as the Free Trade Agreement (FTA). This agreement has forced both countries to acknowledge that renewable resources are freely tradable resources.

Political independence and ethnocentrism, seen most prominently in revolutionary changes of the Eastern Bloc, have emerged at the same time in Canada as the Meech Lake controversy. Issues long thought settled, such as who should own and regulate the nation's water resources, are re-opened. Simplistically, the provincial interests reflected at Meech Lake should oppose the integrative interests represented by the FTA. However, the two influences seem instead to be interacting in a more complex way, as will be discussed below.

To make matters even more complicated, environmental concerns are affecting water resource policies in various new ways. Long-standing concerns with Great Lakes water levels have expanded to include acid rain, global warming, and deforestation. Most but not all of these concerns tend to discourage water resource development.

Finally, advances in irrigation, electrical transmission, and other technologies are changing the costs and trade-offs among water uses. Each change in technology affects trade-offs in a unique way, but the most important recent innovations have tended to favor development of hydroelectric power rather than higher levels of water extraction.

Foreign examples provide small insight concerning these issues because Canada and the United States lead the world in harnessing water resources. Each of the four forces—economic, political, ecological, and technological—needs to be assessed in terms of its change from the past. Each should be seen as changing in popular perception as well as changing in objective reality. And each should be recognized as only a part of the total water resource picture. This paper expands and updates an earlier analysis of these issues.[1]

No one can deny that Canada is a land of unparallelled water potential. It contains 20 percent of all the world's stream flows, but only 1/2 of 1 percent of the world's population. This ratio means that Canadians are 40 times richer in water potential than the average world citizen. Yet according to a report by the Western States Water Council, Canadians consume only 2 percent of their water resources, compared to an average of 10 percent consumption in other nations.[2] Meanwhile, the United States has already developed most of its available water supplies, but its consumption is still increasing at more than 1 percent per year. Accordingly, the prospect of transferring water from Canada appears, at first appraisal, to be an attractive opportunity for both countries.

From pioneer times up to the mid-20th century, water was treated as a resource with infinite supply. However, that assumption was questioned when environmentalists in the 1960s raised new issues, including water salinity, chemical toxicity, and excessive flow diversions. People began to ask if water development might cost more than it was worth. The oil crisis in the 1970s further demonstrated that all resources are finite. Studies such as "The Global 2000 Report to the President" relayed the message that water shortages will become progressively more severe.[3]

In the 1980s, debates concerning such development and environmental issues as water rights and desertification spread to the international arena. Even water development projects that boasted abundant low cost sources, economies of scale, and efficient new technologies faced unexpected barriers. Political regulations became increasingly rigid. Social and financial costs had to be more rigorously identified.

Similar barriers have threatened international electric power transfers, especially those from coal generating plants.[4] New Canadian hydroelectric exports have also become more controversial as both Canadian power projects and environmental opponents have multiplied in recent years.[5] The issues of exporting hydroelectric power, however, differ both from the issues of exporting coal-generated power and the issues of exporting water itself.

Canada has exported hydroelectric power to the United States for more than 100 years. Almost 100 transmission lines extend across the border part of an interconnected grid stretching more than 1,000 miles (1,600 kilometers).[6,7] The market has grown by a factor of eight since 1970. It now amounts to over a billion dollars per year (2 percent of all U.S. consumption) and is expected to continue growing rapidly. Still, one-half of Canadian hydroelectric potential will remain undeveloped by the year 2000.[8] Meanwhile, despite the continued increase in its consumption at more than 2 percent per year, the United States has effectively stopped building power plants because of environmental constraints and faces renewed electrical "brownouts" within a few years.[9] Thus, expanded electrical imports from Canada continue to be logical in terms of the changing economic, technological, political, and environmental forces.

Based on the analysis that follows, the trends for the two types of trade in water resources are projected to diverge. Water transfers from Canada to the United States are unlikely to increase significantly. However, hydroelectric power exports promise relative investment advantages and are likely to grow.

WATER TRANSFERS

Local and regional areas in North America from southern Canada to northern Mexico have long taken water in larger and larger projects. International irrigation proposals are not a new phenomenon; the United States and Canada have discussed joint water management projects for three decades. Although remarkably few of these proposals have actually been implemented to date, people wonder if the FTA will create a flood of new proposals.

Economic Factors

The key economic factor that inhibits new water development projects is price elasticity, defined as the change in demand for a commodity caused by a change in the price. The price elasticity of some commodities, such as wheat, is very low; but the elasticity of others, such as video recorders, is very high. The price elasticity of water is intermediate.

Some planners consider water demands to be fixed because we all need a minimum amount just to live and maintain our life-style. In fact, needs for water and for any economic commodity are usually more flexible than fixed, especially in the long term, because almost none of our needs is absolutely essential. Drinking needs account for less than one out of every 1,000 gallons used.[10] Total cooking, bathing, laundry, toilet, and other domestic needs account for less than 10 percent of all North American water uses. Irrigation, rather than direct people needs, accounts for the largest share—about one-half of all water uses.

Economic estimates indicate that water usage drops fairly rapidly as prices rise. Irrigation use is about inversely proportional to price (according to a rough average of past economic surveys).[11] In other words, doubling the cost of water will cut demand in half. However, a variety of factors often induces water project managers to create excessive demand by setting irrigation prices too low:

- First, water project managers usually set prices based on the project's average cost for water. Modern economic theory, reflected in most commercial practices, supports pricing based on incremental cost for new supplies. Incremental cost is usually greater than average historical cost—as much as seven times greater for some water projects.

- Furthermore, the managers seldom increase prices enough to reflect inflation (a factor of four since 1960).

- U.S. government-sponsored projects usually subsidize interest on capital and many other costs by 80 percent or more, although in the past ten years Congress has made this more difficult by cutting back severely on water development funds.[12]

The U.S. government's Central Valley Project, a typical system that supplies about 40 percent of California's current irrigation needs, illustrates how large these distortions can be. It delivers water through a canal system that averages less than 100 miles from source to destination. The system was founded in 1935 and constructed at costs that averaged only a small fraction of today's costs. Its full current water costs (including capital interest at long-term treasury bond rates) amount to about $25 per acre-foot. Of this total, the farmer pays only $5 and the government $20. An additional $25 or more in federal crop support payments for surplus products grown with the subsidized water are not counted.[13]

A proposed expansion stage of the Central Valley Project is more predictive of future water costs. This next stage (the Auburn-Folsom South Unit) would not require any pumping stations or energy costs for lifting water and would involve only one primary dam, a few support reservoirs, and a main canal extending about 25 miles (40 kilometers). Incremental true costs for this new source of California irrigation water are estimated at more than $300 per acre-foot.[14]

Other, more ambitious new projects could cost much more. But just from the example above, we can calculate very large effects on usage. Raising farmers' average water price from an estimated current $10 per acre-foot (0.8 cents/m^3) to $300 will reduce U.S. irrigation demand from its current 100 million down to a mere 3 million acre-feet per year. In other words, there would be very little demand even for existing irrigation water at unsubsidized prices.

Price elasticity arguments may seem somewhat theoretical. Past experience certainly raises the expectation, as did the Global 2000 Report, that more of all resources will be needed in the future. Growing populations, higher living standards, and efforts to meet pollution standards ("the solution to pollution is dilution") might continue to expand future needs for water, despite higher unit costs. However, the U.S. Bureau of Reclamation has predicted that water demand 50 years from now will be only a small fraction of potentially feasible supplies[15]. If water demands drop because prices increase, conservation and technological measures will be found to adapt to the new realities.

Technological Factors

Many inventions are reducing the resources needed to transfer and use water. Traditional irrigation by flooding, for example, delivered water with only 50 percent efficiency. Then sprinklers raised efficiency to 75 percent, and in recent years drip systems have raised it to 90 percent.[16] Less directly, hybrid grains developed in the "Green Revolution" of the past 25 years have reduced needs for new water by improving existing crop yields around the world. Other innovations such as insect controls help by improving plant productivity. New controls include "integrated pest management" (using good bugs to fight bad bugs), genetic engineering (developing more resistant plants), and mechanical removal (cleaning crops with field vacuum cleaners).

For these and other reasons, U.S. farm production continues to rise even though irrigation water volumes, irrigated land, and total farm acreage are stabilizing or declining. Many farmers in semiarid states have returned to "dry-land farming" because costs of natural gas and other energy used to pump irrigation water have become prohibitive.

Industrial, utility, commercial, and domestic users can all afford to pay higher water rates than can agriculture, so their uses are less elastic. But even these rich buyers cut back their withdrawals as water prices increase. Reduction in industrial water withdrawals apparently is the main cause of declining trends in total U.S. water withdrawals. (See Table 7.1)

In contrast to the reduction in withdrawals (total amounts of fresh water taken), consumption (net amounts lost or polluted during use) is increasing. Clean water standards and higher water costs are encouraging more intensive use and recycling by consumers, Canadian as well as American.[17] (See Table 7.1, Part B, "Consumption".)

The divergent trends of withdrawals and consumption show that plans and policies are no longer being made from the old growth assumptions that more is necessarily better. Rather, they point to two new technological truisms:

1) Whether water uses will increase or decrease is less important than the probability that changes will be small compared to total supplies. The predicted changes will be less than 10 percent of the total amounts used. This means that major new water projects will not be needed in the foreseeable future.

Table 7.1

U.S. Water Use Trends

ECONOMIC USE	A. WITHDRAWALS (Amounts taken from freshwater sources.)				B. CONSUMPTION (Withdrawals less amounts returned to sources.)			
	Volume (mil. A-ft* per year) 1975	2000	Change	% Change	Volume (mil. A-ft* per year) 1975	2000	Change	% Change
Power Plant	100	89	-11	-11%	2	12	+10	+500%
Industry	65	35	-30	-46%	10	20	+10	+100%
Agriculture	180	176	-4	-2%	99	107	+8	+8%
Domestic & Commercial	32	41	+9	+28%	8	11	+3	+38%
Total Volume/Avg. %	377	341	-36	-9%	119	150	+31	+26%

Source: U.S. Water Resources Council, "The nation's Water Resources 1975-2000, vol. 1", Washington, D.C., 1978. Quoted in Perry McCarty, "Water and its Challenges," *The Stanford Engineer,* Fall 1980.
* 1 million acre-feet = 1.23 km^3

2) Future water needs will mainly be met not by the traditional approach of finding and exploiting more sources but by employing new application and conservation technologies to wring more out of existing sources.   Future technologies for cross-border transfers, whether new or old, must demonstrate that they are environmentally sound as well as economically advantageous and politically feasible in both countries.

Environmental Factors

Environmentalists oppose a project in proportion to how much it interferes with nature. They have raised few arguments against the bottling and marketing of glacier water to thirsty Japanese and American consumers or even against proposals for shipping whole tankers full of drinking water. However, they protest vigorously against disrupting Canada's northern environment with widespread reservoirs and extensive canal and power transmission systems. They see flooding, particularly, as causing erosion, creating adverse changes in freshwater and coastal ecosystems, inundating native lands, and threatening health problems.[18]

Environmentalists have been most adamant in their opposition to the larger-scale projects that have been proposed over the years such as the two largest and best known (but never implemented): the Great Replenishment and Northern Development (GRAND) Canal and the North American Water and Power Alliance (NAWAPA) Plan.[19] (See Figure 7.1.)

These two schemes are so vast that only their general outlines can be given here. The GRAND Canal is the earliest and still most prominently discussed major scheme. It would erect a 160-kilometer dam at the shallow opening of James Bay into Hudson Bay. The dam would impound twice the freshwater flow of the entire Great Lakes basin.

A volume perhaps as much as 100 million acre-feet (125 km³) per year would be diverted southward, equivalent to almost one-third of all existing U.S. water withdrawals. It would be pumped up 300 meters and through a 640-kilometer canal system to the Great Lakes and the St. Lawrence River. The power to pump this volume of water would reportedly require four nuclear power stations. The system could add 30 percent more water to the natural Great Lakes supply, allowing further transfers by another canal system to water-short areas in the United States and Canadian midwests, the U.S.West, and even into Mexico.

The NAWAPA proposal, originated in 1964, is designed to divert water from the northwest region of the continent to warmer areas of Canada, the United States, and Mexico.   The watershed region is 3.4 million square kilometers, more than one-quarter of the combined total areas of Canada and Alaska.

Figure 7.1

Two Plans for Water Export from Canada to the United States

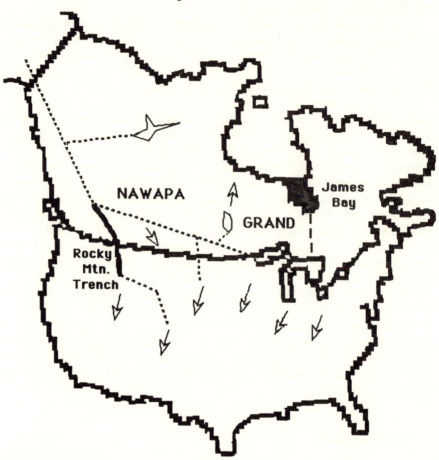

Source: Kendall Moll

The water would flow south through a complex series of canals, tunnels, lakes, dams, and lifts. The regulating reservoir of the system would be in the Rocky Mountain Trench, a natural gorge extending from Canada into northern Montana. The gorge is 700 kilometers long, 16 kilometers wide on average, up to 1500 meters high, and an average of 60 meters deep. Storage capacity is about 507 million acre-feet. From the northern end of the trench, a canal dredged to 10 meters in depth would extend southeast to Lake Superior, furnishing water and transportation to the prairies of southern Canada. The

Dakota Canal, an offshoot, would feed into the upper Mississippi and Missouri rivers. A third canal would lead through Lake Winnipeg northward to Hudson Bay. Annual diversions would amount to 110 million acre-feet, slightly larger than those of the GRAND Canal.[20]

Environmentalists charge that such pervasive irrigation projects will cause widespread flooding, continental-scale climatic alterations, and ecologically unstable cropland "monocultures." In addition, the projects draw fire from "good government" and conservative economic interests, who argue plausibly that such projects can not even be justified in narrow cost/benefit terms.

Certainly the huge costs of these water projects raise many red flags. Total costs of the Grand Canal and the NAWAPA plans have been roughly estimated at $100 to $150 billion each,[21] but historically such preliminary feasibility studies have grossly understated costs.[22] Unit prices required to deliver water to specific users have not been estimated in any detail. However, based on the California irrigation costs described above, they would doubtless be far above the typical prices farmers now pay. Scaled-down projects to obtain northern water would probably be at least as expensive per unit of water, since distance moved and lift are the major cost items.

The benefits of new water for old cropland are equally dubious. For example, two analysts recently referred to the U.S. Homestead Act of 1862, which gave 160 acres of free farmland to settlers, as a "historic error." They proposed that the federal government repurchase five million acres of such land in the Plains states and let it revert to a "Buffalo Commons."[23]

Similar reassessments are occurring in other countries. The Soviet Union suspended work on two ambitious projects to divert four rivers from the Arctic Ocean to southern agricultural areas. The halt, which had been "advocated by wide bodies of public opinion," allowed "more study of the ecological and economic aspects."[24]

Political Factors

Most Canadians seem as concerned about water transfers as about any issue covered by the FTA. The agreement itself is not explicit on water transfers and Canadians atill consider their water as a Canadian, not a continental, resource.[25] Federal and provincial governments in Canada would have to agree before international negotiations could be completed, just as they would for a domestic development project. However, Canadian supplies have not been adequately inventoried and demands for the future have not been properly assessed. Canada feels that it must address its own needs first.[26]

The United States hesitates to enter an agreement that makes it dependent on imported water just as it is reluctant to depend on imported oil (although the FTA shows the United States is learning to accept oil imports). Many Americans would prefer to rely on conservation.

If international water transfers did reach the stage of serious planning, allocation of costs would be controversial. In prospect, these plans show little immediate benefit for Canada, which feels that the United States should pay most of the costs since it would receive virtually all of the benefits. The United States would want to charge a larger proportion of costs to Canada, anticipating long-term irrigation and industrial development potentials there.   U.S. proponents would also have to demonstrate that costs of an international project would be competitive with those of developing alternative water sources within the United States. This could be difficult given the obviously high costs of building and operating such a gigantic long-distance system.

Urban water users in the United States are especially concerned about potential conservation needs, as seen in shortages during droughts and in rapidly ebbing underground water tables.   They have increasingly favored the environment over water in the past 25 years. Whole "wild and scenic" rivers are declared off-limits from any development whatsoever. Most recently, Los Angeles has lost long-established water rights from two major sources in California. Southern California farm irrigators are being threatened with water cutoffs for the first time in memory.   These political trends all involve conservation and regional reallocations among existing users, not an ever-widening search for imports of distant water.

HYDROELECTRIC POWER TRANSFERS

A better method of bringing the benefits of abundant Canadian water resources to the United States is to increase deliveries of hydroelectric power. Hydroelectricity fills an immediate economic need for energy in the expanding American market, and it can supplement unreliable and increasingly expensive nuclear and conventional thermal power.[27] It can use increasingly efficient technology, avoid acid rain and other environmental problems of alternative energy sources, and retain its long-established political acceptance in both Canada and the United States.

Economic Factors

Hydroelectric exports are considerably better accepted by the market and the public than are water transfer projects.   First, the precedent of commercial electrical exports is firmly established among powerful producer and consumer interest groups, whereas there are few transborder water transfers currently in operation.   Second, power transfer networks can be redesigned and relocated more flexibly in order to follow market needs. Third, proposed hydro projects are typically smaller, less bulky, and more dispersed.   Two of the largest hydros, the Site C Dam and the Stikine River Project in British Columbia, would cost only $3 billion and $5 billion, respectively. The existing James Bay Hydro Project in Quebec cost $15 billion. Thus, even the largest hydro projects cost only a small fraction of the cost for either of the proposed international water projects. Fourth, hydroelectricity is often a byproduct of irrigation and other applications, and thus somewhat complementary to rather than competitive with water development proposals. As a result, hydroelectric projects fit more easily into small economic "niches," as new low-head and cogeneration units have demonstrated in recent years. Finally, hydroelectric projects are less vulnerable to charges of foreign exploitation since they do not remove or consume nonrenewable physical goods.

Technological Factors

Recent engineering and scientific advances are making long-distance electrical transmission more feasible than ever.

- Turbine generators now work with improved efficiency. New designs developed during the oil crisis years have been used to fill more niche applications such as low-head generation from canal, river, and tidal flows.

- The high-voltage direct-current transmission lines that have been introduced in the past 20 years can carry electricity farther than 1,000 miles with relatively small losses. In comparison, much shorter conventional alternating-current distribution lines dissipate from 7 to 20 percent of all electricity generated. Also, direct current is not implicated in rising health concerns over power lines (cancer and other hazards have been suggested by recent research on the effects of exposure to electromagnetic fields near alternating-current power lines). Direct-current technology can even open a new Canadian power option: to deliver electricity generated in Alaska to the coterminous United States.

- Very recent research on superconducting materials promises further breakthroughs in the efficiency of electrical generation, distribution, and use. Intercontinental transmission distances may become practical, so that Canada need no longer depend on the monopsonic U.S. energy market. Canada may be able some day to take advantage of a Japanese company's reported offer to build a superconducting power cable from Vancouver to Japan.[28]

Environmental Factors

Except for solar and wind generators, which are not yet economically competitive, hydroelectricity is the cleanest source of power. It creates no radioactive wastes, air pollution, grimy soot particulates, climate-warming carbon dioxide, or toxic or voluminous scrubber wastes. This fact is one of the strongest arguments favoring its further development. Combustion by-products, particularly from coal plants in both the United States and Canada, are the major causes of acid rain, and coal is still increasing its share of electrical power. Even a partial solution to the acid rain problem is not only a top ecological priority but also an economic one. Acid rain has been estimated to create damage in Canada equal to 8 percent of the gross national product. [29]

Hydroelectric facilities require surface developments, including dams, reservoirs, and power lines, but even these are no more obtrusive than comparable water transfer facilities. In fact, hydro projects are typically much smaller, and thus "lower profile," than are irrigation projects because electricity is much easier than water to collect and move. Consequently, hydroelectric projects tend to attract less public attention.

The solution preferred by environmentalists—conservation—is inadequate in the long term. Conservation cannot eliminate all needs for power. Even if power needs decline, new facilities are needed to replace obsolete and environmentally unacceptable plants.

Political Factors

Hydroelectricity should be comparatively invulnerable to protectionist political maneuvers by either exporters or importers because of its long history of international power interties and the new energy provisions of the FTA. Its further development already has political favor as shown by public as well as private initiatives. Although views vary from province to province, they tend to be most favorable in the regions that have the most to export.

For example, Quebec's Premier Bourassa is already on record in favor of further hydroelectric development. [30] Future governments there should also be motivated to continue development policies even if it detaches from national participation, given Quebec's economic needs and political isolation from the rest of Canada.

The FTA opens Canada's gates to American trade on the same basis as domestic trade. If the agreement is implemented as envisioned, trade with America will no longer be as easily blocked by blatant political appeals to local, provincial, or national interests. Beyond these passive protections, the "game rules" of the FTA permit longer-range initiatives for energy development and acid-rain protection.

One political initiative that Canada or its individual provinces might take is to expedite development of hydro power in exchange for U.S. or state government commitments to reduce thermal power pollution. Another might be to offer electric transmission rights for U.S. hydro power generated in Alaska in exchange for U.S. commitments to develop those sources (such as the long-discussed Susitna hydro project near Mt. McKinley) instead of air-polluting thermal sources in the lower 48 states. The United States could also take the leadership in these exchanges.

CONCLUSIONS

Ten years ago there was a great concern that the world was running out of food, that Canada and the United States had to fill the need, and that acreage, crop yields, and water use had to increase to meet the impending shortage. Today, crop production far exceeds market demand, at least in North America. People are still going hungry in the world, but this is due to national food distribution breakdowns rather than food production shortages. Consequently, we have a clearer and more modest view of our real water needs.

Real economic costs for new long-distance irrigation water will be more than $300 per acre-foot. Current U.S. irrigation water prices to farmers average only about $10 at an annual consumption rate of 100 million acre-feet. A major new Canadian source such as the GRAND Canal or the NAWAPA Project could increase U.S. water supplies by as much as one-third, but would have to charge 30 or more times the current average price to cover its costs. Considering the price elasticity of water demand, it could hardly recover more than a very small percentage of these costs. Although some existing irrigation projects reportedly recover as little as zero percent of their costs, anything less than 100 percent cost recovery should be a turn-off in the modern era of economic enlightenment.

Technologically modern conservation methods, which stretch water supplies much further, also discourage new water projects. Many new techniques can reduce water consumption by applying it more sparingly, recycling it more systematically, and diverting it to less-thirsty uses. However, few new techniques have been found to lift and haul water more efficiently. These shifts in comparative advantage toward conservation instead of delivery greatly diminish prospects for large-scale international water transfers.

Nevertheless, Canada's water will not likely be overlooked by international developers. Its potential for generating hydroelectric power is well recognized by Canadian officials and the American utility industry. Furthermore, hydro facilities can provide environmentally less polluting power than can alternative sources. They show special advantages in the intensifying struggle to eliminate acid rain. Finally, they can be used politically to help lead the way toward increased binational cooperation under the FTA.

In summary, the analysis above shows that using water to export energy is more cost-effective than using energy to export water. Furthermore, almost all the foreseeable trends—economic, technological, ecological, and political—favor power as the water resource product with foreign trade growth potential. The situation and trends both show that the wave of future Canadian water resource exports will be hydroelectric, not hydraulic.

NOTES

1.   Kendall Moll and Ned Rosenbrook, "Will Free Trade Release a Flood of Canadian Water?", in *Canada-U.S. Outlook: The Energy-Environment Tradeoff*, Jonathan Lemco, ed., 1, 3/4 (Washington, D.C.: National Planning Association, May 1990).

2.   Western States Water Council, "A Review of Inter-Regional and International Water Transfer Proposals," Salt Lake City (1969), p. 2.

3.   *The Global 2000 Report to the President: Entering the Twenty-first Century*. Vol. 1: *The Technical Report* (Washington D.C., Government Printing Office, 1980).

4.   Everett Cataldo, "Canadian Acid Rain Policy: Institutional, Rational and Societal Perspectives," in *The American Review of Canadian Studies*, 20, no. 1 (Spring 1990).

5.   James Baker, "Whose Power to Which People?" Sierra, (January-February 1987), pp. 22-24.

6.   "Canadian power: what's the real price?" *Electrical World* (November 1987).

7.   Robert N. Macrae, "Canadian Energy Development," *Current History* (March 1988).

8.   James Cook, "Power play," *Forbes,* August 11, 1988.

9.   Peter McNulty, "Get Ready for Power Brownouts," *Fortune*, June 5, 1989.

10.   I. Asimov, "Water, water everywhere, but. . .", *National Wildlife*, 8, no. 12, (1978), p. 26.

11.   Yvonne Levy, "Pricing Federal Irrigation Water," *Economic Review*, (Federal Reserve Bank of San Francisco, Spring 1987), p. 48.

12.   P. K. Rao, "Planning and Financing Water Resource Development in the United States," *American Journal of Economics and Sociology*, 47, no. 1 (January 1, 1988).

13.   *San Jose Mercury*, March 9, 1988.

14.   Levy, op. cit., p. 46.

15.   Western States Water Council, op. cit., p. 5.

16.   Kobe Shoji, "Drip Irrigation," *Scientific American* (November 1977).

17.   John Daly, "The Real Value of A Treasure," *Maclean's*, June 27, 1988.

18. Lionel Haines, "The Green Barrage," *Business Month*, December 1989.

19. Geoffrey R. Weller, "Canadian Water Exports: A Controversy In The Making," *American Review of Canadian Studies*, 16, no. 4 (1986).

20. Western States Water Council, op. cit., p. 9.

21. Weller, op. cit., p. 429.

22. Western States Water Council, op. cit., p. 5.

23. Associated Press, November 12, 1989.

24. "Soviet Union Suspends Plans to Divert Four Rivers," *Science*, 233 (September 5, 1986), p. 1036.

25. John C. Richard and Richard G. Dearden, commentators, *The Canada-U.S. Free Trade Agreement: Final Text and Analysis* (Don Mills, Ont.: CCH Canadian Ltd., 1988).

26. Western States Water Council, op. cit., p. 4

27. McNulty, op. cit.

28. C. K. N. Patel, "Superconductivity," speech to Commonwealth Club, San Francisco, January 27, 1989.

29. Kenneth E. Borst, "Assessing the Effects of Acid Precipitation on Natural Freshwater," talk presented at Association for Canadian Studies in the United States meeting, San Francisco, Noveember 18, 1989.

30. Robert Bourassa, *Power from the North*, (Scarborough, Ontario: Prentice Hall, 1985), portion reprinted in *Canada-U.S. Outlook: The Energy-Environment Tradeoff*, Jonathan Lemco, ed. 1, no. 3/4 (Washington D.C.: National Planning Association, May 1990).

8

Beyond the NIMBY Syndrome in Hazardous Waste Facility Siting: The Albertan Breakthrough and the Prospects for Cooperation in the United States and Canada

Barry G. Rabe

Both Canada and the United States have stumbled badly in recent decades in attempting to design policy that can lead to the safe and efficient disposal of hazardous wastes. These wastes pose a fundamental dilemma for both nations in that any disposal facility will likely impose high costs on those communities surrounding the facility that is constructed. At the same time, the siting and operation of a facility will offer widely dispersed benefits to all who escape these costs and continue to enjoy the advantages of life in a society that generates abundant quantities of these wastes. In both nations, what is commonly referred to as the NIMBY syndrome (Not In My Back Yard) prevails, in which those communities faced with a proposed site take aggressive collective action and thwart the proposal. As a result, the volumes of wastes increase and the types of waste requiring special disposal or treatment proliferate, with the political systems of both Canada and the United States appearing increasingly unable to break through this logjam.

This chapter will consider some of the reasons that prevailing approaches to siting have failed repeatedly to produce agreements. It will also explore alternative policy approaches that may prove more successful in transcending NIMBYism. In particular, the breakthrough case of Alberta, which achieved a siting agreement in 1984 and opened a new, comprehensive waste disposal and treatment facility in 1987, will be examined in considerable detail to determine whether it was a political fluke or if it offers lessons for future siting efforts.

This analysis will draw heavily on the growing body of scholarship on policy cooperation in considering the Alberta agreement and its prospects for replication. As Paul Quirk has noted, political science has generally failed "to identify the conditions for cooperative resolution of policy conflict."[1] However, increasingly mature thinking about policy cooperation, evident in both institutionalist and game theoretic perspectives, has begun to explore this fundamental question with growing sophistication. Applied to cases such as hazardous waste facility siting, it suggests that meeting the following conditions can enhance the prospects for a cooperative outcome: creation of new governmental institutions with capacity for conflict mediation; provision of extensive opportunities for public participation early in the policy-making process; development of economic and related incentives to make cooperation more attractive to integrally involved groups and individuals; recruitment of credible and capable policy professionals to guide policy making on complex policy issues and build public trust; and cultivation of governing norms to guide citizen conduct and assure widespread policy support and compliance.

THE PROBLEM OF HAZARDOUS WASTE
AND ALTERNATIVE APPROACHES TO SITING

Hazardous waste defies precise scientific definition, exact estimation of public health risk through various routes of exposure, or technological agreement on the safest methods for disposal or recycling.[2] All of these factors contribute to the widespread public fear of these wastes and the difficulty in reaching agreement on their safe management. The classification systems for measuring the volumes of these wastes and their toxicity have improved in recent years, particularly in the United States. A series of recent government-sponsored studies suggest that between 250 and 275 million metric tons, about one metric ton per person, of hazardous waste are generated in the United States each year.[3] No comparable estimate exists for Canada. A tabulation of recent provincial estimates suggests that approximately 5 to 7 million metric tons are generated in Canada annually, but this is in all likelihood a significant underestimation of the total volume.

Regardless of the total volume of wastes, it is commonly agreed that disposal and treatment supply fall far short of demand. Many hazardous waste disposal facilities were closed in the 1980s due to revelations of unsafe treatment practices and fears of environmental and public health dangers in the event of continued facility operation. Only a handful of new facilities were opened in either Canada or the United States in the past decade, and the majority of these are relatively modest in scope. Many of these have merely expanded the capacity of existing facilities, as in Michigan, or will treat only select types of wastes, as in Quebec.

Swan Hills, Alberta, a town of 2,396 about 209 kilometers northwest of Edmonton, was the only community in Canada or the United States to accept a comprehensive hazardous waste facility in the 1980s. While it features multiple treatment and disposal methods and has potentially expansive treatment capacity, even this facility cannot handle all Albertan wastes, much less those of neighboring provinces or states. It makes only a modest contribution toward total continental hazardous waste management needs. As one of the most comprehensive surveys of hazardous waste generation and management capacity in the United States noted in 1989: "Once again, almost no new waste management capacity came on-line in the past year . . . . the amount of waste management capacity that has actually become available during the past year is relatively small and is primarily directed at high-energy, liquid wastes. Thus, net waste management capacity for other types of wastes has continued to decrease, albeit more slowly, for a sixth year."[4] With the lone exception of the Alberta facility, the Canadian situation is very similar. As a result the single case of cooperation in Alberta will have to be replicated frequently in future years if adequate disposal capacity is to be developed.

Subnational governments in Canada and the United States dominate siting policy due to the absence of national siting legislation in both nations. Subnational authority remains somewhat more dominant in Canada, consistent with the constitutional deference to provinces on natural resource matters. These moderate differences in degree of decentralization are reflected in Figure 8.1, with the American and Canadian cases representing different parts of cells 2 and 4. The 1988 Canadian Environmental Protection Act may begin to chip away at provincial powers in hazardous waste management, although this remains highly unlikely. The American states must contend with the regulatory structures imposed by the Resource Conservation and Recovery Act (RCRA). This legislation provides uniform national standards and permits guidelines for hazardous waste management, and has attempted to shift states away from land-based disposal methods. However, it operates on a conjoint basis, and more than 40 states have acquired authority to operate RCRA-permitting programs. Moreover, RCRA does not in any way establish a process for hazardous waste facility siting, leaving this matter almost entirely up to the states.

Given this latitude from federal legislation, Canadian provinces and American states have devised a wide array of policies to attempt to overcome this NIMBY dilemma, few of which have demonstrated much promise to date. A fundamental dividing line between the varying approaches that have been adopted by individual provinces and states reflects the extent of governmental involvement, as noted in Figure 8.1. Provinces such as Ontario and states such as Florida, New Jersey, and New York (cell 2) rely upon provincial or state environmental and natural resource agencies to make the main siting decisions and impose them on local communities. Under these "regulatory" approaches, governmental officials weigh a number of siting criteria—technical, economic, social, and political—and decide what type of facility is necessary and where it should be located. Local governments and the general public may be consulted at varying points of the process, but the final decision rests with provincial or state officials. A variety of coercive or consensus-seeking methods may then be used to either force construction of the new facility or gain local support for it. Private corporations may be included on a contractual basis. They may be hired to construct and operate the facility after the provincial or state officials have decided its location, the wastes that will be accepted, and the methods that will be used for their disposal or treatment.

Figure 8.1

Typology of Hazardous Waste Facility Siting Policy

	Centralized	Decentralized
Regulatory	(U.S. HLRW) [1]	Florida New Jersey North Carolina (U.S. LLRW) Ontario Alberta [2]
Market	(Canada LLRW) [2]	Minnesota Manitoba Michigan Massachusetts British Columbia North Carolina Quebec Saskatchewan [4]

Centralized: national government dominant in siting process
Decentralized: state/provincial government dominant in siting process
Regulatory: government agency/agencies make main siting decisions
Market: private-site developers make main siting decisions

On the other hand, provinces such as British Columbia, Quebec, and Saskatchewan, and states such as Massachusetts, Michigan, and North Carolina, give their public officials a far more passive role in the siting process (cell 4). Private-sector initiatives drive the siting process under this "market" approach. After establishing general guidelines for safety, provinces or states wait to receive proposals from private-facility developers to specify the site, the types of wastes to be accepted, and the nature of the facilities to be constructed. These private developers work directly with communities that are potential "hosts" of the site, often negotiating the terms of agreement with little or no direct involvement from provincial or state officials. In the absence of proposals from the private sector, no new facilities are developed.

Both regulatory and market approaches have consistently failed to produce agreements on hazardous waste facility siting in Canada and the United States. Among regulatory approaches, even the existence of a dominant governmental authority is insufficient to overcome local resistance. In fact, it often triggers enormous public distrust of any governmental role in siting. At the same time market approaches that attempt to establish a workable bargaining process in the absence of a substantial governmental role face similarly rigid public resistance. Private-site proponents must repeatedly withdraw their proposals in response to fierce local outcry.

THE EMERGENCE OF COOPERATION IN ALBERTA

The record of governmental efforts to site hazardous waste facilities is a gloomy one, although a few Canadian and American cases have deviated from the NIMBY pattern. The most noteworthy of these involves Alberta's novel approach to facility siting. The Alberta Special Waste Treatment Centre near Swan Hills has proven to be a model of private, provincial, and local government collaboration, antithetical to the pattern common in most other provinces and states that have sought siting approval. As noted in Figure 8.1, the Alberta approach defies categorization in either the regulatory or market cells of the typology, and in many respects constitutes a hybrid strategy. Both Manitoba and Minnesota have modeled their new siting programs after Alberta's, and will be a test of its replicability to other subnational units.

The Swan Hills case is intriguing not only for its seeming transcendence of NIMBYism but also for its alteration of the traditional structure of the siting process and nature of interactions among key participants. Under many current approaches to siting, a conflict emerges that resembles a one-shot, zero-sum game such as prisoner's dilemma. In such cases, interaction between factions ends rapidly, as local communities "defect" rather than pursue cooperative strategies in conjunction with waste facility proponents.

Alberta has countered this pattern by transforming the siting process into an open-ended, non-zero-sum game that, at least in the case of Swan Hills, has resulted in multiparty cooperation. In the parlance of game theory, the case appears to resemble most clearly an assurance game, where both factions prefer negotiation to conflict and both expect to receive optimal payoffs through cooperation. The Alberta case is consistent with the pattern noted by scholars who suggest that, under certain circumstances, it is possible to devise processes that lead to cooperative interaction, even among parties with considerable reason to be skeptical of one another and incentives to take adversarial actions.[5] Although the Alberta siting case may ultimately prove a fluke that cannot be replicated elsewhere, it does indicate that hazardous waste facility siting might not always be an intractable problem. It also suggests that careful attention to the conditions necessary to foster cooperative outcomes may be able to transform the process.

Such conditions are consistent with lessons for policy cooperation drawn from the modest but maturing political science literature on this topic. Some of these lessons are derived from institutionalist analyses that stress creation of new governmental institutions that can mediate factional conflict, establishment of mechanisms for meaningful public participation well before final decisions must be made, and development of competent and credible policy professionals to oversee policy and build public trust. Lessons drawn from game theoretic analyses of cooperation offer some similar insights, but they also emphasize the importance of altering payoffs through incentives that give communities greater reason to consider cooperation and the development of norms to generate a collective sense of responsibility for waste generation as well as guide citizen, corporate, and governmental conduct.

Beyond the Failed Market Approach

Alberta seemed a most unlikely candidate to break through the NIMBY syndrome in the early 1980s. The province began the decade with a market approach to hazardous waste facility siting that closely resembled the policies of British Columbia, Michigan, North Carolina, Quebec, and Saskatchewan. That approach met a familiar political response as Alberta's market-driven efforts resulted in a pair of private-site proposals that were spurned in short order by fierce local opposition. In response, the province placed a moratorium on the siting of hazardous waste facilities in 1980 and established a provincial Hazardous Waste Management Committee to study the problem and devise an alternative siting process.

The committee operated in the absence of any structured process for siting or provincial regulation of hazardous waste management, having been encouraged to design a novel approach. Its report provided the basic structure of the approach that was ultimately embraced by the Alberta legislature. This new approach emphasized voluntarism, as only communities offering to host a site would be considered as candidates. In addition, private developers would be asked to propose facility plans to provincial authorities. At the same time, the new Alberta approach established a major provincial role through establishing siting criteria and educating the public as to the nature of the hazardous waste problem and alternative remedies. It also was designed to allow provincial authorities to make the final decision on site-selection and the private corporations to be involved in construction and operation of the site and ultimately to play a direct role in the management of the facility. This blending of features resulted in a systematic role for government in the hazardous waste siting process that was unprecedented among all other provinces and states.

Siting criteria were applied through constraint mapping, which ruled out parcels of Albertan territory deemed inappropriate for various physical, biological, economic, social, and political reasons. Contrary to siting efforts in other provinces and states that utilized constraint mapping, these efforts in Alberta were shaped through exhaustive consultation with the public. This was an important part of a process that provided for extensive public participation at each stage.

The Alberta approach also involved a potpourri of general informational meetings and frequent sharing of technical and related reports with community organizations. The province established a host of liaison and other committees that were intended to foster regular and direct communication between public, provincial, private corporation, and crown corporation representatives at every stage of the siting process.

In the early stages of the site-selection process, Alberta Environment officials hosted more than 120 meetings in every county, municipal district, improvement district, and special area in the province. These meetings responded to citizen questions, provided briefings on the hazardous waste situation in the province, and offered general information on the types of criteria that can be used in a siting program.[6] Those communities that expressed interest in possible participation continued to have far-reaching access to provincial officials and hazardous waste data. Communities that expressed an interest in this activity were offered a detailed provincial analysis of their area, which could prove useful to them in considering the viability of a hazardous waste site as well as potential landfill sites or other land uses. Fifty-two of a possible 70 jurisdictions requested these assessments, and they were invited to volunteer to explore further the possibility of hosting a site.

Fourteen communities requested further consideration, although nine were subsequently eliminated on either environmental grounds or in response to vocal public opposition. Five communities remained eager to pursue the possibility of further involvement. All of them held plebiscites in 1982 that drew heavy voter turnout and overwhelmingly approved the idea of hosting a hazardous waste facility. Seventy-nine percent of Swan Hills voters supported the facility proposal in a plebiscite in which 69 percent of eligible voters participated. The town was subsequently selected by Alberta Environment as the site for a comprehensive waste facility in March 1984. Community leaders from the town of Ryley, 85 kilometers southeast of Edmonton with 500 residents, were very outspoken in registering their disappointment in not being selected as site host.

Swan Hills proved attractive to provincial policymakers because it was relatively close (209 kilometers) to the major metropolitan area of Edmonton and linked to this area by highway. At the same time, unlike Ryley and other candidate sites, Swan Hills had no immediate neighboring communities, so its acceptance of a facility did not require gaining the support of any nearby towns. Swan Hills also was eager to diversify its economy, which was previously reliant on oil and natural gas extraction, as well as to attract investment for long-term economic development. Like many small Albertan and western Canadian towns of this period, Swan Hills's unemployment and bankruptcy rates increased rapidly in the late 1970s and early 1980s. The other four communities that held plebiscites over siting were also eager for economic development and diversifcation, but were not in as serious an economic downswing as was Swan Hills.

Local political leaders played a pivotal role in building public trust in the provincial siting process and support for pursuing the waste management facility. They emphasized the economic development potential, the voluntary nature of the siting process, and the fact that the proposed facility was part of a comprehensive provincial waste management strategy. Upon initial discussion, many Swan Hills residents expressed alarm and formed citizen opposition groups. "When I brought the idea back to council, I was almost run out of town on a rail," explained Margaret Hanson, the mayor at that time. But after the council embraced the idea, they formed a citizens' committee to hold regular public meetings prior to the plebiscite. These gatherings were held every week over a twelve-week period, and every Swan Hills resident was actively encouraged to attend at least two of them. All relevant provincial and local officials were available at these meetings to discuss any aspect of the proposal. "We became taxi drivers, dishwashers, babysitters, whatever it took to get everyone out," recalled the former mayor of council-led efforts to build support for the proposal. "We divided up the phone book and called everyone in town."[7] Such extensive deliberations also served as a forum to consider and refute claims from national and international environmental groups such as Greenpeace that the facility would pose dire environmental and public health consequences if accepted.

Local leaders also attempted to defuse opposition by highlighting the slipshod, unsafe waste disposal practices previously used in Swan Hills and the province. There had been recent revelations of hazardous wastes being intermingled with garbage in area landfills and extensive dumping of oil industry wastes into ditches and waterways. "It's better to get rid of it properly," explained a local newspaper editor.[8] He emphasized that many Swan Hills residents were very familiar with such shoddy waste disposal practices in Alberta and gradually came to perceive the facility as providing a safer method of addressing a major local problem as well as a potential economic stimulus. These extensive public deliberations differed markedly from those over similar proposals in other provinces and states in their thoroughness, openness, and ability to foster an atmosphere of trust.

They also made possible an extensive public review of potential economic and social advantages associated with the facility. Swan Hills leaders argued that the construction of a facility with an anticipated $45 to $50 million in capital costs and creation of an estimated fifty-five new jobs would boost the area economy and its capacity to attract desired developments, such as a new hospital. In addition, the crown corporation provided $105,000 to cover expenses incurred by Swan Hills for town meetings, consultation with outside experts, and travel expenses; funding to enable the town to hire a permanent consultant to evaluate monitoring data; subsidized housing for approximately 35 family units; and purchase of a van to provide transportation for Swan Hills residents to the site, 20 kilometers northeast of the town. The private corporation responsible for development and operation of the facility supplemented these benefits with approximately $65,000 to support various local activities, including golf course development as well as other educational, sporting, and cultural activities; 400 trees planted for town beautification; and a special medical surveillance program for all facility employees. It has also provided such symbolic forms of compensation as making headquarter offices available for public meetings, sponsoring a hockey school, and donating a bear rug to the town council chambers.

The process of finding a host community went hand in hand with a provincial search for private firms to construct and operate the facility. The Alberta legislature created a provincial crown corporation, the Alberta Special Waste Management Corporation, in 1982 and also began in that year a national and international competition to attract private proposals for site development and management. This resulted in 19 proposals, which were later winnowed to four finalists. One month after Swan Hills was selected as the site acceptable to both provincial and local constituencies, Chem-Security Ltd. (later purchased by Bow Valley Resource Services Ltd.) was selected to build and operate the facility. Representatives from both the private and crown corporations sought a high public profile in Swan Hills, attempting to maintain public trust and support for the project.

The Swan Hills Special Waste Treatment Centre opened in September 1987, with capacity to incinerate organic liquids and solids, treat inorganic liquids and solids, and landfill contaminated bulk solids. The center is expected to process approximately 15,000 to 20,000 metric tons of hazardous waste each year, although its potential capacity is significantly greater. It is the most comprehensive treatment facility ever constructed in Canada or the United States, given the breadth of treatment approaches and types and volumes of wastes that it can handle, and is expected to preclude any future need for an additional major facility in the province. It is designed as the central component in a multifaceted system of provincial hazardous waste management. This system will also include construction of regional facilities for waste storage before ultimate transfer to the central facility as well as promotion of waste recycling, exchange, and reduction so as to minimize the volumes of waste ultimately requiring treatment at Swan Hills.

The Swan Hills experience is unique not only in its ability to foster sufficient cooperation to attain a siting agreement but also in its fundamental transformation of the siting process. It suggests that it may be possible to overcome the problems that have been so rampant in both regulatory and market approaches. In at least the instance of Swan Hills, this alternative approach has transformed siting from a fierce conflict that quickly produces an unresolvable disagreement to a more prolonged bargaining process that culminates in an agreement acceptable to all participants. Some of the most crucial components in this transformation include the following:

Tripartite Management and Governance

New, intermediary institutions have often served to transform highly conflictual situations into more-cooperative ones. For example, Robert Keohane argues that new, multinational institutions have played a pivotal role in fostering international cooperation in an era in which no single nation or institution is likely to enforce agreement through hegemonic power.[9] New institutions may be needed to transform the waste facility siting process as well. These should be distinct from traditional agencies within individual states and provinces that lack public credibility, meet stiff resistance, and repeatedly fail to attain agreement. The introduction of a crown corporation into provincial hazardous waste management appears to have contributed to the cooperative outcome in Alberta. This corporation assumes a number of the important responsibilities generally delegated to either private developers or regulatory agencies in most states and provinces.[10] It provides for direct governmental oversight of facility operation and also affords uniquely direct public financial and technical assistance to private corporations responsible for site development and management. As a 1981 government report endorsing the crown corporation concept noted, the corporation:

> would provide effective evidence of an arm's length position relative to government and industry while allowing various government

departments to continue their particular regulating, inspecting and monitoring functions . . . . [T]he public would be more likely to trust the administration of a crown body. Industry has indicated that if allowed to operate facilities in a free market environment, they too could function efficiently under such administration. Therefore, both concerns are met.[11]

Under this tripartite system, the Alberta Special Waste Management Corporation is responsible for overseeing numerous aspects of the provincial waste management system, including plant design and construction, provision of 40 percent of construction and operating costs plus operating loss subsidies to the private corporation, control of all provincial transfer and collection points, collection of 40 percent of revenues generated by the facility, provision of utilities and highways for the facility, and ongoing research, monitoring, and technological appraisal. It also owns the site, which it leases to the private firm for a minimal fee. In turn, Bow Valley Resource Services provides 60 percent of the construction funds and operating costs and handles day-to-day operation of the facility.

The crown corporation is distinct from Alberta Environment and related provincial agencies, which set regulatory standards that specify the ways in which respective wastes are to be treated. Alberta Environment also provides a system for registering these wastes and punishing regulatory noncompliance by either the crown or private corporations. At the same time that the Swan Hills siting decision and Bow Valley Resource Services selection were made, Alberta was devising one of the more comprehensive hazardous waste regulatory systems of all the Canadian provinces, and it was to be implemented by these agencies. In addition to regulating waste management, provincial agencies provide a number of requirements and incentives for waste generators to alter their production processes to recycle or reduce the volumes (or toxicity) of the wastes that would otherwise be sent to Swan Hills.

Public Participation

The notion of any significant public role in the siting of hazardous waste facilities in Canada and the United States has become synonymous with protests that ultimately thwart siting agreements. Neither regulatory nor market approaches have found mechanisms of public participation that provide citizens with opportunities that enable them to influence policy and encourage them to cooperate. As Gary Davis has noted, common participatory measures such as formal adjudicatory hearings and informal public comment sessions "are usually held too late in the process to really make any differences in the facility siting decision and both tend to create hostility and discourage cooperation."[12]

Creation of meaningful methods of public participation may thus be pivotal to any future siting breakthroughs. Prolonged political dialogue may be essential to defuse the adversarialism so common in NIMBY-type situations and to move toward more unitary processes of conflict resolution.[13] Moreover, multiple participatory mechanisms and outlets may be necessary if participation is to have a significant impact.[14]

The Alberta approach offered a multidimensional system of participation that was clearly more substantial and more likely to build public trust than the ones developed in the other provinces and states that were examined. Ontario and Florida, for example, have attempted to impose sites while providing only perfunctory opportunities for public input. Explosive political conflict has gridlocked both of these siting processes. Alberta also surpassed the limited participatory opportunities provided by market-oriented approaches, such as in British Columbia and Massachusetts, where citizen involvement was minimal or nonexistent until after a community was confronted with a site proposal.

This high level of public participation has continued into the facility's operational stage, through a number of formal and informal mechanisms designed to maintain communication between Swan Hills residents, provincial authorities, and representatives of the crown and private corporations. The Swan Hills Special Waste Liaison Committee was formed in 1985 and meets regularly with members of the Alberta Special Waste Management Corporation and Bow Valley Resource Services. One member of the Swan Hills council is appointed to the crown corporation board and facility managers maintain a high profile in the community and its schools. Observers of the public participation processes consistently emphasize that it was essential to encourage this openness at an early stage of the site proposal and maintain it throughout, making possible a bargaining process that resulted in settlement and has preserved trust in the initial years of operation.[15]

Compensation

Many provincial and state approaches to hazardous waste facility siting have been premised in part on the notion that host communities might agree to accept a proposed site if generous compensation packages were negotiated and provided. Such packages could offer commitments of health and safety protection, economic subsidies, or support for necessary services such as transportation and education.[16] The notion of devising methods of compensation to defuse NIMBYism is consistent with lessons offered by game theorists, who suggest that tinkering with the level of payoffs and the structure for their distribution may result in unexpectedly stable, cooperative outcomes.[17] In the process, highly regulatory and redistributive policies that local communities would normally resist might become more palatable if seen as facilitating local economic and social development.

Merely allowing for compensation to be discussed and provided does not result in cooperation, despite such an assumption by many provinces and states. By contrast, Alberta Environment, the Special Waste Management Corporation, and Bow Valley Resource Services proposed a host of compensatory benefits at a very early stage in the process, and offered them in a very concrete manner, rather than waiting for the advanced stages of deliberation over a specific site. Swan Hills officials contend that the economic impact of the facility has been considerable and has served to solidify public support. The facility has helped Swan Hills overcome declines in oil and gas extraction industries, providing 86 new jobs and luring new industries eager to locate near the comprehensive waste disposal facility. Swan Hills has enjoyed prosperity in the years following facility approval, with major increases in housing starts, a $5 million upgrade of water supply facilities, the opening of a modern, 25-bed hospital, construction of a major new office complex, and plans for a major industrial park in the 1990s. Swan Hills has also begun to lure hundreds of tourists each year, most of them eager to visit the facility. This latter development has proven a completely unexpected aspect of economic development attributable to the agreement.

Policy Professionals

Policies that involve redistribution and regulation invariably lead to political conflict. They often require the guiding hand of nonelected public officials or policy professionals to facilitate bargaining, agreement, and implementation.[18] This is particularly important in hazardous waste facility siting, where political saliency and conflict are extremely high and the credibility of environmental regulatory agencies has often been suspect.[19] As William Lyons and colleagues have noted, "the public has lost faith in those responsible for waste disposal—whether they are private chemical companies or public agencies . . . and is no longer willing to defer responsibility to 'experts'."[20]

The loss of credibility of Alberta environmental officials helped undermine the province's market approach of the 1970s. A 1979 report of the Alberta Environment Research Secretariat indicated that provincial officials were "being seen as aligned with private industry in favour of waste management facilities, as opposed to being neutral."[21] This perception, along with other important factors, served to scuttle facilities proposed in Fort Saskatchewan and Two Hills. This ultimately led to the abandonment of the province's market approach in favor of one that established a crown corporation with functions that could be clearly distinguished from those of environmental regulatory agencies.

The Swan Hills case has resulted in a remarkable coalition between leaders from each of the key components of the tripartite system and local government officials. A major conflict did emerge in 1985 over the role of the crown corporation, resulting in the controversial dismissal of the crown corporation chair by the Alberta Environment Minister. This threatened to return Alberta to the adversarial days of the late 1970s, although the quick appointment of a highly regarded replacement as chair defused the situation.[22] Important leadership has been provided by a number of key provincial officials with extensive experience in natural resources management and considerable public prominence. Elected Swan Hills officials have provided a solid base of support, with the former mayor and council playing a pivotal role in promoting the project and devising a public participation process that could garner trust.

Developing Governing Norms

Norms that guide behavior and lead to a collective willingness to address the problem of hazardous waste management have been notably lacking in most provincial and state siting efforts. A norm functions in a particular social setting insofar as individuals can be expected to act in certain ways and to be punished when they fail to act in these ways. Norms may be buttressed by laws but take on a self-policing characteristic that is often fundamental to cooperative interaction and implementable policy.[23] With regard to hazardous waste, neither Canada nor the United States has devised generally acceptable understandings of what constitutes appropriate and inappropriate conduct either individually or by private or governmental organizations. Moreover, there is as yet no great likelihood of punishment in the event of defection from the norm or refusal to make constructive contributions to resolution of the hazardous waste problem. This has led to extensive illegal dumping in both nations and explains the proliferation of abandoned sites that has necessitated, in the United States, the creation of a multi-billion dollar Superfund to facilitate highly expensive site cleanup. It has also encouraged exportation of wastes to developing nations, which has mired both nations in embarrassing foreign policy conflicts upon revelation of haphazard dumping in heavily populated areas abroad.

Alberta has not resolved this issue but has taken unusual steps to begin to develop governing norms through its massive information and educational efforts. "The public needed to be able to identify with the problem before ever considering any responsibility in developing a solution," noted one analyst.[24] Alongside these efforts, the comprehensive nature of the system to regulate waste management and promote waste reduction is intended to provide an overarching framework in which all Alberta citizens can begin to understand their personal contributions to the problem and their potential role in its resolution. These efforts have only begun to lead to norm development that might facilitate a collective sense of responsibility for the hazardous waste problem, but they appear to surpass those that have been attempted in the other provinces and states that were examined.   Furthermore, Alberta's distinctive political culture may give it certain advantages over many other provinces and American states in developing such norms.   This culture has been highly supportive of natural resource extraction as a tool of economic development and may be more trustful of private and provincial leaders than other, nonwestern provinces or many American states.[25]

LIMITATIONS AND UNCERTAINTIES

The ratification of a siting agreement and the opening of a comprehensive waste treatment center are surprising developments given the acrimonious pattern of hazardous waste facility siting in Canada and in the United States. However, the real tests of the effectiveness of the Alberta approach will be the environmental, economic, and political performance of its hazardous waste management system over time and the experience of other provinces and states that emulate its unique qualities. Some initial concerns that have emerged in the Alberta program suggest that its implementation may indeed be smoother than that of other provinces and states but will not be foolproof. At the same time, the Alberta approach has already begun to diffuse beyond the province's boundaries, having had significant influence on new policies devised in neighboring Manitoba and Minnesota. These cases offer some early indication of the approach's likely effectiveness when it is replicated elsewhere.

The Dangers of Capture

Regulatory theorists have long warned that outward signs of collaboration between regulatory agencies and regulated parties can result in capture of the former by the latter.[26] Canadian environmental regulatory policy in recent decades has been far more deferential to the preferences of private and public organizations that contribute to environmental contamination than has American policy. The relative absence in Canada of environmental advocacy groups or a strong national government authority in regulation has often resulted in harmonious, but arguably captured, regulatory relationships.[27]

This more cooperative form of policy making is, in the eyes of many analysts, more efficient in economic terms and every bit as effective in protecting the environment and public health than the more adversarial American approach.[28] For example, Thomas Ilgen's comparative analysis of chemicals regulation in Canada and the United States emphasizes the relative merits of the Canadian approach.[29] But this regulatory style may not be acceptable in the adversarially oriented American states and those more economically developed provinces, such as Ontario, that have increasingly embraced an American command-and-control approach to environmental regulation. Moreover, this more cooperative style of policy making has regularly failed to overcome NIMBYism in hazardous waste facility siting in a variety of other provinces.

The more cooperative approach may also lead to more superficial forms of public participation than would first seem likely given the proliferation of meetings, outreach efforts, and citizen involvement opportunities in Alberta hazardous waste management. For example, the Alberta Hazardous Chemicals Advisory Committee, which coordinated the assessment of the provincial Hazardous Waste Regulation and its amendments, is dominated by industry representatives. More than half of the committee's members are from the private sector, with the remainder from provincial agencies or municipal associations. This complete absence of environmental advocacy group representation is characteristic of environmental policy making in the province, as the major North American organizations have only a minimal presence in Alberta. It is also consistent with repeated pledges by Alberta environmental officials to consult closely with the regulated community and not allow hazardous waste regulations to thwart economic development. In such a setting, the regulatory agencies could be captured once the political flames of NIMBYism have been contained, particularly if a community such as Swan Hills became economically dependent on the continued operation of the facility.[30]

Planning Pitfalls

The early experience of the Swan Hills facility may underscore the difficulty that a provincial or state government may face in assuming responsibility for all aspects of waste management. Since the facility opened, it has received more incinerable solids and less materials for physical and chemical treatment than had been anticipated. These surprises can be attributed in part to the fact that the province was so eager to get a comprehensive facility sited that the Swan Hills treatment center was "designed, built, and opened before the final hazardous waste regulations were promulgated and before authorities had any reliable data on the waste types and volumes being generated."[31] Moreover, Alberta Environment has continued to prove far more reluctant than have American states (under the prodding of the national Resource Conservation and Recovery Act) to require waste generators to provide detailed waste production data to the province. This has made the projection of waste disposal needs a highly uncertain process.

As a result, Alberta has found its share of treatment center costs to be much higher than originally anticipated. The province provided $32.7 million to Bow

Valley Resource Services to cover operating losses during the first two years of operation, and such subsidies are expected to continue for at least five more years. Moreover, the underutilization of certain components of the comprehensive facility has led Alberta officials to take a more receptive view toward importation of certain nonprovincial hazardous wastes to bring the facility up to capacity and to trim operating losses. An original selling point of the comprehensive facility was its anticipated capacity to give Alberta complete control over its own waste management and the autonomy to restrict waste importation from other provinces and the United States. In fact, a 1985 Ontario highway spill of a truck destined for an Alberta storage facility led the Alberta environment minister to ban further acceptance of out-of-province PCB wastes.[32] This was rescinded, however, when Alberta agreed to incinerate substantial PCB residues from a major 1988 fire in St-Basile-le-Grand, Quebec, a policy shift triggered in part by economic considerations.

The Swan Hills facility is far too new for any definitive analysis of its economic efficiency, capacity to respond to provincial waste disposal needs, or ability to protect the environment and public health. But its early difficulties illustrate some of the potential pitfalls that may occur when an individual province or state attempts to sponsor and manage its own facilities and relies on a comprehensive central facility to serve as the system's focal point.

Replicability

Alberta's unique approach to hazardous waste facility siting will have significance for all of North America only if it proves worthy of emulation elsewhere and can in fact be adopted by other provinces and states. Swan Hills was not particularly unusual among smaller communities of Western Canada, such as the other four Albertan communities that sought the comprehensive hazardous waste facility, in economic terms. It cannot, therefore, be dismissed as an exceptional case in terms of its need for economic development and willingness to accept certain environmental risks in search of such development. In contrast, the province of Alberta may be unusually accepting of the risks posed by a facility by virtue of its distinctive political culture.

The capacity of the Alberta approach to be replicated elsewhere with success is already being tested in a neighboring province and state. Manitoba and Minnesota have abandoned their ineffective siting efforts and borrowed heavily from Alberta in establishing new approaches to siting. Thus far, the Manitoba case is the more promising of the two and may well lead to a major siting agreement in the early 1990s. Like Alberta, it has established a crown corporation and an extensive public participatory process that invites local communities to volunteer as possible hosts for a comprehensive facility. Much like Alberta, Manitoba has a far-reaching system of hazardous waste regulation and offers numerous incentives to stimulate waste reduction. Thus far it has met most of its early timetables without NIMBY-like explosions.

Five communities had expressed strong interest in hosting a facility, although the rural municipality of Rossburn dropped out of contention after a January 1990 referendum was defeated. Among the remaining communities, the city of Winnipeg and the local government district of Pinawa are thought the most likely candidates. The Winnipeg metropolitan area generates more than 80 percent of the province's hazardous waste, and a nearby site would limit the dangers and costs associated with long-distance waste transport. Pinawa, a town of 2,100 located 90 kilometers northeast of Winnipeg, has appeared most eager to acquire the facility. It has a sizable concentration of technically skilled residents accustomed to environmental risk since the primary employer is the Whiteshell Nuclear Research Establishment. Pinawa leaders view the hazardous waste facility as a potential source of economic diversification.

The Minnesota experience suggests, by contrast, that the Albertan model may not be so fully or successfully transportable to American soil. The state abandoned its politically disastrous regulatory approach in 1986 through amendment of the Minnesota Waste Management Act. Much like Alberta's approach, the new legislation sought local voluntarism through a series of public participation mechanisms and compensation packages. It simultaneously pursued the selection of a site and the recruitment of a private firm for site development and management. Although it did not establish an equivalent of a crown corporation, it does provide for state financing and joint ownership of any facility. This would give Minnesota a far greater role in hazardous waste management than most other states. Minnesota also made other adjustments, such as agreeing to eliminate incineration from any comprehensive facility, due to widespread public opposition around the state. It also must operate within the confines of fairly exacting waste management criteria that are imposed by the national RCRA program. This leaves state officials far less bargaining room than is the case in Alberta or Manitoba.[33]

The politics of facility siting under this approach have proven far less harmonious in Minnesota than in Alberta or Manitoba. They seem far less likely to result in a siting agreement. Fifteen Minnesota counties expressed early interest in the possibility of accepting a site. Many of them were economically depressed areas and were attracted by the possible compensation packages and potential economic stimulus that a site might provide. Each of these counties received $4,000 per month from the state, and the four finalists were scheduled to receive $150,000 per year for two years to assist them in technical reviews and in other ways.

A much more adversarial process has emerged in Minnesota than in Alberta. Fourteen of the counties dropped out by early 1990, and the last one that remained, Red Lake in the northwestern part of the state, decided against further involvement through the decisive rejection of a proposed facility contract in a

November 1990 referendum.[34] Local and national environmental advocacy groups proved quite active and encouraged counties to withdraw their offers of participation. Moreover, the staff of the Waste Management Board became divided and suffered major turnover, severely damaging the credibility of the board. Public trust further eroded when the media revealed that the private firm that was selected to build a facility if a site was agreed upon has a suspect environmental safety record in other states. In short, there are strong signs of NIMBYism in Minnesota, despite its emulation of the Albertan process. However, the Minnesota experiment deviated from the Alberta approach in several critical respects, including less-extensive public participation processes, the absence of a crown corporation, and less comprehensive compensation packages. Further experimentation among states is necessary to determine whether the Alberta approach is in fact replicable in the United States.

CONCLUSIONS

Hazardous waste facility siting poses a series of fundamental political problems that are common to Canadian provinces and American states. The prevailing policy approaches of the 1970s and 1980s have repeatedly failed to produce significant siting agreements. By contrast, an alternative approach has been devised in Alberta that has resulted in a major siting breakthrough. This case meets a number of important conditions on the attainment of policy cooperation that are established by the growing body of scholarship on that subject. The Alberta approach may warrant emulation elsewhere and has already served as a model adopted by one neighboring province and one neighboring state. Of course, it should not be viewed at this early stage as either flawless or capable of easy transborder diffusion. While the initial political agreement is noteworthy, the mere construction of a comprehensive facility does not guarantee technological effectiveness, long-term economic efficiency in waste management, or protection of the environment or public health. Nonetheless, the case suggests that the NIMBY syndrome need not be insurmountable and that careful attention to the institutional, economic, and social aspects of the siting process can enhance the likelihood of cooperation.

NOTES

Research for this chapter was supported by a grant from the Canadian Studies Faculty Research Grant Program. Research support was provided by Richard Compton, Margaret Daniel, Laura Flinchbaugh, Elizabeth Lowe, Jessica Miller, Robin Norton, Marion Perrin, and Pamela Protzel. Both sources of assistance are greatly appreciated. I am also grateful to John Gillroy, Philip Mundo, Paul

Quirk, Mark Schneider, Eric Uslaner, Kathy Wagner, and Kenneth Warner for their helpful comments on earlier versions, to Becky Pace for diligent word processing, and to the staff of the University of Michigan Matthaei Botanical Gardens for providing an ideal setting in which to complete revisions.   An earlier version of this chapter was published in the April 1991 edition of *Governance: An International Journal of Policy and Administration.* Permission to reprint was granted by Basil Blackwell Publishers.

1.   Paul J. Quirk, "The Cooperative Resolution of Policy Conflict," *American Political Science Review* 83 (September 1989), p. 908.

2.   The word *hazardous* is generally synonymous with the word *toxic* in both Canada and the United States.   Individual provinces and states tend to define hazardous, as opposed to solid or radioactive wastes, in somewhat differing ways.   Over time, however, the definition provided by the U.S. Resource Conservation and Recovery Act (RCRA) has become dominant.   This legislation defines hazardous waste "as a solid waste or a combination of solid wastes that, because of its quantity, or physical, chemical, or infectious characteristics, may cause, or significantly contribute to, an increase in mortality or an increase in serious irreversible, or incapacitating reversible, illness; or pose a substantial present or potential hazard to human health or the environment when improperly treated, stored, transported, or disposed of, or otherwise managed."   Solid wastes may be deemed hazardous under RCRA if they exhibit one or more of the following four characteristics: ignitability, corrosivity, reactivity, or toxicity.   Richard C. Fortuna and David J. Lennett, *Hazardous Waste Generation: The New Era* (New York: McGraw-Hill, 1987), pp. 26-27.

3.   Conservation Foundation, *State of the Environment: A View Toward the Nineties* (Washington, D.C.:   Conservation Foundation, 1987), pp. 158-160.

4.   "1989 Outlook for Commercial Hazardous Waste Management Facilities: A Nationwide Perspective," in *The Hazardous Waste Consultant* (March/April 1989).

5.   Russell Hardin, *Collective Action* (Baltimore: Johns Hopkins University Press, 1982); Jonathan Bendor and Dilip Mookherjee, "Institutional Structure and the Logic of Ongoing Collective Action," *American Political Science Review* 81 (March 1987), pp. 129-154; Robert Axelrod, *The Evolution of Cooperation* (New York: Basic Books, 1984); Robert O. Keohane, *After Hegemony* (Princeton: Princeton University Press, 1984); Kenneth A. Oye, ed., *Cooperation Under Anarchy* (Princeton: Princeton University Press, 1985). On prospects for cooperation in subnational environmental policy, see Barry G. Rabe, *Fragmentation and Integration in State Environmental Management* (Washington, D.C.:   Conservation Foundation, 1986) and John M. Gillroy, "Moral Considerations and Public Policy Choices: Individual Autonomy and the

NIMBY Problem," paper presented at the Annual Meeting of the Midwest Political Science Association, Chicago (April 1990).

6. Jennifer McQuaid-Cook and Kenneth J. Simpson, "Siting a Fully Integrated Waste Management Facility," *Journal of the Air Pollution Control Association* 34 (September 1986), pp. 1031-1036.

7. Maureen Houston, "Arm-Twisting Recommended," *Winnipeg Free Press* April 14, 1990, p. 3.

8. Glenn Bohn, "Where Waste Finds a Home," *Vancouver Sun* November 22, 1986, p. B1.

9. Keohane, *After Hegemony*.

10. Jeanne Kirk Laux and Maureen Appel Molot, *State Capitalism: Public Enterprise in Canada* (Ithaca, N.Y.: Cornell University Press, 1988).

11. Alberta Hazardous Waste Team, *Hazardous Wastes in Alberta* (Edmonton: Alberta Environment, 1981), p. 22.

12. Gary Davis with Mary English, "Statutory and Legal Framework for Hazardous Waste Facility Siting and Permitting," paper presented at the Workshop on Negotiating Hazardous Waste Facility Siting and Permitting Agreements, Arlington, Virginia (March 1987), p. 29.

13. Jane Mansbridge, *Beyond Adversarial Democracy* (Chicago: University of Chicago Press, 1980); Bruce A. Williams and Albert R. Matheny, *Democracy, Dialogue, and Social Regulation* (forthcoming).

14. Daniel Mazmanian and Jeanne Nienaber, *Can Organizations Change?* (Washington, D.C.: Brookings Institution, 1979); William T. Gormley, Jr., *Taming the Bureaucracy* (Princeton: Princeton University Press, 1989), p. 77; James A. Morone, *The Democratic Wish: Popular Participation and the Limits of American Government* (New York: Basic Books, 1990).

15. C. S. Simons, "Public Participation in Swan Hills—A Success Story," paper presented at the Air and Waste Management Association Annual Meeting, Pacific Northwest International Sections, Whistler, British Columbia (November 1988).

16. Kent E. Portney, "The Potential of the Theory of Compensation for Mitigating Public Opposition to Hazardous Waste Treatment Facility Siting: Some Evidence from Five Massachusetts Communities," *Policy Studies Journal* 14 (September 1985), pp. 81-89; Robert Cameron Mitchell and Richard T. Carson, "Property Rights, Protest, and the Siting of Hazardous Waste Facilities," *American Economic Review* 76 (May 1986), pp. 285-290.

17. Axelrod, *The Evolution of Cooperation*.

18. Paul E. Peterson, Barry G. Rabe, and Kenneth E. Wong, *When Federalism Works* (Washington, D.C.: Brookings Institution, 1986).

19. David E. Price, "Policy Making in Congressional Committees: The Impact of 'Environmental' Factors," *American Political Sciences Review* 72 (1978), pp. 548-574; U.S. Office of Technology Assessment, *Superfund*

Strategy (Washington, D.C.: OTA, 1985), ch. 5; U.S. OTA, *Are We Cleaning Up? 10 Superfund Case Studies* (Washington, D.C.: U.S. OTA, 1988).

20. William Lyons, Michael R. Fitzgerald, and Amy McCabe, "Public Opinion and Hazardous Waste," *Forum for Applied Research and Public Policy* 3 (Fall 1987); 89.

21. Natalia M. Krawetz, *Hazardous Waste Management: A Review of Social Concerns and Aspects of Public Involvement* (Edmonton: Alberta Environment Research Secretariat, 1979), p. 10.

22. William M. Glenn, Deborah Orchard, and Thia M. Sterling, *Hazardous Waste Management Handbook*, 5th ed. (Don Mills, Ontario: Southham, 1988), ch. 3, pp. 4-5.

23. Robert Axelrod, "An Evolutionary Approach to Norms," *American Political Science Review* 80 (December 1986), pp. 1095-1111.

24. Simons, "Public Participation in Swan Hills," p. 4.

25. Roger Gibbins, *Prairie Politics and Society: Regionalism in Decline* (Toronto: Butterworths, 1980); John Richards and Larry Pratt, *Prairie Capitalism: Power and Influence in the New West* (Toronto: McClelland and Steward, 1979).

26. Theodore J. Lowi, *The End of Liberalism* (New York: Norton, 1969); George J. Stigler, *The Citizen and the State* (Chicago: University of Chicago Press, 1975); Grant McConnell, *Private Power and American Democracy* (New York: Knopf, 1966).

27. Barry G. Rabe, "Cross-Media Environmental Regulatory Integration: The Case of Canada," *American Review of Canadian Studies* 19 (Autumn 1989), pp. 261-273.

28. David Vogel, *National Styles of Regulation: Environmental Policy in Great Britain and the United States* (Ithaca: Cornell University Press, 1986); Ronald Brickman, Sheila Jasanoff, and Thomas Ilgen, *Controlling Chemicals: The Politics of Regulation in Europe and the United States* (Ithaca, N.Y.: Cornell University Press, 1985).

29. Thomas Ilgen, "Between Europe and America, Ottawa and the Provinces: Regulating Toxic Substances in Canada," *Canadian Public Policy* 13:3 (1985), 578-590.

30. Matthew A. Crenson, *The Un-Politics of Air Pollution: A Study of Non-Decisionmaking in the Cities* (Baltimore: Johns Hopkins University Press, 1971).

31. Glenn, Orchard, and Sterling, *Hazardous Waste Management*, ch. 3, p. 6.

32. Ibid., pp. 6-7.

33. Dan Reinke, "Development of a Stabilization and Containment Facility in Minnesota," paper presented at the Air Pollution Control Association Annual Meeting, Dallas (1988).

34. Minnesota Office of Waste Management, "Contract Between the State of Minnesota and Red Lake County for the Location, Development, Operation, Closure and Care of a Facility for the Stabilization and Containment of Hazardous Wastes," September 20, 1990.

Selected Bibliography

Acid Rain and Friendly Neighbors: The Policy Dispute Between Canada and the United States. Durham, N.C.: Duke University Press, 1985.

Agnew, Tom. "Canada." *EPA Journal* (January/February 1989).

Alberta Hazardous Waste Team. *Hazardous Wastes in Alberta.* Edmonton: Alberta Environment, 1981, p. 22.

Alston, Julian M., and Brian H. Hurd. "Some Neglected Social Costs of Government Spending in Farm Programs." *American Journal of Agricultural Economics* 72, no. 1 (February 1990).

Ames, Glenn C. W. "US-EC Agricultural Policies and GATT Negotiations," *Agribusiness* 6, no. 4 (July 1990).

Atkinson, Scott E., and Tom H. Tietenberg. "Economic Implications of Emissions Trading Rules for Local and Regional Pollutants." *Canadian Journal of Economics* 20, no. 2 (1987): 370-86.

Axelrod, Robert. "An Evolutionary Approach to Norms." *American Political Science Review* 80 (December 1986): 1095-1111.

-----. *The Evolution of Cooperation.* New York: Basic Books, 1984.

Bendon, Jonathan, and Dilip Mookherjee. "Institutional Structure and the Logic of Ongoing Collective Action." *American Political Science Review* 81 (March 1987): 129-154.

Bhagwati, Jadish N. "United States Trade Policy at the Crossroads." *World Economy* 12, no. 4 (December 1989).Bluestone, Barry, and Bennett Harrison. *The Deindustrialization of America.* New York: Basic Books, 1982, pp. 6 and 40.

Bohi, Douglas R. *Energy Price Shocks and Macroeconomic Performance.* Washington, D.C.: Resources for the Future, 1989.

Brickman, Ronald, Sheila Jasanoff, and Thomas Ilgen. *Controlling Chemicals: The Politics of Regulation in Europe and the United States.* Ithaca, NY: Cornell University Press, 1985.

Canada, House of Commons. *Still Waters: The Chilling Reality of Acid Rain.* Committee on Fisheries and Forestry, Subcommittee on Acid Rain, Ottawa: Minister of Supplies and Services, 1981.

Carroll, John E. *Environmental Diplomacy: An Examination and a Prospective of Canadian-U.S. Transboundary Environmental Relations.* Ann Arbor: University of Michigan Press, 1983.

Carson, Richard T., and Robert Cameron Mitchell. "Property Rights, Protest, and the Siting of Hazardous Waste Facilities." *American Economic Review* 76 (May 1986): 285-290.

Chandler, W. U., H. S. Geller, and M. R. Ledbetter. *Energy Efficiency: A New Agenda.* Springfield, Va. GW Press, 1988, p. 21.

Changnon, Stanley A. "Climate Change and Hydrologic and Atmospheric Issues: Lessons of the Past." *Impacts of Climate Change on the Great Lakes Basin.* National Climate Program Office/NOAA and the Canadian Climate Centre, 1989, pp. 79-83.

Cleveland, Culter J., Robert Stanza, Charles A. S. Hall, and Robert Kaufman. "Energy and The U.S. Economy: A Biophysical Perspective. " *Science* 225 (August 1984): 891-893.

Cohen, Stewart J. "Influences of Past and Future Climates On The Great Lakes Region of North America." *Water International* 12 (1987): 163-169.

-----. "The Effects of Climate Change on the Great Lakes." *Effects of Changes in Stratospheric Ozone and Global Climate.* vol. 3: Climate Change. October 1986, pp. 163-183. United Nations Environment Programme and United States Environmental Protection Agency.

-----. "How Climate Change in the Great Lakes Region May Affect Energy, Hydrology, Shipping and Recreation." *Preparing for Climate Change: A Cooperative Approach*, Conference Proceedings. Government Institutes, Inc., 1988, pp. 460-471.

-----. "Responses to Climate Change: A Challenge to the Energy and Transportation Sectors." In *Impacts of Climate Change on the Great Lakes Basin.* 1989, pp. 102-108. National Climate Program Office/NOAA and Canadian Climate Centre.

-----. "Great Lakes Levels and Climate Change: Impacts, Responses, and Futures." In *Societal Responses to Regional Climatic Change: Forecasting by Analogy.* Glantz, Michael H., ed. Boulder, Colo: Westview Press, 1988.

Collins, Keith, and James Vertrees, "Decoupling and U.S. Farm Policy Reform." *Canadian Journal of Agricultural Economics* 36, no. 4 (December 1988).

Congressional Budget Office. *Curbing Acid Rain: Cost, Budget, and Coal-Market Effects.* Washington, D.C.: Congress of the United States, 1986.

Conservation Foundation, *State of the Environment: A View Toward the Nineties*. Washington, D.C.: Conservation Foundation, 1987, pp. 158-160.

Cowling, Ellis B. "Acid Precipitation in Historical Perspective," *Environmental Science and Technology* 16, no. 2 (1982): 110A-123A.

Crenson, Matthew A., *The Un-Politics of Air Pollution: A Study of Non-Decisionmaking in the Cities*. Baltimore: Johns Hopkins University Press, 1971.

Crissman, Randy D. "Impacts on Electricity Generation in New York State." *Impacts of Climate Change on the Great Lakes Basin* (January 1989): 109-118. National Climate Program Office/NOAA and Canadian Climate Centre.

Crosson, Pierre. "Climate Change and Mid-Latitudes Agriculture: Perspectives on Consequences and Policy Responses." *Climatic Change* 15 (1989): 51-73.

Davis, Gary, and Mary English. "Statutory and Legal Framework for Hazardous Waste Facility Siting and Permitting." Paper presented at the Workshop on Negotiating Hazardous Waste Facility Siting and Permitting Agreements, Arlington, Va (March 1987): 29.

Dennis, Robin. Selected Applications of the Regional Acid Deposition Model, An Appendix of the SOS/T Report No. 4, in *Acidic Deposition: State of Science and Technology*, Summary Compendium Document, Summaries of NAPAP, 1989.

Doern, G. Bruce, and Glen Toner. *The Politics of Energy: The Development and Implementation of the NEP*. Toronto: Methuen, 1985.

Dunkerly, J. "Energy Use Trends in Industrial Countries." *Energy Policy* 8 (June 1980).

Ferguson, H. L. "Luncheon Address." Report of the First U.S.-Canada Symposium on Impacts of Climate Change on the Great Lakes Basin. U.S. National Climate Program Office/NOAA and Canadian Climate Centre, 1989.

Fitzgerald, Michael R., William Lyons, and Amy McCabe. "Public Opinion and Hazardous Waste." *Forum for Applied Research and Public Policy* 3 (Fall 1987): 89.

Fortuna, Richard C., and David J. Lennett. *Hazardous Waste Generation: The New Era*. New York: McGraw-Hill, 1987, pp. 26-27.

Fox, Annette Baker. "Environmental Issues: Canada and the United States." In: The Atlantic Council Working Group on the United States and Canada, *Canada and the United States: Dependence and Divergence*, Lanham, Md: University Press of America, 1986.

Furtan, W. H., "The Future of the Canadian Grain Economy." *Canadian Journal of Agricultural Economics* 38, no. 2 (July 1990).

Gibbins, Roger. *Prairie Politics and Society: Regionalism in Decline*. Toronto: Butterworths, 1980.

Gilroy, John M. "Moral Considerations and Public Policy Choices: Individual Autonomy and the NIMBY Problem." Paper presented at the Annual Meeting of the Midwest Political Science Association, Chicago, April 1990.

Glantz, Michael H., ed. *Societal Responses to Regional Climatic Change: Forecasting by Analogy*. Boulder, Colo: Westview Press, 1988.

Glenn, William M., Deborah Orchard, and Thia M. Sterling. *Hazardous Waste Management Handbook* 5th ed. Don Mills, Ontario: Southam, 1988, ch. 3, pp. 4-7.

Gormley, Jr., William T. *Taming the Bureaucracy*. Princeton, N.J.: Princeton University Press, 1989, p. 77.

Grotch, Stanley L. "Regional Intercomparisons of General Circulation Model Predictions and Historic Climate Data." Report DOE/NBB-0084. Livermore, Calif.: Lawrence Livermore National Laboratory, 1988.

Hahn, Robert W. "Economic Prescriptions for Environmental Problems: How the Patient Followed the Doctor's Orders." *Journal of Economic Perspectives* 3 no.2, (1989): 95-114.

Hannon, B. "Analysis Of the Energy Cost of Economic Activities: 1963 to 2000." *Energy Systems and Policy Journal* 6, no. 3 (1982): 261.

Hardin, Russell. *Collective Action*. Baltimore: Johns Hopkins University Press, 1982.

Hare, F. Kenneth. "Vulnerability to Climate." The Impact of Climate Variability and Change on the Canadian Prairies. Workshop Proceedings, Alberta Research Council, Alberta, 1987.

Hare, F. Kenneth, and Stewart J. Cohen. "Climatic Sensitivity of the Great Lakes System." *Impacts of Climate Change on the Great Lakes Basin*. National Climate Program Office/NOAA and Canadian Climate Centre 1989. pp. 49-60.

Hoekman, Bernard M. "Agriculture and the Uruguay Round." *Journal of World Trade* 23, no. 1 (March 1989).

Houghton, G. J., Jenkins and J. J. Ephraums, eds. *Climate Change: The IPCC Scientific Assessment*. New York: Cambridge University Press, 1990.

Hutton, S., and M. Trebilcock. "An Empirical Study of the Application of Canadian Anti-Dumping Laws: A Search for Normative Rationales." *Journal of World Trade* 24, no. 2 (June 1990).

Ilgen, Thomas. "Between Europe and America, Ottawa and the Provinces: Regulating Toxic Substances in Canada." *Canadian Public Policy* 13, no. 3 (1985): 578-590.

Kelly, H. C., P. D. Blair, and J. H. Gibbons. "Energy Use and Productivity: Current Trends and Policy Implications." *Annual Review of Energy* 14 (1989): 345.

Kennedy, Kevin C. "The Canadian and U.S. Responses to Subsidization of International Trade: Toward a Harmonized Countervailing Duty Legal Regime." *Law and Policy in International Business* 20 (1989).

Krawetz, Natalia M. *Hazardous Waste Management: A Review of Social Concerns and Aspects of Public Involvement.* Edmonton: Alberta Environment Research Secretariat, 1979, p. 10.

Laidlaw, Angus. "Notes on Climate Impacts on Transportation." *Impacts of Climate Change on the Great Lakes Basin.* In National Climate Program Office/NOAA and Canadian Climate Centre, 1989, pp. 119-121.

Larson, Eric D., Marc Ross, and R. H. Williams. "Materials, Affluence, and Industrial Energy Use." *Annual Review of Energy* (1987): 114.

Linder, Kenneth P., and Michael J. Gibbs. "The Potential Impacts of Climate Change on Electric Utilities: Project Summary." *Preparing for Climate Change: A Cooperative Approach.* Conference proceedings. Government Institutes, Inc., 1988, pp. 284-293.

MacCracken, Michael C. "Scenarios for Future Climate Change: Results of GCM Simulations." In *Impacts of Climate Change on the Great Lakes Basin.* National Climate Program Office/NOAA and Canadian Climate Centre. 1989, 43-48.

Magnuson, J. J. "Potential Effects on Great Lakes Fishes. In *Impacts of Climate Change on the Great Lakes Basin.* National Climate Program Office/NOAA and Canadian Climate Centre, 1989, pp. 147-148.

Marta, Tim J. "Societal Implications of Climate Change: A Review of the Canadian Perspective." *The Operational Geographer* 7, no. 1 (March 1989): 8-12.

McQuaid-Cook, Jennifer, and Kenneth J. Simpson. "Siting a Fully Integrated Waste Management Facility." *Journal of the Air Pollution Control Association* 34 (September 1986): 1031-1036.

Melo, O. T. "Electricity Supply and Demand in Ontario." In *Impacts of Climate Change on the Great Lakes Basin.* National Climate Program Office/NOAA and Canadian Climate Centre, 1989, pp. 134-143.

Minnesota Office of Waste Management. "Contract Between the State of Minnesota and Red Lake County for the Location, Development, Operation, Closure and Care of a Facility for the Stabilization and Containment of Hazardous Wastes." September 20, 1990.

Moll, K., and N. Rosenbrook, "Will Free Trade Release a Flood of Canadian Water?" *Canada-U.S. Outlook* 1, nos. 3/4 (1990): 47-59.

Monrone, James A. *The Democratic Wish: Popular Participation and the Limits of American Government.* New York: Basic Books, 1990.

Morton, Colleen S. "Subsidies Negotiations and the Politics of Trade." *Canada-U.S. Outlook* 1, no. 1 (July 1989). Entire issue.

NAPAP/RMCC. Joint Report to the Bilateral Advisory and Consultative Group: Status of Canadian-U.S. Research in Acidic Deposition. Prepared by the

U.S. National Acid Precipitation Assessment Program Washington, D.C. and Canadian Federal-Provincial Research and Monitoring Committee Downsview, Ontario, 1987.

National Acid Precipitation Assessment Program. Acidic Deposition: State of Science and Technology, Summary Compendium Document, Summaries of NAPAP State-of-Science/Technology Reports 1-28, Washington, D.C., 1989.

Oye, Kenneth A. ed. *Cooperation Under Anarchy.* Princeton, N.J.: Princeton University Press, 1985.

Palmeter, N. David. "Agriculture and Trade Regulation: Selected Issues in the Application of U.S. Antidumping and Countervailing Duty Laws." *Journal of World Trade Law* 23, no. 1 (1989).

Peterson, Paul E., Barry G. Rabe, and Kenneth E. Wong. *When Federalism Works.* Washington, D.C.: Brookings Institution, 1986.

Phillips, D. W. "Climate Change in the Great Lakes Region." In *Impacts of Climate Change on the Great Lakes Basin.* National Climate Program Office/NOAA and Canadian Climate Centre, 1989, pp 19-42.

Placet, Marylynn. Emissions Involved in Acidic Deposition Processes, SOS/T Report 1, in *Acidic Deposition: State of Science and Technology*, Summary Compendium Document, Summaries of NAPAP State-of-Science/Technology Reports 1-28, National Acid Precipitation Assessment Program, Washington, D.C., 1989.

Portney, Kent E. "The Potential of the Theory of Compensation for Mitigating Public Opposition to Hazardous Waste Treatment Facility Siting: Some Evidence from Five Massachusetts Communities. *Policy Studies Journal* 14 (September 1985): 81-89.

Quinn, Frank H. "Likely Effects of Climate Changes on Water Levels in the Great Lakes." *Preparing for Climate Change: A Cooperative Approach*, Conference Proceedings. Government Institutes, Inc., 1988, pp. 481-487.

Quirk, Paul J. "The Cooperative Resolution of Policy Conflict." *American Political Science Review* 83 (September 1989): 908.

Rabe, Barry G. *Fragmentation and Integration in State Environmental Management* Washington, D.C.: Conservation Foundation, 1986.

----. "Cross-Media Environmental Regulatory Integration: The Case of Canada." *American Review of Canadian Studies* 19 (Autumn 1989): 261-273.

Raoul, Joseph, and Zane M. Goodwin. "Climatic Changes—Impacts on Great Lakes Levels and Navigation." *Preparing for Climate Change: A Cooperative Approach*, Conference proceedings, Government Institutes, Inc., 1988, pp. 488-501.

Reinke, Dan. "Development of a Stabilization and Containment Facility in Minnesota." Paper presented at the Air Pollution Control Association Annual Meeting, Dallas, 1988.

Richards, John, and Larry Pratt. *Prairie Capitalism: Power and Influence in the New West*. Toronto: McClelland and Steward, 1979.

Ritchie, Joe T. "Summary: Effects on Corn and Soybean Production." In *Impacts of Climate Change on the Great Lakes Basin*. National Climate Program Office/NOAA and Canadian Climate Centre, 1989, p. 196.

Rosenberg, Norman J., and Pierre R. Crosson. "A Methodology for Assessing Regional Economic Impacts of and Responses to Climate Change—The Mink Study." Resources for the Future. Washington, D.C., 1990.

Ryan, George J. "Impacts on Great Lakes Shipping." In Impacts of Climate Change on the Great Lakes Basin. National Climate Program Office/NOAA and Canadian Climate Centre, 1989, pp. 122-125.

Sanderson, Marie. "Implications of Climatic Change for Navigation and Power Generation in the Great Lakes." *Climate Change Digest*, (September 1987). Environment Canada and Canadian Climate Institute.

Schlesinger, Michael. "Likely Climate Changes in the Western Hemisphere." Paper presented at the Annual Meeting of the American Association for the Advancement of Science, New Orleans, 1990.

Schmandt, Jurgen, Hilliard Roderick, and Judith Clarkson, eds. *Acid Rain and Friendly Neighbors: The Policy Dispute Between Canada and the United States*. Revised edition, Durham, N.C.: Duke University Press, 1988.

Schwartz, Steven E. "Acid Deposition: Unraveling a Regional Phenomenon," *Science* 243, no. 10 (February 1989): 753-63.

Scott, Anthony. "The Canadian-American Problem of Acid Rain," *Natural Resources Journal* 26 (Spring 1986): 338-58.

Seitzinger, Ann Hillberg, and Philip L. Paarlberg. "A Simulation Model of the U.S. Export Enhancement Program for Wheat," *American Journal of Agricultural Economics* 72, no. 1 (February 1990).

Simons, C. S. "Public Participation in Swan Hills—A Success Story." Paper presented at the Air and Waste Management Association Annual Meeting, Pacific Northwest International Sections, Whistler, British Columbia, November 1988.

Smit, Barry. "Implications of Climatic Change for Agriculture in Ontario." *Climate Change Digest*. Environment Canada and Canadian Climate Institute, (April 1987).

Stakhiv, Eugene Z., and James R. Hanchey. "Policy Implications of Climate Change." In *Impacts of Climate Change on the Great Lakes Basin*. National Climate Program Office/NOAA and Canadian Climate Centre, 1989, pp. 162-173.

Strommen, Norton D. "Climate and Agriculture: Case of the Fruit Belt in Lower Michigan." *Impacts of Climate Change on the Great Lakes Basin*. National Climate Program Office/NOAA and Canadian Climate Centre, 1989, pp. 194-195.

Sweden. "Air Pollution Across National Boundaries: The Impact on the Environment of Sulfur in Air and Precipitation," Stockholm: Royal Ministry for Foreign Affairs, Royal Ministry of Agriculture, 1972.

Timmerman, Peter. "Everything Else Will Not Remain Equal: The Challenge of Social Research in the Face of a Global Climate Warming." In *Impacts of Climate Change on the Great Lakes Basin*. National Climate Program Office/NOAA and Canadian Climate Centre, 1989, pp. 61-78.

Toronto Conference Report. *The Changing Atmosphere: Implications for Global Security.* June 1988.

U.S. Environmental Protection Agency. Clean Air Act Amendments: Cost Comparisons, Office of Air and Radiation, Washington, D.C., 1990.

U.S. Office of Technology Assessment. *Acid Rain and Transported Air Pollutants: Implications for Public Policy.* OTA-0-24, Washington, D.C., U.S. Government Printing Office, 1984.

Van Duren, Erna, and Larry Martin. "The Role of Economic Analysis in Countervailing Duty Disputes: Cases Involving Agriculture." *Canadian Public Policy*, 15, no. 2 (June 1989).

Variyam, Jayachandran N., Jeffrey L. Jordan, and James E. Epperson. "Preferences of Citizens for Agricultural Policies: Evidence from a National Survey." *American Journal of Agricultural Economics* 72, no. 2 (May 1990).

Vogel, David. *National Styles of Regulation: Environmental Policy in Great Britain and the United States.* Ithaca, N.Y.: Cornell University Press, 1986.

Walker, W., "Information Technology and The Use of Energy," *Energy Supply* (October 1985): 460-461.

Wall, Geoffrey. "Implications of Climatic Change for Prince Albert National Park Saskatchewan." *Climate Change Digest*, 1989. Environment Canada and Canadian Climate Institute.

Winham, Gilbert R., "Dispute Settlement in the Canada-U.S. Free Trade Agreement." *Canada-U.S. Outlook* 2, no. 1 (June 1990).

Index

About the Contributors

AMY ABEL is an Analyst in Energy Policy at the Library of Congress, Congressional Research Service.

LISA CHERNIN is a Consultant working in Houston, Texas.

GREGORY P. MARCHILDON is an Assistant Professor of Canadian Studies at the Paul Nitze School of Advanced International Studies of The Johns Hopkins University.

FREDRIC C. MENZ is a Professor of Economics and Director of the Center for Canadian-U.S. Business Studies at Clarkson University.

KENDALL D. MOLL is a Professor of Management at San Francisco State University.

LARRY B. PARKER is a Specialist in Energy Policy at the Library of Congress, Congressional Research Service.

BARRY G. RABE is an Assistant Professor of Health Policy in The School of Public Health at The University of Michigan.

JURGEN SCHMANDT is a Professor of Public Affairs at the L.B.J. School of Public Affairs of The University of Texas at Austin.

ALAN M. SCHWARTZ is a Professor of Environmental Studies at St. Lawrence University.

ANDREW W. WYCKOFF is a Senior Analyst at the Congressional Office of Technology Assessment (OTA).

About the Editor

JONATHAN LEMCO is a Senior Fellow at the National Planning Association and adjunct professor of Canadian Politics at the Paul Nitze School of Advanced International Studies of The Johns Hopkins University. His books include *Canada and the Crisis in Central America, Political Stability in Federal Governments* and *State and Development* (co-edited).